Studies in Leading and Organizing Schools

A Volume in
Research and Theory in Educational Administration

Series Editors: Wayne Hoy and Cecil Miskel

Studies in Leading and Organizing Schools

Edited by
Wayne Hoy
Ohio State University

and

Cecil Miskel
University of Michigan

INFORMATION AGE PUBLISHING

80 Mason Street • Greenwich, Connecticut 06830 • www.infoagepub.com

Library of Congress Cataloging-in-Publication Data

Studies in leading and organizing schools / edited by Wayne Hoy and
Cecil Miskel.
    p. cm. – (Research and theory in educational administration)
Includes bibliographical references.
  ISBN 1-931576-98-X (pbk.) – ISBN 1-931576-99-8 (hardcover)
  1. School management and organization–United States. 2. Educational
leadership–United States. I. Hoy, Wayne K. II. Miskel, Cecil G. III.
Series.
  LB2805.S817 2003
  371.2'00973–dc21

                                     2003003794

Printed in the United States of America

CONTENTS

CONTRIBUTORS

Janice R. Fauske is Associate Professor in the Department of Educational Leadership and Policy at the University of South Florida. She teaches organizational theory and related courses on school administration and conducts research on collaboration theory in school governance, the cognition of school administrators, and organizational learning in schools.

Wayne K. Hoy is Novice Fawcett Chair in Educational Administration at Ohio State University. His research interests include the structure and climate of organizations, especially school characteristics that enhance teaching and promote student learning.

Bob L. Johnson, Jr., is Associate Professor and Director of Graduate Studies in the Department of Educational Leadership and Policy at the University of Utah. He teaches graduate courses in organizational theory and research logic and design, the politics of education, and education policy studies. Dr. Johnson's research interests focus on such issues as schools as organizations, reform and change, educational policymaking, arena politics, evaluation policy, and public choice theory.

Robert Miller is a Doctoral Candidate in Educational Administration and Policy at the School of Education, University of Michigan. His main fields of interest are educational policy, organizational theory, and the analysis of school effectiveness.

Studies in Leading and Organizing Schools, pages vii–viii

Cecil Miskel is Professor of Educational Administration and Policy at the University of Michigan. He maintains an active program of research and scholarship and currently is investigating state and national reading policy issues and processes.

Nancy S. Nestor-Baker is Assistant Professor and Program Coordinator of the Educational Administration Program at the University of Cincinnati. Her research focuses on the tacit knowledge of school administrators and on public school governance. Recent publications include "Knowing When to Hold 'Em and Fold 'Em: Tacit Knowledge of Place and Career Bound Superintendents" in the *Journal of Educational Administration.*

Jennifer King Rice is Associate Professor in the Department of Education Policy and Leadership at the University of Maryland. Her research draws on the discipline of economics to explore education policy questions concerning the efficiency and equity of U.S. public schools and school systems. Her current work focuses on teachers as a critical resource in the education process, with specific attention to issues of productivity, equity, and adequacy.

Brian Rowan is Professor of Education at the University of Michigan and Principal Researcher in the Consortium for Policy Research in Education. His scholarly interests focus on the organizational analysis of schooling, paying special attention to the ways in which schools organize and manage instruction and affect student learning.

Celia Sims is a graduate student at the University of Michigan concentrating on federal educational policy. At present, she is serving as a special assistant in the Office of Elementary and Secondary Education at the U.S. Department of Education.

Linda Skrla is Assistant Professor in the Educational Administration and Human Resource Development Department at Texas A&M University. She is a former public school teacher and administrator. Her research focuses on educational equity issues in school leadership, including accountability, high success districts, and women superintendents. Her published work has appeared in numerous journals, including *Educational Researcher, Educational Administration Quarterly,* and *Phi Delta Kappan.*

Megan Tschannen-Moran is Assistant Professor at the College of William and Mary. Her research interests center on the social psychology of schools including trust, collaboration, and self-efficacy beliefs.

EDITORS' COMMENTS

Wayne K. Hoy and Cecil G. Miskel

This book is the second in a series dedicated to advancing our understanding of schools through empirical study and theoretical analysis. Scholars both young and established are invited to publish original analyses, but we especially encourage young scholars to contribute to *Studies in Leading and Organizing Schools.*

This volume provides a mix of beginning and established scholars and a range of theoretical perspectives. Eight separate but related analyses were selected for publication this year. The book begins with a chapter by Sims and Miskel, which examines national reading policy as part of a broader federal government agenda on children's literacy. Using a model of punctuated equilibrium, they trace the peaks of congressional and media attention to literacy. Their findings reveal that the broad level of literacy has remained a rather active and durable policy issue for more than three decades. When, however, the analysis shifts to different targets, that is, from elementary and secondary school students to adults and youth to LEP individuals, there are distinct patterns of punctuation and equilibrium. The researchers conclude that the specific issue of children's literacy in the 1990s is the latest version or episode of literacy policy produced by shifting images and venues.

The next five chapters focus on administrators. In Chapter 2, Skrla develops the case that principals can and do play productive roles as mediators of accountability policy, and in the process influence student achieve-

Studies in Leading and Organizing Schools, pages vii–ix
Copyright © 2003 by Information Age Publishing
All rights of reproduction in any form reserved.

ment in their schools. She offers evidence from four highly successful, highly diverse school districts that principals can mediate accountability policy by influencing the goals, structure, people, and culture of their schools. In Chapter 3, Miller and Rowan examine the sources and consequences of organic management in schools using a contingency theory that argues schools will be effective when they develop the appropriate match between task environments and managerial forms. Their data only partially confirmed their theory. They found that management arrangements did vary by school level. Elementary schools had higher levels of supportive leadership and staff collaboration than secondary schools, but secondary schools had higher levels of teacher authority over decision making than elementary ones. The findings suggest that many factors *other than* differences in task environment contribute to patterns of organic management. Moreover, organic forms of management in schools are not strongly related to student achievement. The problem of finding organizational properties, other than socioeconomic status, that are consistent and strong predictors of student achievement remains elusive.

The next two chapters deal with cognitive processing of information by administrators. In Chapter 4, Fauske and Johnson focus on cognitive processes that guide principals' responses to the environment of their schools, that is, what do principals act upon, how do they explain their action, and what underlying mental models guide their actions. Their data suggest that principals have frameworks and routines that reflect an implicit belief that their school environment has three related challenges that they continually scan, monitor, and react to: the dependence of their schools on their communities, uncertainty, and their own vulnerability. In Chapter 5, Nestor-Baker introduces the concept of tacit knowledge as personal knowledge so grounded in experience that it allows an administrator to know when to adapt to the environment, when to shape the environment, and when to select a new one. Tacit knowledge reflects the practical abilities to navigate successfully through everyday life; it is informal, impressionistic, and self-regulatory. Tacit knowledge has been used to study successful behavior in the military, in medicine, and in business, but it has been neglected in the study of educational administration. Nestor-Baker explores the utility of the concept in educational administrative contexts, the role of tacit knowledge in socialization, the development and transfer of tacit knowledge, and the use of tacit knowledge in the preparation of educational administrators.

In Chapter 6, Tschannen-Moran challenges the assumption that transformational leadership is the path to organizational citizenship in schools, that is, that principal transformational leadership encourages teachers to work beyond their formally prescribed role responsibilities and give their very best to the task at hand. Her research suggests that teacher trust in the principal, but not the transformational leadership of the principal, is a key in the development of strong organizational citizenship among faculty; in fact, transformational leadership was unrelated to teachers' willingness to work beyond formally established roles. Trust seems to be critical in the development of productive schools, and in Chapter 7, Hoy and Tschannen-Moran provide a comprehensive conceptualization of trust in schools. Building on a multidisciplinary trust literature in diverse organizations, they identify five facets of trust: benevolence, reliability, competence, honesty, and openness to define trust. Then in a series of factor analytic studies they use the multifaceted definition to develop a reliable and valid measure of trust in schools. The Omnibus Trust Scale is a short, 26-item scale that measures three referents of trust in both elementary and secondary schools—faculty trust in the principal, in colleagues, and in students and parents.

The current demand for quality teachers has generated many efforts to reform the preparation and continuing professional development of teachers. Cost is always a constraint in such endeavors, but unfortunately no comprehensive framework exists for the cost elements that must be considered when planning and implementing professional development activities for teachers. In the final chapter, Rice develops such a framework for estimating the cost of teacher professional development.

Studies in Leading and Organizing Schools is about understanding schools. We welcome articles and analyses that explain school organizations and administration. We are interested in the "why" questions about schools. To that end, case analyses, surveys, large database analyses, experimental studies, and theoretical analyses are all welcome. We provide the space for authors to do comprehensive analyses where that is appropriate and useful. We believe that *Studies in Leading and Organizing Schools* has the potential to make an important contribution to our field, but we will be successful only if our colleagues continue to join us in this mission.

CHAPTER 1

THE PUNCTUATED EQUILIBRIUM OF NATIONAL READING POLICY

Literacy's Changing Images and Venues[1]

Celia Sims and Cecil Miskel

ABSTRACT

As children's literacy found a place on the federal government's agenda in the late 1990s, the question of why children's literacy should command such high agenda status has arisen. This research, examining the broader domain of federal literacy policy and utilizing the agenda-setting model of punctuated equilibrium, offers one explanation to this question concerning children's literacy. Successfully redefining the literacy policy domain in the 1990s to focus on children, policy entrepreneurs, who were dissatisfied with the status quo, garnered the attention of policymakers, who, deeming the issue of children's literacy serious, stripped the issue of children's literacy from policy subsystems and placed children's literacy on the federal government's agenda where major policy changes occur.

Studies in Leading and Organizing Schools, pages 1–26
Copyright © 2003 by Information Age Publishing

1

PROBLEM AND PURPOSE

The issue of children's literacy found a place on the federal government's agenda during the 1990s. Both Presidents Bill Clinton and George W. Bush have offered forth policies aimed at improving the reading skills of America's young. President Clinton proposed the America Reads program, whereby, armed with a citizen army of one million volunteers, Clinton (1996) hoped to lead the nation to reaching a "critical national goal: All America's children should be able to read on their own by the third grade, every single one of them." More recently, for George W. Bush, children's literacy has also become political fodder. At a campaign event in March 2000, Bush declared that "America must confront a national emergency. ... Illiteracy of our children impacts the whole nation. And therefore it requires a national response in its reach" (as quoted in LaGanga, 2000). Thus, he unveiled his Reading First initiative that would provide scientifically based reading programs and teacher training in reading. Besides Presidents, Congress, as well, has entered into the children's literacy arena, first in 1998 passing into law the Reading Excellence Act (P.L. 105-277) and most recently in 2001 enacting the Reading First and Early Reading First programs as part of the newly reauthorized Elementary and Secondary Education Act (P.L. 107-110).

While the rise of children's literacy on the federal government's agenda is clearly evident, the reasons why are not. In recent years, the reading research community has begun to explore the area of children's reading policy and attempted to answer such questions as why the federal government is increasingly involving itself in reading policy and who the actors are advocating the need for a government policy (Allington, 1999; Coles, 2000; Goodman, 1998; Taylor, 1998; Weaver & Brinkley, 1998). Unfortunately, the work so far conducted on children's literacy policy continues, as Shannon lamented in 1984, to offer "few sophisticated answers to even the most basic policy questions that could be posed about federal, state, and citizen influences on the organization and processes of reading instruction...and few reading researchers have tackled these complex, yet vital, concerns through systematic inquiries" (pp. 159–160).

Current investigations of reading policy have pointed to a slew of potential influences—the media, fundamentalist Christians and far right-wing conspiracies, a misinformed public, a rampant crisis mentality concerning education—as the cause for reading rising on the agenda. However, because many of these investigations have relied heavily upon anecdotal evidence and have weak theoretical and empirical groundings, they have been unable to integrate all these possible influences into a coherent and systematic investigation of the policy process. Thus, while a rampant crisis mentality concerning education may be one important facet to explaining the current agenda status of children's literacy, on its own and disconnected from the broader policy processes at work, such an explanation is rather simplistic and myopic. For it does little to explain why children's literacy should have gained the government's attention over other educational issues or why children's literacy should have gained prominence over other literacy issues such as adult literacy and bilingual education. Furthermore, such an explanation offers little in the way of explaining why children's literacy, an issue generally viewed to be under the purview of state and local governments, should have found a place on the very crowded agenda of the federal government. Therefore, the purpose of the present research is to offer an explanation, firmly grounded in agenda-setting theory and methodologies, for why children's literacy today commands such a high place on the federal government's agenda.

SOCIAL PROBLEMS

Agendas—media, public, and policy—are composed of issues and problems, which have captured people's attention and which the public spheres have taken up for discussion and redress. Yet, not every bad condition becomes an agenda item. Rather, a selection process exists whereby a society chooses some problems and not others for amelioration.

When the National Assessment of Educational Progress (NAEP) released the results of its 1994 reading assessment, many began to speak of a children's reading problem or crisis. As measured by the 1994 NAEP, only 28 percent of American fourth-graders nationally were reading at proficient and advanced levels and 41 percent were reading at a level below basic. The perception of a reading problem was particularly profound in California where fourth-graders scored well below the national average and ranked with students from Mississippi and Louisiana, states with notorious histories of poor academic achievement. The low scores of California's students prompted statements from the California Reading Task Force (1995) such as "there is a crisis in California that demands our immediate attention" and from the *Los Angeles Times* that the "failure to teach our children to read is a catastrophe of epic proportions" (Willes & Park, 1998, p. A1).

Although the NAEP scores, an objective measurement of children's reading abilities, were certainly important for bringing attention to children's literacy, the NAEP scores in and of themselves did not catapult reading onto the national agenda. For example, the results of the 1994 NAEP math assessment were similarly poor, with only 29 percent of American fourth-graders performing at proficient and advanced levels and 40 percent scoring below basic. Yet President Clinton did not propose an "America Adds and Subtracts" initiative to accompany his America Reads program and Congress did not pass a "Math Excellence Act" to accompany its Reading Excellence Act. The problems that policymakers, the media, and the public take up for redress are dependent on more than objective indexes (Gusfield, 1981; Kingdon, 1995) and "it is a grave mistake to assume that any kind of malignant or harmful social condition or arrangement in a society becomes automatically a social problem for that society" (Blumer, 1971, pp. 301–302).

John Kingdon (1995) distinguishes between conditions and problems. Conditions, for example poverty, illiteracy, and disease, are all around us; however, "conditions become defined as problems when we come to believe that we should do something about them" (p. 109). The problems, therefore, that a society addresses are social constructions or, in the terms of Hilgartner and Bosk (1988), "projections of collective sentiments rather than simple mirrors of objective conditions" (p. 53). Social problems, thus, have both objective and subjective elements (Fuller & Myers, 1941) and cognitive and moral elements (Gusfield, 1981, p. 9). For example, an objective condition such as illiteracy may be regarded as a social problem in one society but not in another. Additionally, child abuse, something that today we all define as a social ill, was only in the last half of the 20th century regarded as a social problem, not being reported on in either the popular or research literature until 1962 (Nelson, 1984). Furthermore, objective measures are sometimes negatively correlated with a society's attention to various social conditions. When America launched its war on drugs in the 1980s, drug use was actually falling (Dearing & Rogers, 1996). Hence, the issue of children's poor reading abilities as a social problem exists because our society collectively chooses to define it as a problem in need of redress.

The possible number of conditions that a society may choose to define as social problems is immense. Yet, only some conditions are defined as problems. Blumer (1971) writes, "Many push for societal recognition but only a few come out of the end of the funnel" (p. 302). What all social conditions, which exit this funnel defined as problems, share is legitimacy (Blumer, 1971; Spector & Kitsuse, 1977). Legitimacy is evidenced when the public sphere—for example, government, the media, and civic organizations—take up an issue for discussion or action.

Those problems that the media, the public, and policymakers take up are similar in at least two regards. First, society defines the problem in terms of the public rather than the private individual. Baumgartner and Jones (1993) write: "When a student drops out of school before learning to read or write...that is a private misfortune. When businessmen complain that the collective lack of training in the workforce is making the United States less able to compete in the international marketplace, that is a public problem that calls for governmental response" (p. 27). Indeed, much of the current rhetoric regarding children's literacy shows this appeal to the public realm. "As the Nation begins to enter the 21st century," Senator Barbara Mikulski (1997) exhorted, "we cannot have our young people—our future—lagging behind in basic skills. This affects our Nation as a whole. It affects our Nation's productivity. It affects our work force."

Second, to socially legitimate problems society attributes both a "causal responsibility" and a "political responsibility" (Gusfield, 1981, pp. 13–14). In Stone's (1989) terms, social problems are defined "as amenable to human action. Until then difficulties remain embedded in the realm of nature, accident, and fate" (p. 281). Thus, to craft public policy in response to the student who drops out of school without being able to read and write, the student's illiteracy must be defined in terms of human causation, for example, the result of poor instruction in school, rather than in terms of the student being fated or naturally and genetically predisposed to illiteracy. Scheberle's (1994) agenda-setting study of radon and asbestos demonstrates the importance of human causation for successfully defining a social problem. Whereas asbestos, a manufactured substance, had manufacturers, culpable human parties, to whom blame could easily be assigned, radon, a natural substance, had no easily discernible culprits and thus was a much more difficult issue to move onto the agenda. Furthermore, Stone's work reveals how policy actors strategically manipulate the causal responsibility of problems and the critical importance of this maneuver for moving an issue to a position of prominence. For example, Stone shows how Ralph Nader transformed the issue of car crashes from a conversation about unforeseeable mechanical failures and careless drivers, accidents and inadvertent incidents, to a conversation about automobile manufacturers skimping on safety features and design, intentional human actions. The critical effect, therefore, of attributing causal responsibility to problems is that a society can pin blame on someone or something and fashion solutions for "a problem is a problem only if something can be done about it" (Wildavsky, 1979, p. 42).

Finally, along with this causal responsibility a society also pins political responsibility to social problems or a belief that government should intervene (Gusfield, 1981; Kingdon, 1995). In their study of Congressional attention to issues surrounding work, family, and gender between 1945 and 1990, Burstein and Bricher (1997) found that policies advocating equal employment opportunity and family and medical leave were rather new phenomena. For example, in 1945 no member of Congress introduced legislation requiring that employers treat men and women equally in the workplace or hold workers' jobs when they temporarily left the workplace due to the birth of a child or to care for a sick family member. The absence of such proposals in 1945 and their preponderance in later decades, Burstein and Bricher posit, is not due to the existence of sex discrimination in later years and not in the 1940s and 1950s. "Rather, the problems did not exist in the sense that difficulties people faced were not viewed as public problems—as conditions the government could, and should, do something about" (p. 136). Hence, when the problem of equal employment opportunity rose in the 1970s and 1980s, it did so because society now viewed the issue as having a cause (employers favoring men over women) and now believed that it was the government's responsibility to do something (pass laws requiring employers to treat men and women equally).

THE POLICY AGENDA

Once a society legitimizes a given social problem, that problem is still far away from entering the government's agenda. Just as social ills pass through a funnel that permits only a few to exit defined as social problems (Blumer, 1971), social problems must pass through additional funneling processes if they are to achieve government agenda status. Cobb and Elder (1983) distinguish between two agendas, the systemic agenda and the institutional agenda. The systemic agenda "consists of all issues that are commonly perceived by members of the political community as meriting public attention and as involving matters within the legitimate jurisdiction of existing governmental authority" (p. 85). To reach the systemic agenda, a problem must meet three prerequisites. First, people must be aware of and their attention drawn to the problem. This attention is usually acquired through mass media coverage. Second, consensus must exist that acting upon the problem is both possible and necessary. Third, people must believe that addressing the problem is legitimately within the purview of the government. Cobb and Elder argue that meeting this third requirement is often the greatest obstacle for an issue reaching the systemic agenda. For example, for a long period of time child abuse was denied systemic agenda status because most did not believe that the government had the authority to intervene in the traditionally held private sphere of the family (Nelson, 1984). If an issue reaches the systemic agenda, it must then pass through yet another funneling process to reach the institutional agenda, the narrowest agenda and the place where governmental action takes place.

Cobb and Elder (1983) define the institutional agenda as the "set of items explicitly up for active and serious consideration of authoritative decision makers" (p. 86). Because the government, as any organization, has a limited processing capacity (Cobb & Elder, 1983; Simon, 1983; Walker, 1977), only a very small number of issues reach the institutional agenda. The issues composing the institutional agenda are divided between old and new items (Cobb & Elder, 1983) or between required and discretionary items (Walker, 1977). Constituting the bulk of the formal

government agenda, the old or required items are consistently and period-
ically recurring items such as budget appropriations and program reautho-
rizations. With the scope and size of the federal government continuing to
grow and balloon since the 1960s, required items have likewise grown and
taken up a greater proportion of policymakers' attention. Those few items
that make up the discretionary agenda, Walker (1977) argues, are determined by three factors. First, the issue must affect large numbers of people.
Second, convincing evidence must exist that the legislation being proposed addresses a serious problem. Third, the issue or problem has an easily understood solution. Using the Reading Excellence Act (P.L. 105-277),
which in 1998 legislated a new federal children's literacy program, a discretionary item, as an example, we might say that the success of this issue
reaching the agenda was achieved by the issue affecting all elementary
school students, by the 1994 NAEP reading assessment convincingly indi-
cating a serious problem with 40 percent of American fourth-graders reading below the level of basic, and by research coming out of the National
Institute of Child Health and Human Development explaining that children's reading performance could be improved by schools and teachers
employing research-based techniques for reading instruction.

In addition to the three factors addressed above, another critical factor
for an issue reaching the discretionary institutional agenda is whether the
issue can overcome the seemingly inherent bias of political organizations
(Cobb & Elder, 1983). Beginning with Schattschneider's (1960) contention
that "some issues are organized into politics while others are organized
out" (p. 71) and observations that for long periods of time policymaking in
America was the politics of subsystems and policy monopolies, groups of
elites who held sway over the various policy domains and supported the status quo, policymaking theories have emphasized the incremental, conservative, and static nature of policymaking. However, concomitantly,
longitudinal case studies indicated that conservatism and support for the
status quo did not well describe policymaking in certain domains. Bosso
(1987), in his study tracing pesticide and agricultural policy over a 50-year
period, found both periods of stasis in which policy monopolies led to governmental policy supporting the development and use of pesticides and
periods of change in which these monopolies were overthrown by outside
environmentalist groups. This overthrow of the vested interests of pesticide
producers and farmers resulted in an abrupt change in governmental policy, a change from support of pesticides to restriction of pesticide use. In
contrast to Bosso, Nelson (1984), in her study of child abuse, found a long
period of conservatism in which child abuse was never considered to be an
issue for policy followed by a period of dramatic and rapid attention to
child abuse by policymakers. Thus, a conundrum for policy studies has
been how to explain both the stability and change in policymaking.

PUNCTUATED EQUILIBRIUM
AND THE POLICYMAKING PROCESS

Baumgartner and Jones (1991, 1993), dissatisfied with theories and models that only explained the stasis in policy and longitudinal case studies that showed rapid and large-scale change within certain policy domains, searched for a single explanation for both the long periods of stability, when entrenched interests firmly command the policy domain, and the shorter, often abrupt periods of rapid change, when outsiders wrest control from traditional policy elites. Having investigated a series of policy issues over extended periods of time, the explanation Baumgartner and Jones found for both the stability and change, and upon which their model of punctuated equilibrium rests, is the interaction of policy images and policy venues.

A policy image refers to "how a policy is understood and discussed" (Baumgartner & Jones, 1993, p. 25). Important to Baumgartner and Jones' theory is a recognition that how elites, the public, and the media define and discuss particular issues over time changes and is not static (Rochefort & Cobb, 1994). Throughout the history of any given issue, the public and policymakers can be seen shifting their attention from one particular aspect of an issue to another, sometimes with the shift being quite dramatic (Baumgartner & Jones, 1994). In their study of the image of civilian nuclear power, Baumgartner and Jones (1991) showed how following World War II people's fascination with nuclear power was one that afforded the nuclear industry a positive image—nuclear power was cheap, clean, technology at its best. However, beginning in the 1960s perceptions changed and all were then discussing the negative images of nuclear power—nuclear power was unsafe, a cause of cancer. Swings, not so dramatic in their shift from positive to negative, but dramatic nonetheless in their yo-yo motion of attention from one aspect of an issue to another, is seen in Sharp's (1994) study of federal antidrug policy. Within the antidrug policy domain, attention has shifted from law enforcement, to counseling and therapy, to education, and then back again to enforcement. Within the issue of literacy, we might speculate that over time attention has shifted from an image that has focused on immigrants to one that takes adults as its focus and then to an image that sees children as its focus. These changes in the discussions of issues become critical for determining what types of policies have a chance of moving up on the policy agenda (Petracca, 1992; Rochefort & Cobb, 1994; Stone, 1989). For example, when the public is currently focusing on the potential harms of nuclear power, proposals for building nuclear power plants have a fairly negligible chance of reaching the policy agenda, whereas policies that advocate closer and more thorough inspections of nuclear plants have a far greater chance of rising on the agenda. Likewise, when increasing attention is being given to children's literacy, policy proposals that aim to improve the reading skills of the prison population are being blotted off the agenda.

This process of problem definition and strategic issue manipulation has important implications for the policy process (Rochefort & Cobb, 1994). Stone (1989) writes, "the different sides of an issue act as if they are trying to find the "true" cause, but they are always struggling to influence which side is selected to guide policy. Political conflicts...are fights about the possibility of control and the assignment of responsibility" (p. 283). Thus, when a policy entrepreneur such as Ralph Nader argued for a different definition of car crashes—car crashes were the result of faulty car design rather than the result of careless drivers—Nader was fighting a battle to determine if consumer protectionists would control the policy agenda or the more traditional holders of the agenda, car manufacturers and industrialists, would be the ones setting the agenda and the policies (Stone, 1989). Therefore, the policy image becomes a crucial means for disrupting the status quo. If those outside the system of policy elites can manage to alter an issue image, the opportunities for policy change or punctuation are greatly enhanced.

While a policy image is important for explaining the policy change, Baumgartner and Jones (1991, 1993) also argue it is critical for explaining the incrementalism and equilibrium that exist in policy, for an image is just as important for wresting control from a group or venue of policy control as it is for supporting the existing control. As defined by Baumgartner and Jones (1993), policy venues are "institutions or groups in society...[that] have the authority to make decisions concerning the issue" (p. 31). These venues may include federal agencies, state and local authorities, interest and professional groups, families, the open market, and a host of other institutions, and may be controlled by one institution or a combination of institutions. Typically, when these venues are government and interest groups, they are referred to as policy subsystems, policy monopolies, policy whirlpools, or iron triangles. For Baumgartner and Jones, the most compelling reason for the vast array of various venues rests upon theories of bounded rationality and the idea that no single institution or individual is capable of processing all the information and making all the decisions within a given policy domain. Because of this limiting factor in decision-making capabilities, governments must often parcel the work out to others and these others are often the subsystems and monopolies mentioned above.

Important to Baumgartner and Jones's punctuated-equilibrium model is the work of Simon (1983; 1985). In his work on decision making, Simon characterized the processes by which individuals and organizations make decisions as being parallel or serial. Parallel processing best describes a decision-making process in which many different decisions are made at the same time. Serial processing, on the other hand, describes decision-making processes in which only a small number of issues are decided upon at any given time. While individuals and organizations engage in both types of processes, the cognitive abilities of individuals within organizations usually limit them to serial processing (Jones, 1994; Simon, 1983). As Simon (1983) writes, "by and large, with respect to those needs that are intermittent, that aren't constantly with us, we operate very much as serial, one-at-a-time, animals. One such need is about as many as our minds can handle at one time" (p. 21). However, macro political institutions such as the federal government cannot execute the services and duties that are expected from them if they rely on serial processing alone—social security checks must be mailed out; the military must be trained, equipped, and paid; money must be distributed to schools; treaties must be negotiated and ratified; budgets must be decided; and so on. Thus, to carry out all its duties, a government must find some means also to engage in parallel processing and attend to many issues simultaneously.

Jones (1994) has argued that delegating decision-making authority to policy subsystems or monopolies is how the federal government enables itself to engage in the parallel processing necessary for its functioning. Also referred to as policy whirlpools and iron triangles, a policy subsystem or monopoly, as defined by Baumgartner and Jones (1993), is "a definable institutional structure...responsible for policymaking...that limits access to the policy process" and that may additionally be characterized by "a powerful supporting idea...associated with the institution" (p. 7). The idea that enables a policy monopoly to retain its power is often a policy image that confers the status of expert, one who is best capable of making the decisions, to those within the monopoly or subsystem (Baumgartner & Jones, 1993; Elder & Cobb, 1983). In literacy, the International Reading Association (IRA) and the National Council of Teachers of English (NCTE) may be thought of as members of subsystems, since to these groups, groups of professors and teachers, the "experts," the power of determining how best to teach a child or an adult to read, has at times been bequeathed.

While delegating such authority to the "experts" in subsystems may be a rational and sensible act as it permits those with the supposed expertise to make decisions and it allows the government to carry out all its duties, such delegation has a price. Placing power in the hands of subsystems may result in long periods of stasis or incrementalism in policymaking, since individuals with similar beliefs, values, and wants control the subsystems. These periods of incrementalism Baumgartner and Jones (1993) term "equilibrium." Thus, a successful subsystem or monopoly is one that keeps outsiders who might question its authority from entering its closed circle and disrupting the status quo or the equilibrium (True, Jones, & Baumgartner,

1999). For example, in Bosso's (1987) study of pesticide and agricultural policy, the pesticide manufacturers and farmers were a successful policy monopoly so long as they were able to keep the environmentalist groups at bay and continue to keep governmental policy favorable to the use of pesticides. Additionally, in literacy policy, the policy subsystem composed of the IRA and NCTE would be deemed successful for those periods of time in which it was able to exclude outside groups with variant ideas about the teaching of reading from the policymaking process. However, as True and colleagues (1999) write, "policy monopolies are not invulnerable forever" (p. 100).

At certain times, those outside a policy subsystem may begin to question the status quo that a subsystem has so successfully set up. In so doing, these outsiders call into question the "expert" status of the subsystem or redefine and expand the issue domain into areas outside the expertise of the present subsystem (Baumgartner & Jones, 1993; Cobb & Elder, 1983; Jones, 1994). Therefore, to break a subsystem's control, outsiders expand the issue by attracting other outsiders to their cause and attempt to alter the policy image so as to newly define themselves as the "experts." Thus, for example, if the present discussion of literacy by a policy subsystem is one that emphasizes deriving meaning from context, those outside the policy subsystem, if they wish to break the control the subsystem has over the literacy policy, may begin to expand the issue to include discussion of literacy in terms of the acquisition of specific decoding skills. Yet, for outsiders to break the present subsystem, they must attract, often through the media, the attention of legislators or the executive branch. If the outsiders successfully garner this attention and those in the government deem the problem serious enough, an issue previously handled exclusively by the parallel processing of a subsystem may be wrested from the subsystem and given over to the serial processing of the government where major changes in policy occur. It is this occurrence Baumgartner and Jones (1993) term the "punctuation." After the punctuation, however, those outsiders who have now taken control of the policy image themselves establish the boundaries of the new policy venue and subsystem and reestablish the equilibrium, thus returning the policy domain to a period of conservative and incremental change, which a new outside group may later punctuate.

Following from the literature discussed above and moving the discussion on the policy changes in literacy from speculation to empirical evidence, we conducted an investigation, employing Baumgartner and Jones's punctuated-equilibrium theory of the policy process, to assess the following three propositions.

1. Across time, literacy, as a policy issue, can be characterized by periods of equilibrium or government and media inactivity followed by shorter periods of punctuation or government and media activity.

2. As the policy domain undergoes periods of equilibrium and periods of punctuation, the policy image for literacy shifts and changes.

3. As the policy domain undergoes periods of equilibrium and periods of punctuation, the roster of participants changes.

METHODOLOGY

This study closely followed the procedures of Baumgartner and Jones (1993) to assess the three propositions. Covering the time period of 1975 to 1999, the study utilized two archival data sources, media coverage of literacy and Congressional hearings, to assess the propositions.

To assess the first proposition, we measured the frequency and intensity of media and government activity in literacy. Media activity and coverage of literacy were measured by counting articles indexed in the *New York Times Index* under the subject headings of illiteracy, reading, reading and writing skills, bilingual education, and dyslexia. We subsequently recorded for comparison and graphical representation the valuations for each year. While the data set for media coverage drew from only one source, the *New York Times*, studies by Patterson and Caldeira (1990) and Mazur (1981), comparing media coverage of various issues across several different media outlets, have shown that, although the absolute number of stories and reports varies from outlet to outlet, the general trends of upward and downward attention to issues vary little. Furthermore, Baumgartner and Jones (1993), when comparing media coverage of child abuse over a 25-year period in the *New York Times* and the *Readers' Guide to Periodical Literature*, found that attention peaked at exactly the same times in both data sources and followed similar patterns for decline as well, with a Pearson correlation between the two indices of .88.

We constructed a measure of government activity in literacy from Congressional hearings. We identified Congressional hearings covering the topic of literacy between 1975 and 1999 by conducting a search in the Congressional Information Service (CIS) Congressional Universe database. The CIS subject terms illiteracy, reading, and bilingual education were used to locate relevant hearings. As with media coverage, we analyzed congressional hearings to determine the frequency with which they had been held across the time period of investigation.

Since the work of Baumgartner and Jones (1991, 1993) argues that the public and policymakers alike attend rather narrowly to issues at one given time, to assess Proposition two and to determine the change in policy images for literacy across time as conveyed in articles in the *New York Times*, we read and coded the abstracts of each article for their focus on various populations. Initial population codes included children, adults, individuals with limited English proficiency (LEP), and families. After a first reading of the abstracts, we found that these initial codes did not well capture the populations upon which articles in the *New York Times* focused. Therefore, for final coding, the initial codes were refined to include elementary/secondary schoolchildren, youth/adults (e.g., individuals who had dropped out of school, individuals in the workforce, and college students), LEP individuals, families, individuals in countries outside the United States, and general, a category to capture both articles addressing the issues of literacy and reading without specifying a particular population of focus and articles addressing rather amorphous issues surrounding reading such as the correct placement of lamps for reading.

We used the Congressional Information Service's summaries of Congressional hearings to identify the target populations for literacy issues in Congressional hearings. We coded Congressional hearings similarly to *New York Times* articles for their attention to various target populations. However, we did not employ the code for individuals outside the United States for Congressional hearings, since this population was not addressed in Congressional hearings. Furthermore, the code of general for Congressional hearings worked somewhat differently from that for *New York Times* articles. For Congressional hearings, we used the general code only for hearings addressing the issue of literacy in general terms, for example, adults, schoolchildren, and families; the rather amorphous issues of the placement of lamps while reading did not surface in Congressional hearings.

To assess proposition 3 to determine whether, as literacy policy undergoes periods of equilibrium and punctuation over time, the roster of the participants and the composition of policy subsystems changes, we again used Congressional hearings. From these hearings, we created a data set that included the following information for each hearing: the committee(s) or subcommittee(s) holding the hearing, the date of the hearing(s), the names of all witnesses, and the witnesses' group affiliations. We subsequently tracked across time the individuals and groups testifying at the hearings.

FINDINGS

Assessing Propositions 1 and 2

During the time period of the study, 1975 to 1999, Congress held 115 hearings on the topic of literacy and the *New York Times* published 1,522 articles. As may be seen in Figure 1.1, we found only partial support for proposition

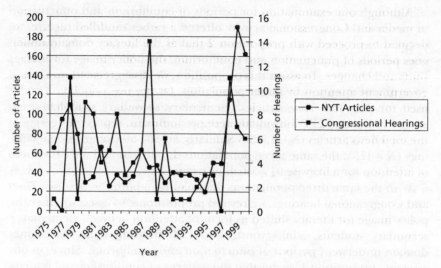

Figure 1.1.   Congressional and media attention to literacy, 1975–1999.

1 that across time literacy can be characterized by periods of equilibrium or government and media inactivity followed by periods of punctuation or periods of media and government activity. Looking at literacy as a whole, proposition 1 held far better for media activity alone than for government activity alone or for media and government activity together. For media activity, we do see two very discernible peaks occurring in 1977 and 1998, brief periods of activity, and a relatively long and less active period intervening. While media activity also peaked moderately in 1981 and 1986, these peaks, respectively representing 66 and 61 articles on literacy annually, were far less intense than the 1977 peak (109 articles) and the 1998 peak (190 articles). Thus, using media activity as a measurement, we may characterize literacy by short periods of activity followed by longer periods of inactivity.

The characterization for Congressional activity, however, is quite different. Instead of a long period of relative inactivity buttressed by two short periods of punctuation, government activity, as measured by the number of Congressional hearings, was chaotic and wild. This was especially so for the period of 1975 to 1991, when peak after peak of activity was followed by approximately equal troughs of inactivity. Only between 1991 and 1994 do we see a somewhat long period of decline, four years, following on the heals of a peak of activity in 1990. Therefore, contrasting the pattern of punctuation and equilibrium exhibited by media activity, government activity is better characterized by a yo-yo–like pattern of sharp and short increases in activity ensued by sharp and short decreases in activity.

Although our examination for periods of equilibrium and punctuation in media and Congressional activity offered a rather muddled picture, we decided to proceed with proposition 2 that as the literacy domain undergoes periods of punctuation and equilibrium, the policy image for literacy shifts and changes. To assess this proposition, we disaggregated media and government attention by target population. Of the five population codes used for *New York Times* articles, elementary/secondary schoolchildren, adults/youth, and LEP individuals were predominant, representing 91% of the total news articles (N = 1,522). Similarly, among all Congressional hearings (N = 115), the same three populations dominated and were the focus of attention for a likewise 91% of all hearings.

With the same three populations dominating in both the *New York Times* and Congressional hearings, we revised proposition 2 to assess whether the policy image for literacy shifted its focus of attention between elementary/secondary students, adults/youth, and LEP individuals as the literacy domain underwent periods of punctuation and equilibrium. Since, in our assessing proposition 1 we saw that the patterns of equilibrium and punctuation differed for media and government activity, in assessing proposition 2 we examined each peak of activity separately, whether media or government, to determine what if any population dominated. As may be seen in Figure 1.2, which displays the dominant populations of focus for each major peak, we found that for the majority of peaks of activity a single population dominated attention.

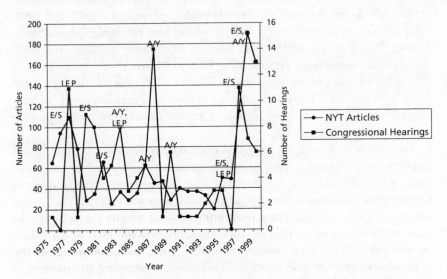

Figure 1.2.   Peaks of Congressional and media attention by population of focus.

Most interestingly, when one looks closely at these peaks of attention, one sees media and government activity clustering around individual target populations. Specifically, attention to elementary/secondary school students clusters and is pronounced in the late 1970s and early 1980s and again in the late 1990s; attention to adults/youth is pronounced throughout the 1980s; and attention to LEP individuals is evidenced in the late 1970s, mid-1980s, and mid-1990s. These clusters of attention by target population and the moderately long intervening periods of time between returning attention to a given population offers strong evidence for proposition 2 that as the literacy policy domain undergoes periods of punctuation and equilibrium, the image for literacy shifts between attention to elementary/secondary students, adults/youth, and LEP individuals.

Additionally, in seeing these clustering patterns, we returned again to proposition 1 and surmised that the muddled pattern of punctuation and equilibrium that we saw when examining literacy in the aggregate may have been due to these individual populations having separate and unique patterns of activity, thus masking the evidence of periods of punctuation and equilibrium when examining literacy as a whole. Therefore, separately for elementary/secondary students, adults/youth, and LEP individuals, we analyzed media and congressional attention to test for patterns of short periods of activity or punctuation followed by longer periods of inactivity or equilibrium.

When examining media and Congressional activity for each of the specific target populations, we found clearer patterns of punctuation and equilibrium than when we examined literacy in the aggregate. This was especially true for elementary/secondary students, a population for whom a very distinct pattern of punctuation and equilibrium occurred. As may be seen in Figure 1.3a, two short periods of punctuation were present in the late 1970s and early 1980s and in the mid- to late-1990s and bound a rather long and protracted period of decreased activity lasting for most of the 1980s and into the early to mid-1990s. Patterns of equilibrium and punctuation are also discernible for adults/youth (Figure 1.3b) and LEP individuals (Figure 1.3c), though not as clear as that for elementary/secondary students. While media and government activity in the area of elementary/secondary school literacy tracked one another very closely, presenting a very crisp portrayal of punctuation and equilibrium, in the case of adults/youth, media activity most often preceded Congressional activity and in the case of LEP individuals, Congressional activity most often preceded media activity. When such time lags are taken into account, a pattern of punctuation and equilibrium emerges for both adults/youth and LEP individuals. This pattern for adults/youth includes a period of equilibrium in the mid- to late 1970s, followed by a period of punctuation in the 1980s, another period of equilibrium throughout most of the 1990s, and a final short

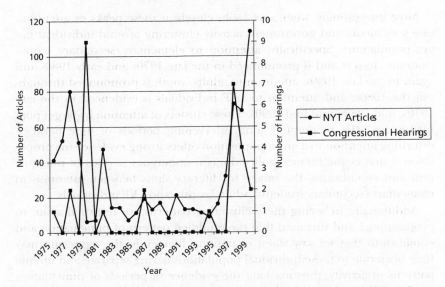

Figure 1.3a.   Congressional and media attention to elementary/secondary students.

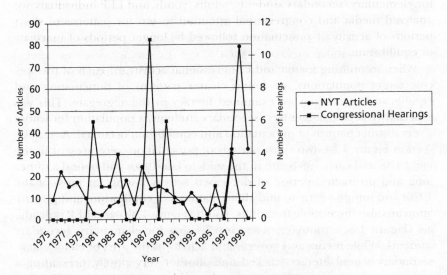

Figure 1.3b.   Congressional and media attention to adults/youth.

period of punctuation in the late 1990s. For LEP individuals, the pattern is a period of punctuation in the late 1970s and early 1980s, followed by a period of equilibrium lasting from the mid-1980s to the mid-1990s, and another short punctuation in the late 1990s. Therefore, although we found only partial support for our first proposition when examining literacy in the aggregate, when we disaggregated our data by the three dominant pop-

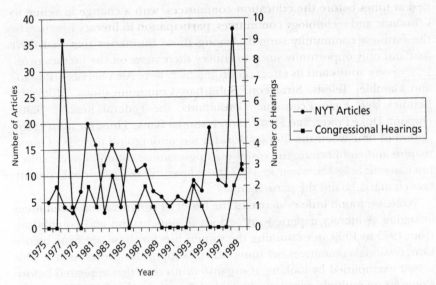

Figure 1.3c.   Congressional and media attention to limited English proficient individuals.

ulations of attention, we found strong support for the existence of patterns of equilibrium and punctuation for the specific literacy domains of elementary/secondary students, adults/youth, and LEP individuals.

Assessing Proposition 3

In proposition 3 we proposed that as the literacy domain undergoes periods of punctuation and equilibrium, the roster of participants changes. To assess this proposition, we tracked both the Congressional committees holding hearings on literacy and the witnesses who testified along with their organizational affiliations. The House and Senate education committees were the convening authority for the vast majority of literacy hearings. Of the 115 literacy hearings between 1975 and 1999, 72 (63%) were under the auspices of the House education committee and 29 (25%) were under the Senate education committee. The five other Congressional committees holding literacy hearings included the House Judiciary committee (one hearing), the Senate Judiciary committee (three hearings), the House Science, Space, and Technology committee (one hearing), and the Joint Economic committee (eight hearings). Of the 14 hearings outside the education committees, the Joint Economic and House Science, Space, and Technology committees convened nine in 1987 and took adults/youth as their focus. Although representatives from the business community testified at times before the education committees, with a change in venue to economic and technology committees, participation in literacy hearings by the business community surged. Among those businesses that had their first and only opportunity since to convey their views on the literacy problem among adults and its effect on productivity were ARA Services, Proctor and Gamble, Telesis, Stratecon, Suburban Communications, Motorola, Bendick and Egan Economic Consultants, the Federal Reserve Bank, Dupont, Duke Power, and First Union National Bank. Thus, for most of the period of time when the literacy domain was undergoing periods of punctuation and equilibrium, the roster of congressional committees remained unchanged; however, when in 1987 the convening congressional committees changed, so did the participants.

While we found little evidence of the roster of congressional committees changing as literacy experienced periods of punctuation and equilibrium from 1975 to 1999, in examining the witness lists for those testifying before Congressional committees, we found strong support for proposition 3. This is best exemplified by looking at organized interests that appeared before Congress on multiple occasions. In Table 1.1, we have listed the 32 organiza-

Table 1.1.   Organizations Appearing on Multiple Occasions at House and Senate Literacy Hearings

Groups Entering in Late 1970s and Leaving in Late 1980s	*Years Appearing*
American Federation of Teachers	1977, 1979, 1980, 1983, 1987
Center for Applied Linguistics	1977, 1982
National Council of La Raza	1977, 1982, 1986, 1989
National Education Association	1977, 1979, 1980, 1983, 1987
Groups Entering and Leaving in 1980s	*Years Appearing*
American Association of Community and Junior Colleges	1983, 1987
American Vocational Association	1980, 1983
Business Council for Effective Literacy	1987, 1989
Committee for Economic Development	1983, 1987
Council of Chief State School Officers	1980, 1983, 1985
Council of Great City Schools	1980, 1983
IBM	1987, 1989
International Reading Association	1979, 1983, 1985, 1986, 1987
Laubach Literacy	1981, 1989
League of United Latin American Citizens	1981, 1982, 1984, 1986
National Association of State Boards of Education	1983, 1986
National School Boards Association	1980, 1983, 1984

Table 1.1.   Organizations Appearing on Multiple Occasions at House and Senate Literacy Hearings (Cont.)

Groups Entering in Late 1980s and Present in 1990s	Years Appearing
AFL-CIO	1987, 1997
American Association of Adult and Continuing Education	1987, 1989, 1995
Mexican American Legal Defense and Education Fund	1986, 1987, 1993, 1998
National Center for Family Literacy	1992, 1995, 1999
National Institute for Literacy	1994, 1995, 1997, 1998, 1999
Toyota Motor Sales	1995, 1997
United Auto Workers	1990, 1997

Groups Spread throughout 1975 to 1999	Years Appearing
American Association of School Administrators	1980, 1983, 1997
Correctional Education Association	1983, 1989, 1995, 1997
Literacy Volunteers of America	1981, 1984, 1997
National Assessment of Educational Progress	1975, 1981, 1998, 1999
National Association for Bilingual Education	1977, 1982, 1984, 1986, 1987, 1993, 1999
National Council of State Directors of Adult Education	1982, 1986, 1987, 1989, 1995, 1997
Parent Teacher Association	1978, 1996
Reading Is Fundamental	1975, 1985, 1994, 1999
US English	1983, 1998

tions that were represented at Congressional hearings on more than one occasion. Among these 32 organizations, four distinct patterns emerge: groups that entered the literacy scene in the late 1970s and that left by the late 1980s (e.g., American Federation of Teachers, National Council of La Raza, National Education Association); groups that both entered and left in the 1980s (e.g., International Reading Association, Council of Chief State School Officers, League of United Latin American Citizens); groups that entered in the late 1980s and were still present in the 1990s (e.g., American Association of Adult and Continuing Education, National Center for Family Literacy, National Institute for Literacy); and groups that were present throughout the greater part of 1975 to 1999, though some with long periods of time between appearances (e.g., American Association of School Administrators, National Association for Bilingual Education, Reading Is Fundamental). Therefore, while a few groups maintained a presence at Congressional hearings between 1975 and 1999, most organized interests did not, subsequently altering the roster of participants as the literacy domain underwent periods of punctuation and equilibrium.

DISCUSSION

The impetus for this study was the rise of children's literacy on the federal government's agenda beginning in 1996 with President Clinton's America Reads proposal and continuing today with President Bush's Reading First proposal. The question we confronted was how children's literacy gained such a level of prominence. To answer this question, we turned to the literatures on problem definition and agendas and constructed a study to assess Baumgartner and Jones's (1993) punctuated-equilibrium model of agenda setting.

Baumgartner and Jones (1991, 1993) argue that the explanation for both an issue's rise and fall on the governmental agenda lies with the interaction of policy images and venue. An issue's policy image, how the issue is defined and discussed, is critical for understanding which issues policymakers are likely to take up for action. The fact that children's reading abilities are a component of the broader policy domain of literacy and the fact that the federal government had previously taken up the issue of children's literacy helped the rise of children's literacy on the agenda in the 1990s. First, the issue of low literacy levels has for some time now been defined as a socially legitimate problem (Blumer, 1971), as evidenced in our study by literacy never leaving the media agenda. Second, the problem of illiteracy over the course of American history has come to be defined as a serious problem affecting large numbers of people and a problem upon which the government must act because of the ramifications for the public as a whole (Cobb & Elder, 1983; Stone, 1989; Walker, 1977). Thus, for example, when Senator Barbara Mikulski in 1997 exhorted that a child's poor reading ability "...affects our Nation as a whole...our Nation's productivity...our work force," she was simply reiterating a well-defined and crystallized public definition of the illiteracy problem, one that was similarly used 10 years earlier, when Representative James Scheuer (1987), speaking of adult illiteracy, stated "...the adverse impact on business and the Nation's competitive position is so clear and so serious and such a clear and present danger that we must develop practical and workable solutions to this massive national problem." Third, the issue of children's literacy is not a new issue for the federal government. As seen in our study, children's literacy experienced a peak of Congressional attention in the late 1970s and was taken up again sporadically for action in the years intervening before its second great peak of activity in the late 1990s. Therefore, because of its being part of the broader policy domain of literacy, an issue very well defined as being an area of legitimate government action, and because of its previous agenda status, children's literacy, when returning to the agenda in the 1990s, had already successfully made it through the many funneling processes that new issues must pass before gaining admittance to the government's agenda (Blumer, 1971; Cobb & Elder, 1983; Walker, 1977).

As evidenced in our study, between 1975 and 1999 the very broad issue of literacy has remained a rather active issue, never quite undergoing the periods of punctuation and equilibrium we had anticipated with our first proposition. The pattern of the broad literacy domain, it appears, is similar to the pattern of activity Sharp (1994) observed with federal antidrug policy. When taken in the aggregate, the problem of illiteracy, like drugs, has proven to be a very durable issue. Durable issues, issues that do not fade from the agenda, share three characteristics: dramatic potential, proximity, and novelty (Rochefort & Cobb, 1994; Sharp, 1994). For example, the problem of illiteracy easily appeals to our sense of drama and crisis, such as signaling impending doom for the nation's economic well-being. Furthermore, because of its proximal or everyday existence in our lives, we can easily imagine the hardships illiteracy poses for those who cannot read and write. Finally, literacy, because of its effect on every person, young and old, individuals and families, native speakers and non-native speakers, is an issue that lends itself to novelty and transformation and as such can easily shift its focus to different populations. Therefore, in examining the durable issue of literacy in the aggregate, we should not see periods of punctuation and equilibrium, as was the case in our study. Instead, with a policy image shifting from one problem or target population to another, it is only when we disaggregate a durable policy domain such as literacy by population of focus that we should expect to see a pattern of punctuation and equilibrium. As occurred with our study, when analyzing separately the three dominant target populations, elementary/secondary school students, adults/youth, and LEP individuals, we observed distinct and independent patterns of punctuation and equilibrium. And in the specific case of children's literacy, the punctuation that occurred in the late 1990s, gives evidence for the durable policy issue of literacy having been redefined and shifted in its focus away from adults/youth, the defined problem population of the 1980s, and toward children, the newly defined problem population of the 1990s.

Yet, durable issues cannot remain on the agenda forever in the absence of policy entrepreneurs, individuals who expend time and effort to redefine the policy issue and to garner the support of others, most importantly policymakers, in this redefinition (Baumgartner & Jones, 1993; Kingdon, 1995; Sharp, 1994). In attracting others to their side and their problem definition, policy entrepreneurs are attempting to expand, disrupt, and ultimately overthrow the present venue of control. Thus, as the literacy domain, broadly speaking, shifts its focus from one problem population to another and as the individual population domains fluctuate between short periods of punctuation and long periods of equilibrium, we should see the roster of participants change as well. In our examination of literacy policy, we did indeed see the participants changing. For example, the National Education Association and the National Council of La Raza, which were on the literacy scene in the late 1970s, left in the mid- to late-1980s; the American Vocational Association and the National Association of State Boards of Education both entered and retreated from the literacy scene in the 1980s; and the National Center for Family Literacy and the National Institute for Literacy newly traversed the literacy scene in the 1990s. Furthermore, when the specific domain of elementary/secondary schoolchildren experienced a punctuation in the late 1990s, the roster of participants differed from that of the late 1970s, when the domain also underwent a period of punctuation. With the policy image having been redefined and the venue having been expanded in the 1990s, the specific issue of children's literacy came to dominate other literacy issues and found a place on the federal government's agenda.

Therefore, given the patterns of punctuation and equilibrium of the literacy domain with their shifting images and venues, the specific issue of children's literacy in the 1990s may best be characterized as the latest version or episode in the literacy policy domain. And the operative or important word here is *version*. When the literacy issue peaks anew, we are not replaying and rehashing an issue identical to the one before. The issue has been redefined and transformed, for example, from one that focuses on adults to one that focuses on children. Furthermore, when the more specific issue of children's literacy reappeared in the 1990s, it was a different version from the issue of children's literacy that appeared in the 1970s and was not simply a swing in the pendulum back toward what had been before. For with the roster of participants being different for the two episodes, those fighting to push children's literacy on the governmental agenda in the 1990s differ from those of the 1970s with respect to their beliefs and values and thus propose different solutions and approaches to ameliorating children's reading difficulties. Thus, the only things we can expect to remain the same when these differing versions of the literacy issue arise are the basic and fundamental characteristics of the problem of illiteracy that has allowed it time and time again to be taken up for governmental action—its acceptance as a socially legitimate problem, its affecting large numbers of the public, its being amenable to human action, and its being viewed as under the purview of the federal government for attention and action.

Borrowing from the literatures on problem definition and agendas and utilizing Baumgartner and Jones's punctuated-equilibrium model of agenda setting have proven useful and beneficial endeavors for exploring the issue of national literacy policy generally and the issue of national children's literacy policy specifically. The sound basis of our study is a positive step forward, we believe, in moving the work on reading policy away from anecdotal evidence and toward systematic and coherent explanations, grounded in theory and empirical evidence, of the policy process. Additionally, with the literatures on problem definition, agendas, and punctuated equilibrium having shown their applicability to the domain of literacy policy, we hope that others will undertake similar investigations in other educational policy domains as well, domains, which similar to literacy policy, are often plagued by weak theoretical and empirical underpinnings.

NOTE

1.   This research was conducted as part of CIERA, the Center for the Improvement of Early Reading Achievement, and supported under the Educational Research and Development Centers Program (PR/Award No. R305R70004), as administered by the Office of Educational Research and Improvement, U.S. Department of Education. However, the contents of the described report do not necessarily represent the positions or policies of the National Institute on Student Achievement, Curriculum, and Assessment, the National Institute on Early Childhood development, or the U.S. Department of Education, and you should not assume endorsement by the federal government.

REFERENCES

Allington, R. L. (1999). Critical issues: Crafting state educational policy: The slippery role of research and researchers. *Journal of Literacy Research, 31*(4), 457–482.

Baumgartner, F. R., & Jones, B. D. (1991). *Agenda dynamics and policy subsystems. Journal of Politics, 5*(4), 1044–1074.

Baumgartner, F. R., & Jones, B. D. (1993). *Agendas and instability in American politics.* Chicago: University of Chicago Press.

Baumgartner, F. R., & Jones, B. D. (1994). Attention, boundary effects, and large-scale policy change in air transportation policy. In D. Rochefort & R. Cobb (Eds.), *The politics of problem definition: Shaping the policy agenda* (pp. 50–66). Lawrence: University Press of Kansas.

Blumer, H. (1971). Social problems as collective behavior. *Social Problems, 18*(3), 298–306.

Bosso, C. J. (1987). *Pesticides and politics: The life cycle of a public issue.* Pittsburgh, PA: University of Pittsburgh Press.

Burstein, P., & Bricher, M. (1997). Problem definition and public policy: Congressional committees confront work, family, and gender, 1945–1990. *Social Forces, 76*(1), 135–168.

California Reading Task Force (1995). *Every child a reader: Report of the California Reading Task Force* [Online]. Sacramento: California Department of Education.

Retrieved February 29, 2001, from the World Wide Web: http://www.cde.ca.gov/cilbranch/eltdiv/ everychild1.htm

Clinton, W. J. (1996, September 2). Remarks in Wyandotte, Michigan. *Weekly Compilation of Presidential Documents, 32*[Online], 1495–1588. Retrieved February 2, 1999, from 1996 Presidential Documents Online via GPO Access, on the World Wide Web: http://www.access.gpo.gov/nara/nara003.html

Cobb, R., & Elder, C. (1983). *Participation in American politics: The dynamics of agenda-building* (2nd ed.). Baltimore: Johns Hopkins University Press.

Coles, G. (2000). *Misreading reading: The bad science that hurts children.* Portsmouth, NH: Heinemann.

Dearing, J. W., & Rogers, E. M. (1996). *Agenda-setting.* Thousand Oaks, CA: Sage.

Elder, C. D., & Cobb, R. W. (1983). *The political uses of symbols.* New York: Longman.

Fuller, R. C., & Myers, R. R. (1941). The natural history of a social problem. *American Sociological Review, 6*(3), 320–329.

Goodman, K. (1998). *In defense of good teaching: What teachers need to know about the reading wars.* York, ME: Stenhouse.

Gusfield, J. R. (1981). *The culture of public problems: Drinking-driving and the symbolic order.* Chicago: University of Chicago Press.

Hilgartner, S., & Bosk, C. L. (1988). The rise and fall of social problems: A public arenas model. *American Journal of Sociology, 94*(1), 53–78.

Jones, B. D. (1994). *Reconceiving decision-making in democratic politics: Attention, choice, and public policy.* Chicago: University of Chicago Press.

Kingdon, J. W. (1995). *Agendas, alternatives, and public policies* (2nd ed.). New York: HarperCollins.

LaGanga, M. L. (2000, March 29). Bush vows to end illiteracy in U.S. children. *Los Angeles Times,* p. A1.

Mazur, A. (1981). Media coverage and public opinion on scientific controversies. *Journal of Communication, 31,* 106–116.

Mikulski, B. (1997, April 29). Senator Mikulski of Maryland speaking on the *America Reads Challenge Act,* S. 664, 105th Cong., 1st sess., *Congressional Record,* S.3801. Retrieved June 30, 2000, from the Library of Congress Thomas database on the World Wide Web: www.thomas.loc

Nelson, B. J. (1984). *Making an issue of child abuse: Political agenda setting for social problems.* Chicago: University of Chicago Press.

Patterson, S. C., & Caldeira, G. A. (1990). Standing up for Congress: Variations in public esteem since the 1960s. *Legislative Studies Quarterly, 15,* 25–47.

Petracca, M. P. (1992). Issue definitions, agenda-building, and policymaking. *Policy Currents, 2,* 1, 4.

Rochefort, D. A., & Cobb, R. W. (1994). Problem definition: An emerging perspective. In D. Rochefort & R. Cobb (Eds.), *The politics of problem definition: Shaping the policy agenda* (pp. 1–31). Lawrence: University Press of Kansas.

Schattschneider, E. E. (1960). *The semisovereign people: A realist's view of democracy in America.* New York: Rinehart and Winston.

Scheberle, D. (1994). Radon and asbestos: A study of agenda setting and causal stories. *Policy Studies Journal, 22*(1), 74–86.

Scheuer, J. (1987, April 28). Representative Scheuer of New York speaking on the *Trade and International Economic Policy Reform Act of 1987,* H.R. 3, 100th Cong.,

1st Sess., *Congressional Record*, H.2548. Retrieved June 29, 2000, from the Lexis-Nexis Congressional Universe database.

Shannon, P. (1984). Politics, policy, and reading research. In P. Pearson, R. Barr, M. Kamil, & P. Mosenthal (Eds.), *Handbook on reading research* (Vol. 2, pp. 147–167). New York: Longman.

Sharp, E. B. (1994). Paradoxes of national anitdrug policymaking. In D. Rochefort & R. Cobb (Eds.), *The politics of problem definition: Shaping the policy agenda* (pp. 98–116). Lawrence: University Press of Kansas.

Simon, H. A. (1983). *Reason in human affairs.* Stanford, CA: Stanford University Press.

Simon, H. A. (1985). Human nature in politics: The dialogue of psychology with political science. *American Political Science Review, 79,* 293–304.

Spector, M., & Kitsuse, J. I. (1977). *Constructing social problems.* Menlo Park, CA: Cummings.

Stone, D. A. (1989). Causal stories and the formation of policy agendas. *Political Science Quarterly, 104,* 281–300.

Taylor, D. (1998). *Beginning to read and the spin doctors of science: The political campaign to change America's mind about how children learn to read.* Urbana, IL: National Council of Teachers of English.

True, J. L., Jones, B. D., & Baumgartner, F. R. (1999). Punctuated-equilibrium theory: Explaining stability and change in American policymaking. In P. Sabatier (Ed.), *Theories of the policy process* (pp. 97–115). Boulder, CO: Westview Press.

Walker, J. L. (1977). Setting the agenda in the U.S. Senate: A theory of problem selection. *British Journal of Politics, 7,* 423–445.

Weaver, C. & Brinkley, E. H. (1998). Phonics, whole language, and the religious and political right. In K. Goodman (Ed.), *In defense of good teaching: What teachers need to know about the reading wars* (pp. 127–141). York, ME: Stenhouse.

Wildavsky, A. (1979). *Speaking the truth to power: The art and craft of policy analysis.* Boston: Little, Brown.

Willes, M. H., & Parks, M. (1998, October 18). Reading by 9: To our community: We all need to help teach our children. *Los Angeles Times,* p. A1.

CHAPTER 2

PRODUCTIVE CAMPUS LEADERSHIP RESPONSES TO ACCOUNTABILITY

Principals as Policy Mediators

Linda Skrla

ABSTRACT

This chapter presents evidence that campus principals can play productive roles as mediators of accountability policy and thereby influence student achievement on their campuses. The discussion is based on research interview data collected in four school districts that had demonstrated sustained, district-wide success in improving student performance and in closing historic achievement gaps.

> *Our principal was the only one that came to me and said, "What can I do to help you so you're not feeling this [accountability] pressure?"... It was just nice to know there's somebody out there that actually wants to help me instead of just saying, you can do it, don't worry about it, you can do it.*
>
> —elementary school teacher

Studies in Leading and Organizing Schools, pages 27–50
Copyright © 2003 by Information Age Publishing

At a time when accountability is reaching its zenith as the predominant force in U.S. educational policy, there is a critical need for research that carefully considers the full range of complexity associated with formulation, implementation, and modification of such policy, especially as these impact the education of groups of students who historically have benefited least from our schools—children of color and children from low-income families. To this end, several colleagues and I (both collaboratively and independently)[1] for the past five years have researched the implementation of accountability policy in a group of school districts that have demonstrated substantial, sustained, district-wide success in improving achievement and in closing achievement gaps.

Our focus in this research has been on learning from these positive examples of district-wide success how the belief systems, roles, and actions of district leaders, campus leaders, and teachers operate to improve schooling within the context of high-stakes accountability. We have reported in other venues various portions of our findings, including those related to superintendents and teachers (see Skrla, 2001b; Skrla & Scheurich, 2001; Skrla, Scheurich, & Johnson, 2000). The focus of this chapter, however, is on a group of leaders whose pivotal role in the mediation of accountability policy heretofore has received limited attention—campus principals. Understanding of the ways in which principals interact with accountability policy, particularly how they interpret and implement it productively to promote improved and more equitable student achievement, is sorely needed, given the present national focus on accountability, and given what past research has shown to be the central importance of the principal's role in school improvement. From earlier research, we know that principals influence a wide range of campus factors from the degree to which teachers accept direction (Kunz & Hoy, 1976) to students' engagement with school (Leithwood & Jantzi, 2000), to campus inclusiveness of diversity (González, 1998; Riehl, 2000), but their role in mediating current generation accountability policy has yet to be explored to any significant degree. This chapter is intended, then, as an exploratory step toward needed understanding of how principals use accountability policy in productive ways. This discussion begins with a brief review of relevant literature, which is followed by a section describing the studies from which the findings have been drawn. This is followed by a discussion of four areas in which principals mediate and utilize accountability policy to positively serve their schools and thereby improve student performance. The final section contains a brief conclusion.

BACKGROUND

Accountability and the Single Truth Wars

Accountability is the topic currently at the very forefront of research and debate in U.S. education policy circles. Its rising prominence throughout the decade of the 1990s has been further accelerated by the passage of the No Child Left Behind Act of 2001 (NCLB), the far-reaching federal legislation that heavily emphasizes accountability at the school, district, and state levels (Linn, Baker, & Betebenner, 2002). The success or failure of any such accountability policy, however, including NCLB, in improving student performance depends on a long and complicated succession of interpretation and implementation between the statehouse and classroom (Keating, 2000). Failure to attend to this great complexity in policy enactment can be counterproductive to the quality and credibility of scholarly debate around such issues, as Cohen and Hill (2001) point out:

> Policies that aim to improve teaching and learning depend on complex chains of causation.... Policy research that fails to make such distinctions [among extensive variations in types of implementation] can quite seriously mislead everyone about the nature and effects of policy. (pp. 8, 11)

Unfortunately, much of the recent debate about accountability policy in both the educational and popular press has given insufficient attention to these vagaries of implementation and has been instead polarized and often polemic, caught up in what Glickman (2001) called the "single truth wars" (p. 149).[2]

Accountability policy in these recent policy debates has been characterized as either a major success or, more commonly, as an complete failure, especially with respect to its impact on student achievement for children of color and children from low-income homes (see, e.g., Grissmer, Flanagan, Kawata, & Williamson, 2000; Haney, 2000; McNeil, 2000; Orfield & Wald, 2000). This type of dichotomized discourse does not allow for reasoned discussion of the full range of accountability policy's complex effects, nor does it acknowledge the possibility that negative effects can, and most often do, exist side-by-side with positive effects, as Adams and Kirst (1999) point out,

> When observers describe accountability mechanisms as problematic (Darling-Hammond, 1989), invalid and trivial (Sagor, 1996), or ineffective (Wilson, 1996), one wonders whether education's growing preoccupation with accountability might be counterproductive to the goals of school improvement. Though perhaps reasonable at first glance, that conclusion would be premature. Consider, for instance, the efficacy of educational accountability

mechanisms to ensure probity in school district accounts, depth of program offering, equity in resource distribution, or progress on desegregation. Similarly, accountability mechanisms have opened educational governance to public scrutiny. (p. 481)

The positive effects of accountability policy that Adams and Kirst cite are but a few among many that require more careful consideration than has been given in the past by researchers, policymakers, and practitioners, a point that my colleagues and I have argued at length elsewhere (see Skrla, 2001a; Scheurich & Skrla, 2001; Scheurich, Skrla, & Johnson, 2000).

Principals as Policy Mediators

All too often, regrettably, the discussion of campus principals' interaction with accountability policy has been characterized by the same type of polarization as has the larger accountability discourse. In the relatively small amount of discussion about principals and accountability that has appeared in the research literature and in the popular media, negative viewpoints have been predominate. This negativity has taken two main forms. One has been reports of the negative pressure accountability places of the job security of principals, on the perceived desirability of the role, and on the quality and quantity found in applicant pools (see, e.g., Gallegos, 2000; Keller, 1998). The second has been oft-repeated horror stories of heavy-handed principal behavior in response to accountability policy that resulted in squandered resources, narrowed curricula, and "deskilled" teachers. These latter portrayals of principals' responses to accountability have been, unfortunately, characterized as the unilateral and inevitable result of such policy (see McNeil, 2000, for a prominent example). In contrast, much less attention has been paid to unpacking the particular ways in which successful principals may utilize accountability policy in service of the educational aims of their schools and the ways in which such productive leadership responses might contribute to student success and increased educational equity.[3]

This is, then, an important area for research. As was emphasized earlier, accountability is a huge force in U.S. education at present, and the need for research-based understanding of how to differentiate between productive (as opposed to ineffective, inept, or even destructive) responses to it at all levels is enormous (Forsyth & Tallerico, 1998). However, achieving such understanding with respect to what principals do in relation to accountability policy is not a simple or easily accomplished task. In fact, pinning down what principals do to contribute to school improvement, in general, has been one of the ongoing challenges of educational leadership research. Though the basic belief that the leadership of campus principals has a major impact on schools and on student achievement within them is deeply imbedded in the conventional wisdom of the educational administration profession (Heck & Hallinger, 1999), it has only been recently that empirical evidence has begun to accumulate in support of that belief. Since about 1980, with the advent of improved research designs and increasingly sophisticated statistical methods, research has shown that principal leadership does have measurable effects on student performance—albeit small and mainly indirect ones (Hallinger & Heck, 1998; Leithwood & Jantzi, 2000; Riehl, 2000). These findings, however, "do not resolve the most important theoretical and practical issues concerning the means by which principals achieve an impact on school outcomes and how contextual forces influence the exercise of leadership in the schoolhouse" (Hallinger & Heck, 1998, p. 157). In other words, we continue to have limited understanding of the mechanisms by which principals exercise their leadership for the positive benefit of the students in their schools and how these mechanisms operate in relation to important contextual forces such as current configurations of accountability.

Though our understanding of specifics in this area may be limited, research conducted on earlier generations of educational policy provides useful background. For instance, we have learned that principals can play important roles as mediators in the interpretation and implementation of policy originating at all levels—district, state, and federal. Principals, thus, can be considered "street-level bureaucrats" (a term coined by Lipsky, 1972, 1980) in that they, like other public-sector workers who interact directly with citizens, "exercise considerable discretionary power in implementing public policy" (Haynes & Licata, 1995, p. 21). For example, Haynes and Licata (1995), in applying Lipsky's concept of street-level bureaucrat specifically to campus principals, characterized principals' roles in mediating policy as the practice of "creative insubordination." The authors defined this term as "a conscious effort by principals to ameliorate any negative consequences of a decision, policy, or programme that was developed at a higher level and adapt it in the most constructive way to the school's environment" (pp. 22–23). The principals Haynes and Licata studied, in other words, appropriated any policy coming to their campus from a higher level and ignored it, changed it, or used it as they thought best fit their campus's needs.

It seems likely that principals continue to practice street-level bureaucracy (or the art of creative insubordination) at present in what Adams and Kirst (1999) described as a time of "new educational accountability," in which accountability has "shifted from districts to schools, from compliance regarding inputs and practices to student performance, from comparative performance to performance against a standard of achievement" (p. 472).

Recent research has provided a few tantalizing clues about the ways in which principal mediation of this current incarnation of accountability policy may operate in a range of ways—from negatively to neutrally to positively. For example, McNeil (2000) related the story of a principal who left stacks of standardized test practice materials on teachers' desks and ordered teachers to suspend their regular curriculum in favor of test drills until further notice. Teachers in this school, understandably, felt deep frustration with what they saw as a leadership response to accountability that devalued their teaching skills and diminished their professionalism.

In contrast, a starkly different, more positive view of the mediation of accountability policy by principals appeared in the work of Hall (2001):

> There was no evidence in the women head-teachers study[4] of them feeling that they and their teacher colleagues were being forced to set aside their own value systems to respond to the demands of [accountability].... One explanation is that these women approached leading and managing schools in ways that protected teachers from feeling de-skilled and reinforced teachers' sense of professionalism.... I saw the women leaders using power, managing staff, and transforming some of the externally generated reforms for the benefit of the school. (pp. 19–20)

The principals in Hall's study, contrary to what the researchers had expected to find, were able to not only protect teachers from feeling deskilled due to the pressure of accountability policy but also to transform the pressure of external reform in ways that benefited the school.

Clearly, there is great need to understand better not only that positive mediation of accountability policy such as what the principals in Hall's study demonstrated is possible, but *how* it is possible (Hogan, 2001; Riester, Pursch, & Skrla, 2002). One potentially useful framework within which to achieve such understanding was developed by Hallinger and Heck (1998), who drew on earlier work by Ogawa and Bossert (1995) and Leithwood (1994). Based on the results of an extensive analysis of research conducted between 1980 and 1995 on principals' effect on student achievement, Hallinger and Heck suggested four "avenues of influence" (p. 171) through which principal leadership influences both individuals in schools and the organizational system in which the individuals work, thereby exerting indirect influence on school outcomes. These four areas were (a) purposes and goals, (b) structure and social networks, (c) people, and (d) organizational culture. These four avenues of influence form an analytic framework within which the role of principals as productive mediators of accountability policy can be examined. I have used these avenues of principal influence to frame the discussion that follows (after a brief section on methods) of how principals in four highly successful, highly diverse school districts used accountability policy for the positive benefit of their schools.

METHODS

The findings about principals' mediation of accountability policy discussed in this chapter have been drawn from a larger body of findings from a multiyear, multiphase, grant-funded research project with successful Texas public school districts.[5] This project had three phases—a pilot study conducted in 1997, a main study conducted in 1999–2000, and a follow-up study conducted in 2000–2001. The different phases involved collaborative research by professors and doctoral students from Texas A&M University, The University of Texas at Austin, and the University of Michigan.

Pilot Study

The pilot phase consisted of a set of exploratory interviews conducted onsite in 1997 with district officials (superintendents, school board members, central office staff, and principals) in each of 11 Texas public school districts (out of 1,045 districts in Texas, not including charter schools) that were identified for the pilot study using two screening criteria. The first criterion was a district enrollment over 5,000 students; the second was that one-third or more of high poverty campuses (schools at which more than 50% of students were eligible for federal free or reduced-price lunch assistance) in the district earned a "Recognized" or "Exemplary" rating in the state accountability system. To earn a Recognized rating in the Texas system, at least 80% of all students, as well as 80% of African American, Hispanic, white, and low-income students, must pass each section (reading, writing, and mathematics) of Texas Assessment of Academic Skill (TAAS) and meet additional dropout and attendance standards. To be rated Exemplary, schools and districts must have a 90% pass rate for all groups in all subjects tested on TAAS and meet attendance and dropout standards. The pilot study resulted in a report (see Ragland, Asera, & Johnson, 1999) that guided the design of the main study that followed.

Main Study

Site selection. Based on the results of the pilot study, grant funding was secured and a research project was designed to focus in-depth on four districts. The districts ultimately selected for the main study phase had student populations ranging from 8,000 to 50,000. These districts were chosen for study because they all had demonstrated significant improvement by children of color and children from low-income homes over a six-year period on Texas state achievement tests and because they had closed achievement gaps between the performance of these children and that of white and middle- and upper-income students. These districts were also selected based on a broad range of other quantitative evidence of improvement in academic performance for all student groups, including African American, Hispanic American, white, and economically disadvantaged students.

The selection process was multiphase, beginning with the same two criteria used for the pilot study, which, in 1997, produced a list of 11 districts. In 1999, when the main study began, this same initial screening process produced a list of 36 districts. The list was reduced to 17 by applying a third criterion—that at least two secondary (middle school or high school) campuses earned Recognized or Exemplary ratings.[6] A fourth criterion was then applied—the elimination of districts that had test exemption rates, dropout rates, or ninth-grade retention rates that were above the mean rates for other schools with similar demographic characteristics. This left 11 districts under consideration. For these 11 districts, disaggregated student performance data from 1994 through 1998 on indicators other than TAAS was evaluated for evidence of improved achievement and narrowed performance gaps among groups. These indicators included passing rates on Algebra end-of-course tests,[7] percentage of students taking advanced placement courses and scoring above the criterion for earning college credit on the exams, percentage of students completing the college-preparatory Texas Recommended High School Program,[8] and percentage of students taking SAT/ACT exams and exceeding the criterion score for admission to a Texas state college or university.[9]

None of the districts still under consideration in this phase had demonstrated the same degree of improvement on these higher-end academic measures as they had on TAAS, but seven of the 11 districts remaining on the list for consideration had made significant progress in at least one of these areas. From this list of seven finalists districts, four were selected to include the racial, geographic, economic, and district size diversity of Texas as much as possible. The four districts selected were Aldine Independent School District (ISD), Brazosport ISD, San Benito Consolidated Independent School District (CISD), and Wichita Falls ISD. Only one district (Brazosport) chosen for study was also included in the pilot study. Aldine was identified as one of the 11 high-success districts in 1997, but did not participate in the pilot phase of the project. Brief profiles of the four districts follow.

Participant districts. Aldine ISD is one of the 12 largest school districts in Texas, with 60 campuses and almost 53,000 students. It is located in the northwest Houston metropolitan area and covers 111 square miles. Its schools serve a variety of communities, including rural, suburban, commercial, and industrial areas. The student population is 52% Hispanic, 35%

African American, 10% white, and 71% economically disadvantaged. The district earned a Recognized accountability rating in 2001–2002 for the sixth consecutive year.

Brazosport ISD is located on the Texas gulf coast, 50 miles southwest of Houston, and serves a diverse group of small towns and communities. About 50,000 residents live in the area, and the school district's enrollment is 13,161 students. The children in Brazosport ISD are 54% white, 36% Hispanic, 10% African American, and 41% economically disadvantaged. Brazosport has been rated Exemplary for the past five years and was rated Recognized for the two previous years.

San Benito CISD is located in the Rio Grande Valley area of South Texas, seven miles east of the small city of Harlingen. The primary industry for the area is agriculture. The town of San Benito has a population of 26,350; the school district serves 8,864 pupils. The students in San Benito CISD are 97% Hispanic, 3% white, and 87% economically disadvantaged. The district has held a Recognized accreditation rating for seven consecutive years, beginning in 1995–1996.

Wichita Falls ISD is located in northwest Texas, approximately 100 miles north of the Dallas–Fort Worth metroplex. The city of Wichita Falls has approximately 100,000 residents and is home to Sheppard Air Force Base, Midwestern State University, and a variety of petroleum- and agriculture-based industries. Wichita Falls ISD has 15,031 students; 62% are white, 19% are Hispanic, 16% are African American, and 46% are economically disadvantaged. In 2001–2002 WFISD earned a Recognized rating for the second time.

Data collection and analysis. A team of six researchers (three professors and three doctoral students) conducted onsite, qualitative research in the four districts in fall 1999 and spring 2000. While in the districts, the researchers interviewed board members, superintendents, central office staff, principals, teachers, parents, newspaper staff, and business leaders. They also shadowed district staff and principals, observed classrooms, and attended community functions. The research team audio-recorded over 200 individual and group interviews and collected thousands of pages of observation notes and documents. Data analysis began on the first day of the first site visit, included twice daily team-debriefing sessions, and continued for six months following the completion of site visits. The research team also utilized qualitative research software, Folio Views 4.2, to assist in the identification of findings from the large volume of interview transcripts and documents. For a longer, more in-depth discussion of the study methodology, see Skrla, Scheurich, and Johnson (2000)

Follow-Up Study

A follow-up study with one of the participant districts, Aldine, was conducted during 2000–2001, which focused specifically on the relationship between teachers' perceptions of collective efficacy and student performance in an urban district making significant progress in closing achievement gaps. I conducted this follow-up study in collaboration with a colleague from the University of Michigan and two doctoral students. The research had both quantitative and qualitative phases; the findings will be reported in forthcoming papers (Goddard & Skrla, 2002; Skrla & Goddard, 2002).

RESULTS

The four districts that were the focus of study were not (and still are not) average or typical school districts. They were, in fact, selected for study for that very reason—they had all demonstrated progress in improving achievement and in closing historic achievement gaps to a greater degree than had other districts serving diverse student populations in Texas. Some critics of this study have suggested that these districts are, in fact, "outliers" and are, therefore, not useful examples of what kind of progress can be made toward the realization of educational equity goals since the majority of other, similar, districts have not made the same kind of progress under similar circumstances (see Valencia, Valenzuela, Sloan, & Foley, 2001). My colleagues and I emphatically reject this outlier characterization of the districts we studied. Labeling districts that are successful in educating children of color and children from low-income families outliers is a form of deficit thinking (Valencia, 1997). That is, it is based on the assumption that schools and districts serving racially and economically diverse students will inevitably perform at the bottom of achievement rankings and that any school or district (and the school personnel and children in it) that departs from this norm is automatically suspect (see Scheurich & Skrla, 2001). Edmonds's (1979, 1986) groundbreaking work on effective schools received the same type of criticism; in fact, this sort of criticism has been a typical response whenever research has reported on classrooms and schools in which children of color perform at high levels (Skrla, 2001a).

Though this deficit-oriented labeling of schools that are successful in educating for children of color as outliers may be a typical criticism, it is not a valid one. The four Texas districts that were the focus of our research, in the view of my colleagues and I, were not outliers found at the extreme end of a bell curve on which all possible school districts were arranged. They were, instead, a new, different model of a school district, one in which the district as an institution had shifted away from the traditional, business-as-usual focus on maintenance of the appearance of success (Rowan & Miskel, 1999) toward a genuine organizational commitment to producing both excellence and equity in educational outcomes for the children of all families in the district. Rorrer (2002), based on her award-winning research,[10] has described new model school districts such as the ones in our study as organizations that have "institutionalized new equity scripts."

The discussion of principals as productive policy mediators contained in this chapter is, then, based on data collected in a particular context—districts focused on educational excellence and equity. That districts can and do play an important role in contributing to successful policy implementation has been documented by other researchers such as Spillane (1998, 2002). Thus, the interviews that served as the basis for the discussion contained in this chapter were conducted with principals and teachers in a district context that was success oriented. Each of the four districts had had multiple-year success in increasing student achievement and in closing historic achievement gaps. For example, the Wichita Falls district had raised passing rates district-wide on the mathematics portion of TAAS for African American students from 34% in 1994 to 87% in 2002. In Aldine, the passing rate for Hispanic students on the rigorous Algebra end-of-course exam had risen from 16% in 1994 to 70% in 2001, a figure that was 32 percentage points higher than the 38% passing rate for Hispanic students statewide that same year. In addition, the lowest passing rate for any group (African Americans, Hispanics, whites, economically disadvantaged students) on any portion of TAAS (reading, writing, and mathematics) was 94.1% in 2002 in Brazosport. In San Benito in 2000, 80% of students classified as economically disadvantaged (who comprised 87% of all students in the district) graduated from high school (with a regular diploma, not including those earning a GED) in four years, compared to a 73% graduation rate for the same students statewide.

It is important to remember this type of district context in making sense of how our interviewees thought about accountability and how principals in these districts acted as policy mediators to productively serve their schools. These districts were exemplars of success, and from them there is much to learn. I turn now to a discussion of the ways in which principals in the study districts productively mediated accountability policy, using the avenues of principal influence identified by Hallinger and Heck (1998).

Avenue of Influence #1: Purposes and Goals

According to Hallinger and Heck (1998), "Principals' involvement in framing, conveying and sustaining the schools' purposes and goals represent an important domain of *indirect* influence on school outcomes [emphasis original]" (p. 171). The concept that principals' work in setting and communicating challenging goals for their schools can positively impact student success is not new. In fact, the phrase "high expectations," taken from Edmonds (1979, 1986) and Lezotte's (1992) correlates of effective schools, has passed into the vernacular of the profession to such a degree that it is found somewhere in the mission statement of virtually every school. Parroting the rhetoric of high expectations and actually having them are two distinctly different things, however, and principals who successfully appropriate the tools accountability provides to help set and reinforce school purposes and goals that include high expectations for the success of literally all students do so in particular ways that other principals do not.

First of all, the principals in our study districts themselves accepted the responsibility for equitably educating all of their students, and they appreciated the role that accountability played in setting the expectation of achievement for every child. This point was compellingly articulated by an elementary principal at a majority low-income campus who participated in our interviews:

> Part of the change [in the district] is obviously accountability. I think that's one positive thing about the assessment system in Texas is that people finally are being held accountable for teaching kids that are in poverty.... There is a yardstick that's going to measure all kids and that's going to not take the excuse that "Well, their home situation isn't the same so we're not going to have the expectation from them."... The expectation is there. The expectation is the same, regardless of color, regardless of economic status. There is a high expectation for achievement for every student.

This principal stated clearly her view that accountability was useful in leveraging the goal that she held for her own school—teaching all students and not making excuses. She did not hold a deficit view of the educability of the children in her school, and she welcomed the role the state assessment played in holding people accountable for the education of children who formerly were not expected to learn.

How principals such as the one quoted above view accountability and its relationship to appropriate (and achievable) goals for their schools is extremely important because principals' opinions have additional weight in the campus discourse, as Riehl (2000) pointed out:

> Schools are, in effect, constructed around the meanings that people hold about them. Real organizational change occurs not simply when technical changes in structure and process are undertaken, but when persons inside and outside of the school construct new understandings about what the change means. In this regard, the role of the school principal is crucial.

Although meanings are negotiated socially, that is through a shared process (Miron, 1997), leaders typically have additional power in defining situations and their meanings.

This point—that principals have extra power in defining meanings (in this case, goals) in schools—was well illustrated by the numerous statements made by teachers in the study districts in response to a question asked in teacher focus groups about what had changed on their campuses from the time when students were less successful and achievement gaps were larger. For example, a middle school teacher told us:

I think the positive outlook of our principals has made a big difference. Just that we've decided that all kids can learn. Not that we ever not believed that, but we enforce it to the kids and say, "You have to know this. You have to learn it." I think that's the biggest difference.

Another teacher at this same campus described the link between leadership, accountability, and campus goals this way:

We have instructional leaders who focus on the data.... I guess what we've done is say, "Okay, the state of Texas has said to us and mandated that we will teach this to the seventh grade." And instructional leaders, principals...all sat down [with us] and said, "Let's decide what our goals are. Not just on paper but what they are really. What is it going to take to achieve those goals?" Then we set up a machine that achieves those goals. Our motto is, "Whatever it takes."

Another, similar comment was made by an elementary teacher at a Title I distinguished school in a different district:

It [the belief that all students can be successful] trickles down from the top, our principal.... I know that I would jump off the Empire State Building for him. Because I know what he wants. And I know he expects it, and he believes that we can do it. And it kind of just makes you work harder and do it.

And, finally, a high school teacher in a third district had this to say about the principal's role in using accountability measures to set and communicate goals for the school:

I'll say one thing [that has changed] is the push from the principal's office. Student performance is their major concern. They are concerned about the dropout rates; they're concerned about the attendance rate and it filters down. Sometimes not so gently, but it filters down.

Clearly, the teachers in these districts understood that the primary goal on their campuses was student success for all students and all student groups. These teachers also defined this success in terms of elements monitored by the accountability system (test performance, attendance, dropout rates), and they attributed the origination of these student success goals based on accountability measures, at least in part, to their principals.

Avenue of Influence #2: Structure and Social Networks

The second avenue of principal influence that Hallinger and Heck (1998) identified as impacting student achievement was structure and social networks. They argued that "Leadership enhances organizational performance and survival by affecting social structures, the regularized aspects of relationships existing among participants in an organization" (p. 173). In this area, principals' leadership can affect school outcomes positively by influencing the relationships and patterns of interactions among other adults involved in the schooling process, such as teachers and parents. For example, principals can have positive influence in this area by "providing support for individual teachers, fostering cooperation, and assisting them to work together toward the fulfillment of identified school goals" (p. 174).

Principals in the high performing schools in our study utilized accountability policy in this area in several ways. For instance, the research team heard repeatedly from teachers about the ways in which campus leaders had restructured teachers' work days to allow collaborative planning time. During this planning time, teachers worked together to collaboratively address the learning needs of their students. These needs were in each instance defined by individual students' progress toward curriculum standards measured by the state assessment or by other measures reported through the state accountability system such as the Algebra end-of-course test or the attendance rate or the dropout rate.

This point is illustrated by the following comment from an intermediate school teacher about the new organizational structure of her school that resulted from increased focus on student achievement created by accountability:

> We've become more focused on what we want to achieve.... Block scheduling and academic teaming has had a lot to do with a good portion of our success. When I say that, first of all, as a team we're able to work with a smaller group in math and language. I can reach 75 [students each day] more effectively than I can reach 150. I've got more time and energy to devote to their needs. In an area where it's high poverty, you just cannot give 150 the kind of attention you can give 75. The second thing, as a team we communicate what's going on in math to the science teacher. So when the science teacher is teaching something that can impact what I do, it's a team effort to work with that 75.... With double dosing, seeing them every day for 90 minutes, you're

able to spend more time on a concept while you have them as a captive audience to teach to mastery rather than hitting and missing.

As this teacher described the situation at her school, the teachers used both block scheduling and academic teaming (two commonly recommended "best practices" for middle schools) not for the sake of having trendy practices, but because the benefits of these arrangements (collaboration among teachers and time to teach to mastery) allowed them to help each student on their team succeed on clearly delineated learning goals that were tied to curriculum standards and the state assessments.

Another exchange among a research interviewer and a group of elementary teachers at a campus with a very high percentage of students from low-income families illustrates the type of talk that was common in our interviews about how the campus leadership's structuring of campus interaction to meet the demands of accountability increased collaboration and a fostered a sense of accomplishment among teachers who formerly had worked mainly in isolation:

Researcher: Going back to the high expectations, the pressure of what's expected of you as a teacher. How is that working for you compared to in the past? You all said that the expectations have gone up a lot. How are you all experiencing the pressure of that?

Teacher #1: Well, there's lots of pressure, but there are also more rewards for doing more, going the extra step. That's a way of dealing with it.

Teacher #2: I just see, as a special ed teacher, I see more collaborative effort between regular teachers. I work with all regular teachers that my kids are in their class, and I see them, when one is getting really bogged down or really stressed over this, how to incorporate this or how to maneuver around all this stuff that we're doing now, they pull together more. And then I get in there and we all pull together as a team. I see more collaboration between teachers and support between teachers, pulling together.

Teacher #3: Collaboration—that's the key word. There is pressure. I will venture to say we teach harder than any teachers I know, but it's a good pressure. It's a good pressure. The teamwork...I was at a meeting and I made this comment about my school; I said I wouldn't miss it for the world. I wouldn't miss this for the world, what I'm going through. It's made me a much better teacher. It's made

> me really care about the kids, each child. I don't want
> them to fail. The children pick up on this.... The inclu-
> sion students coming out of content mastery, they're
> motivated now. Our kids are motivated. It's a fact now,
> we're motivated. Work, yes it is a lot of work for us, but
> it's a good work.

This exchange stands in sharp contrast to other portrayals in the research
literature of teachers who felt deskilled or oppressed by the responses to
the requirements of accountability on their campuses. Rather than feeling
deskilled, this group of teachers felt stronger connections to one another
and a deep pride of accomplishment that resulted from the new organization of their work to meet the demands of accountability.

Avenue of Influence #3: People

A third avenue of principal influence on school outcomes, according to
Hallinger and Heck (1998), is through the people in the organization: "A
major impact of principal efforts is to produce changes in people.... Principal effects are achieved through fostering group goals, modeling desired
behavior for other, providing intellectual stimulation, and individualized
support" (p. 175). This differs from the second avenue of principal influence discussed above, structure and social networks, in that the concern in
this "people" dimension is the principal's relationships with and influence
on individuals rather than on the relationships and structures between and
among others in his or her school.

The examples of the ways in which principals in our study districts used
accountability policy to influence people in order to positively impact their
schools were numerous. For instance, a high school teacher commented
favorably about specific, positive feedback from principals on not only
areas in which teachers needed improvement but on areas in which they
were doing well:

> I think the positive attitudes of the principals we have now [are important];
> they are constantly saying, "Thank you, staff. You're doing a good job. We
> appreciate you." And, you know, I really believe that people work harder
> when they think they're appreciated, than when they're told what they're
> doing wrong. Not that we don't all need to know how we can progress, but, if
> we feel we're appreciated, that makes people work even harder.

In addition to using accountability measures as a basis for specific cor-
rective feedback on and praise of teachers' work as in the example above,
principals in our study used curriculum standards and assessment data to

support a dialogic form of supervision that not only assessed teachers' progress but also allowed principals to provide support and assistance to teachers in a more focused way than had been typical in the past. An example of how this sort of supervision worked was provided by a middle school principal of a campus serving virtually 100% Hispanic students from low-income homes that was one of the first campuses in his district to achieve a Recognized rating:

> I'll meet with my teachers five or six times throughout the year just to see, individually with them, just to see how they're doing with their students. And I basically ask them, "What's your plan to do this?" And they'll give me their plans. And then throughout the year, at least once in each six weeks we'll sit down and we'll meet and I'll say, "How are your students progressing? Do you need extra help? Do I need to assign somebody to help you?" And we have the instructional coaches that work in the central office area that come in and help the teachers. So, it is a lot easier than before accountability, and I've been in this business for 23 years. Before the state accountability came in, it was sort of a hit-or-miss situation.

Still another example of how principals in these study districts used accountability measures to positively influence the people on their campuses was provided in the extended quote below from a high school principal talking about how he addressed a problem that is extremely common at the high school level—intellectual elitism among department chairpersons:

> I've stressed to the teachers that we don't have any second class citizens; kids are what we have, and everybody deserves a fair chance, whether he or she is Hispanic, black, or white, it doesn't matter. I've seen a change this year. ... And probably the world's worst was our math department chairperson. She teaches all AP classes, and she fought adamantly for SAT/ACT, National Merit Scholar, everything because that's all she knew, that's all she taught. Her philosophy last year held down the rest of the faculty, but this year I finally convinced her that we can do both. We can do TAAS and SAT and National Merit Scholars, we can do both. And I think probably just since November of this year, her attitude has changed completely and that's affected everybody. She's helped us tremendously on TAAS this year. Last year, she absolutely refused; she wasn't going to do TAAS.

> How I got this change was at several faculty meetings, I emphasized that we have the highest SAT scores of any district around us; we have more National Merit Scholars than any high school in Texas except one.... And I looked at her every time I said it.... She wrote me a letter saying, "Thanks so much for bringing up the fact that our scores are so high." She had felt like all the emphasis was being placed on the lower level kids; she felt like the upper level had been neglected.... And I think I finally convinced her that you can

do both. You can have teachers who are AP teachers and teach that curriculum up there on a college level where they can get in A&M or Texas and do well. But at the same time, you have these kids who've been struggling and failing all of their lives. They've got to have a chance to do as well as they can do. So she's finally turned around. And I've worked on her for quite a bit too...because I knew she was the key. She was the department head; she'd been there 25 years.

This example of a principal appropriating the force of state accountability to make a positive change with a teacher who held great power and influence on his campus is particularly noteworthy. This principal, consciously and deliberately, used positive data on a high-end accountability measure (SAT scores and National Merit Scholars) as leverage (in addition to measures more traditionally focused on such as state achievement test results) to encourage a resistant teacher to become more cooperative with campus efforts to improve student performance for students this campus had formerly failed to serve well.

Avenue of Influence #4: Organizational Culture

According to Hallinger and Heck (1998), drawing from Leithwood, Jantzi, Silins, and Dart (1993), school culture can be conceptualized as "widespread agreement about norms, beliefs, and values" (p. 177). The importance of school leaders in creating a campus culture that supports high and equitable student success has been explored in depth and detail elsewhere by a number of scholars, among them Deal and Peterson (1999) in their excellent book *Shaping School Culture: The Heart of Leadership.*

The importance of the avenue of influence, though, cannot be overemphasized. The creation of a school culture that respected, valued, and expected achievement from literally all of its students was an essential ingredient in the success of the schools we studied. One elementary principal of a high performing school serving mainly African American children described the culture—the shared agreement about norms, beliefs, and values—on her campus this way:

I think it's just a feeling you get when you walk through the doors of our building. It's the belief. It's what you see from the children when you enter the classrooms. It's the attitudes of the teachers and how much energy they're putting into everything that they do. It's the demeanor they have with the children. It's the attitude of whatever it takes to make children successful, we're willing to do that. It's just everything we do focuses on one thing and that's student success and believing that they can do it.

As this principal so clearly articulated, at her school everything focused on success for all students, and this permeated all aspects of the school culture.

The links between this type of school culture that was focused on success for all students, principal leadership, and the state accountability system were also clearly articulated by two high school teachers in a focus group interview. The first teacher described these linkages this way:

> It [focus on student success] came down from the principals.... They said, "This is what's expected, and our students can do this." And so the people who had always felt that felt very encouraged. And the people that didn't feel that way were kind of on the outs because this is the new philosophy we're having and those really strong teachers who always expected that of their kids really overpowered the people that weren't interested. So it became that the accepted thing to do was to have the high expectations. And the unaccepted thing to do would be the slacker teacher.

The second teacher elaborated on the change in culture at this high school:

> I've been with this school since the fall of 1973. So I've seen a *huge* number of changes in attitude. And I think the thing I like the best in the last few years that I've seen is the sense that we are all in this together. That we are all here to help each other. That it is not my department or my subject matter, but that we all work together. That what we do in our department affects the success or failure rate in other departments. That we need to each improve. That we need to each encourage students skill-wise, attitude-wise. Also, I see on this campus a lot more genuine concern about students and about what happens to them. About what their life is going to be like when they leave high school.

That the school culture at this high school had changed due to the influences of campus leadership and state accountability was not in question for either of these teachers. Furthermore, these quotes are even more compelling when one considers that they were taken from an interview with teachers at an urban high school that held a Recognized accountability rating and was peopled almost entirely by children of color. The culture at this campus had changed, due to leadership and accountability, from one of isolation and negativity toward the children it served to one of collaboration and commitment to the success of all students.

CONCLUSION

The accountability road that begins with the passage of policy initiatives in statehouses and ends with implementation in classrooms is a long, winding one that is filled with shortcuts, detours, and obstacles. Along the way, however, there are numerous individuals and groups that can erect additional barriers, stand idly by, or help pave the way. Insufficient attention has been paid thus far in education policy research to those in the latter category. Principals, especially, are important and opportune positions to help pave the way for the positive benefits of accountability to reach their intended destination—students whose learning might improve and become more equitable.

In this chapter, I've offered evidence, based on research interview data collected in four highly successful, highly diverse school districts, that principals can act as productive mediators of accountability policy to benefit student achievement and equity in their schools. Through four avenues of influence—(a) purposes and goals, (b) structure and social networks, (c) people, and (d) organizational culture—principals can appropriate the force of accountability and use it to influence both individuals and the organizational structure of their schools and, thereby, raise achievement and narrow achievement gaps. If, truly, no child in U.S. schools is to be left behind, then it is critically important that principals in all schools learn how to interact with accountability policy and to use it for the benefit of their campuses in the same way that the campus leaders profiled in this chapter learned to do.

NOTES

1. The colleagues to whom I refer here include James Joseph Scheurich at the University of Texas at Austin; Joseph F. Johnson, Jr., of the U.S. Department of Education; and James W. Koschoreck at the University of Cincinnati.

2. Accountability is not the only topic about which U.S. educational debates have been polarized. Glickman (2001) notes that research and policy analysis about standards, student motivation, learning theory, and reading instruction, among other topics, have been similarly dichotomized.

3. For exceptions, see Bushman, Goodman, Brown-Welty, and Dorn (2001) and George (2001).

4. "Head teacher" is the terminology used in the United Kingdom for the role known in the United States as campus principal.

5. Funding for the project was provided by the Sid W. Richardson Foundation, a private foundation located in Fort Worth, Texas, and by a Seed Grant from the Texas A&M College of Education.

6. The great majority of Texas campuses earning Recognized or Exemplary ratings in both 1997 and 1999 were elementary schools. The requirement of evidence of secondary school success was intended to ensure that improvement was occurring district-wide rather than falling off after sixth grade.

7. This test has a high level of difficulty; the percentage of all Texas students passing this test in 1999 was 43.4 (Texas Education Agency, 1999).

8. The Recommended High School program requires students to take a more rigorous set of courses than the minimum high school program, including four credits of English, three credits of mathematics (Algebra, Geometry, Algebra II), three credits of science, four credits of social studies and economics, two credits of a language other than English, and a variety of other coursework including speech, technology applications, physical education, fine arts, and electives in specialized areas (Title 19 Texas Administrative Code, Part II, §74.12).

9. The criterion scores used by the Texas Education Agency for these measures are 1110 on SAT and 24 on SAT.

10. Rorrer's (2002) research with successful school districts serving children from low-income families in Texas and North Carolina won the 2002 AERA Division A Dissertation of the Year award.

REFERENCES

Adams, J. E., & Kirst, M. W. (1999). New demands and concepts for educational accountability: Striving for results in an era of excellence. In J. Murphy & K. S. Louis (Eds.), *Handbook of research on educational administration* (2nd ed., pp. 463–490). San Francisco: Jossey-Bass.

Bushman, J., Goodman, G., Brown-Welty, S., & Dorn, S. (2001). California testing: How principals choose priorities. *Educational Leadership, 59*(1), 33–36.

Cohen, D. K., & Hill, H. C. (2001). *Learning policy: When state education reform works.* New Haven, CT: Yale University Press.

Darling-Hammond, L. (1989). Accountability for professional practice. *Teachers College Record, 91,* 59–80.

Deal, T. E., & Peterson, K. D. (1999). *Shaping school culture: The heart of leadership.* San Francisco: Jossey-Bass.

Edmonds, R. R. (1979). Effective schools for the urban poor. *Educational Leadership, 37*(1), 15–18, 20–24.

Edmonds, R. R. (1986). Characteristics of effective schools. In U. Neisser (Ed.), *The school achievement of minority children: New perspectives* (pp. 93–104). Hillsdale, NJ: Erlbaum.

Forsyth, P. B., & Tallerico, M. (1998). Accountability and city school leadership. *Education and Urban Society, 30*(4).

Gallegos, K. (2000). Paying the price to put students first. *Thrust for Educational Leadership, 29*(4), 33.

George, P. S. (2001). A+ accountability in Florida. *Educational Leadership, 59*(1), 28–32.

Glickman, C. D. (2001). Dichotomizing education: Why no one wins and America loses. *Phi Delta Kappan, 83*(2), 147–152.

Goddard, R., & Skrla, L. (2002, November). *The influence of school composition on teacher perceptions of collective efficacy.* Paper presented at the annual convention of the University Council for Educational Administration, Pittsburgh, PA.

González, M. L. (1998). Successfully educating Latinos: The pivotal role of the principal. In M. L. González, A. Huerta-Macías, & J. V. Tinajero (Eds.), *Educat-*

ing Latino students: A guide to successful practice (pp. 3–29). Lancaster, PA: Technomic.

Grissmer, D., Flanagan, A., Kawata, J., & Williamson, S. (2000). *Improving student achievement: What NAEP state test scores tell us.* Santa Monica, CA: RAND.

Hall, V. (2002). Reinterpreting entrepreneurship in education: A gender perspective. In C. Reynolds (Ed.), *Women and school leadership: International perspectives.* Albany: State University of New York Press.

Hallinger, P., & Heck, R. H. (1998). Exploring the principal's contribution to school effectiveness: 1980–1995. *School Effectiveness and School Improvement, 9*(2), 157–191.

Haney, W. (2000). The myth of the Texas miracle in education. *Education Policy Analysis Archives, 8*(41) [Online]. Available: http://epaa.asu.edu/epaa/v8n41/

Haynes, E. A., & Licata, J. W. (1995). Creative insubordination of school principals and the legitimacy of the justifiable. *Journal of Educational Administration, 33*(4), 21–35.

Heck, R. H., & Hallinger, P. (1999). Next generation methods for the study of leadership and school improvement. In J. Murphy & K. S. Louis (Eds.), *Handbook of research on educational administration* (2nd ed., pp. 141–162). San Francisco: Jossey-Bass.

Hogan, D. D. (2001). *Principals as change agents: Campus leadership in Texas public school districts achieving district-wide success serving children of color and children of poverty.* Doctoral dissertation, Texas A&M University.

Keating, P. (2000, April). *Understanding standards.* Paper presented at the annual meeting of the American Educational Research Association, New Orleans, LA.

Keller, B. (1998). In age of accountability, principals feel the heat. *Education Week, 17*(36), 1–2.

Kunz, D. W., & Hoy, W. K. (1976). Leadership style of principals and the professional zone of acceptance of teachers. *Educational Administration Quarterly, 12*(3), 49–64.

Leithwood, K. (1994). Leadership for school restructuring. *Educational Administration Quarterly, 30,* 498–518.

Leithwood, K., & Jantzi, D. (2000). Principal and teacher leadership effects: A replication. *School Leadership and Management, 20*(4), 415–434.

Leithwood, K., Jantzi, D., Silins, H., & Dart, B. (1993). Using the appraisal of school leaders as an instrument for school restructuring. *Peabody Journal of Education, 68,* 85–109.

Lezotte, L. W. (1992). "Principal" insights from effective schools. *Education Digest, 58*(3), 14–16.

Linn, R. L., Baker, L., & Betebenner, D. W. (2002). Accountability systems: Implications of requirements of the No Child Left Behind Act of 2001. *Educational Researcher, 31*(6), 3–16.

Lipsky, M. (1972). Toward a theory of street-level bureaucracy. *Journal of Politics, 34,* 3–25.

Lipsky, M. (1980). *Street-level bureaucracy.* New York: Russell Sage Foundation.

McNeil, L. M. (2000). Creating new inequalities: Contradictions of reform. *Phi Delta Kappan, 81*(10), 728–734.

Miron, L. F. (1997). *Resisting discrimination: Affirmative strategies for principals and teachers.* Thousand Oaks, CA: Corwin.

No Child Left Behind Act of 2001, Pub. L. No. 107-100. Retrieved August 20, 2002, from http://www.ed.gov/legislation/ESEA02/

Ogawa, R. T., & Bossert, S. T. (1995). Leadership as an organizational quality. *Educational Administration Quarterly, 31*(2), 224–243.

Orfield, G., & Wald, J. (2000, June 5). Testing, testing. *The Nation* [Online]. Available: www.thenation.com/issue/000605/0605orfield.shtml

Ragland, M. A., Asera, R., & Johnson, J. F. (1999). *Urgency, responsibility, efficacy: Preliminary findings of a study of high-performing Texas school districts* [Online]. Retrieved August 18, 2002, from http://www.starcenter.org/pdf/urgency.pdf

Riehl, C. J. (2000). The principal's role in creating inclusive schools for diverse students: A review of normative, empirical, and critical literature on the practice of educational administration. *Review of Educational Research, 70*(1), 55–81.

Riester, A. F., Pursch, V., & Skrla, L. (2002). Principals for social justice: Leaders of school success for children from low-income homes. *Journal of School Leadership, 12*(3), 281–304.

Rorrer, A. K. (2002, April). *Leadership and equity: From reproduction to reconstruction.* Paper presented at the annual meeting of the American Educational Research Association, New Orleans, LA.

Rowan, B., & Miskel, C. G. (1999). Institutional theory and the study of educational organizations. In J. Murphy & K. S. Louis (Eds.), *Handbook of research on educational administration* (2nd ed., pp. 359–383). San Francisco: Jossey-Bass.

Sagor, R. (1996). *Local control and accountability: How to get it, keep it, and improve school performance.* Thousand Oaks, CA: Sage.

Scheurich, J. J., & Skrla, L. (2001). Continuing the conversation on equity and accountability. *Phi Delta Kappan, 83*(4), 322–326.

Scheurich, J. J., Skrla, L., & Johnson, J. F. (2000). Thinking carefully about equity and accountability. *Phi Delta Kappan, 82*(4), 293–299.

Skrla, L. (2001a). Accountability, equity, and complexity. *Educational Researcher, 30*(4), 15–21.

Skrla, L. (2001b). The influence of state accountability on teacher expectations and student performance. *UCEA Review, XLII*(2), 1–4.

Skrla, L., & Goddard, R. (2002, November). *Accountability, equity, and collective efficacy in an urban school district: A mixed-methods study.* Paper presented at the annual convention of the University Council for Educational Administration, Pittsburgh, PA.

Skrla, L., & Scheurich, J. J. (2001). Displacing deficit thinking in school district leadership. *Education and Urban Society, 33*(3), 235–259.

Skrla, L., Scheurich, J. J., & Johnson, J. F. (2000). *Equity-driven, achievement-focused school districts: A report on systemic school success in four Texas school districts serving diverse populations* [Onine]. Available: www.utdanacenter.org/products/equity-districts.pdf

Spillane, J. P. (1998). A cognitive perspective on the role of the local educational agency in implementing instructional policy: Accounting for local variability. *Educational Administration Quarterly, 34*(1), 31–57.

Spillane, J. P. (2002). Local theories of teacher change: The pedagogy of district policies and program. *Teachers College Record, 104*(3), 377–420.

Texas Education Agency (TEA). (1999). *Academic Excellence Indicator System 1998-1999 state performance report* [Online]. Retrieved August 21, 2002, from http://www.tea.state.tx.us/ perfreport/aeis/99/state.html

Valencia, R. R. (1997). *The evolution of deficit thinking.* London: Falmer.

Valencia, R. R., Valenzuela, A., Sloan, K., & Foley, D. E. (2001). Let's treat the cause, not the symptoms: Equity and accountability in Texas revisited. *Phi Delta Kappan, 83*(4) 318–326.

Wilson, T.A. (1996). *Reaching for a better standard: English school inspection and the dilemma of accountability for American schools.* New York: Teachers College Press.

CHAPTER 3

SOURCES AND CONSEQUENCES OF ORGANIC MANAGEMENT IN ELEMENTARY AND SECONDARY SCHOOLS[1]

Robert J. Miller and Brian Rowan

ABSTRACT

We examined the causes and consequences of organic management patterns in elementary and secondary schools within a contingency theory framework, using hierarchical linear modeling (HLM) and data from the National Education Longitudinal Study (NELS: 88), Prospects: The Congressionally-Mandated Study of Educational Opportunity, and the Schools and Staffing Survey (SASS: '93–'94). Focusing on indicators of administrative support, staff cooperation, and teacher control, we found that managerial arrangements vary by schooling level, although the effects were not consistently in the direction hypothesized by contingency theory. Elementary schools tended to have higher levels of supportive leadership and staff collaboration than secondary schools, but secondary schools had higher levels of teacher

Studies in Leading and Organizing Schools, pages 51–89

authority over decision making than elementary schools. Additionally, we found limited support for the propositions from contingency theory that suggest these properties of organic management improve student achievement. Our research calls attention to the limitations of contingency theory for the study of the organizational design of schools.

ORGANIC FORMS OF MANAGEMENT

A great deal of research on educational administration focuses on what Rowan (1990) called "organic" forms of management in schools. As discussed in the general literature on organizations, this form of management involves a shift away from conventional, hierarchical patterns of bureaucratic control toward what has been referred to as a network pattern of control. This is a pattern of control in which line employees are more involved in organizational decision making, staff cooperation and collegiality supplant the hierarchy as a means of coordinating work flows and resolving technical uncertainties, and supportive (as opposed to directive) patterns of administrative leadership emerge to facilitate line employees' work.

Many different lines of research in educational administration reflect an interest in some or all of these elements of organic management in schools. There is, for example, a large body of research on teachers' participation in school decision making, as well as research on related management innovations such as site-based management and teacher empowerment initiatives that seek to replace more centralized forms of decision making with decentralized forms (see, e.g., Conley, 1991; Conway, 1984; Duke, Showers, & Imber, 1981; Malen, Ogawa, & Kranz, 1990; Marks & Louis, 1999; Smylie, 1994; Smylie, Lazarus, & Brownlee-Conyers, 1996; Taylor & Bogotch, 1994). There also is a growing body of literature on teachers' professional communities in schools, a literature in which network patterns of teacher collaboration and collegiality are seen as critical to promoting both instructional coordination and teachers' professional development (Bird & Little, 1986; Bryk, Camburn, & Louis, 1996; Grossman, Wineburg, & Woolworth, 2001; Little & McLaughlin, 1993; Louis, Marks, & Kruse, 1996; McLaughlin & Talbert, 2001). And finally, a great deal of attention has been given in research on educational administration to supportive (as opposed to directive) forms of school leadership, in part based on the view that supportive leadership is central to successful school improvement (Blase, 1993; Blase & Blase, 2002; Bossert, Dwyer, Rowan, & Lee, 1982; Rosenholz, 1985; Weiss & Cambone, 1994).

This interest in organic forms of management has many sources. Surely, the historic American commitment to democratic forms of organizational governance is relevant here, as is the firm belief on the part of most education professors in the benefits of teacher professionalism and the professional control of schools. But also important in this literature is a naive assumption on the part of (at least some) theorists that "organic" forms of management inexorably promote workplace commitment, on-the-job learning, and improved organizational outcomes. There is a problem with this naive view, however. As several analysts have noted (e.g., Conway, 1984; Rowan, 1990; Smylie et al., 1996), empirical evidence on the efficacy of organic management in education is surprisingly uneven. As a result, there is a continuing need for scholarship on both the sources and consequences of organic management in K–12 schools.

PURPOSES AND BACKGROUND

In this chapter, we use a theoretical perspective known as contingency theory to integrate the various, and often separate, streams of research on school leadership, staff collaboration, and participatory decision making into a coherent theoretical perspective on "organic" management in schools. Moreover, we present two separate, but related, empirical studies to test the logic of this synthesis. In the first analysis, we examine organic management as a dependent variable, presenting hypotheses and empirical data relevant to the question of why different kinds of schools develop patterns of organic management. Here, we look at variations in organic management that occur across different types of schools, and at variations in organic management that occur within schools as a result of teachers' different locations within a school's academic division of labor. In a second analysis, we shift our attention from factors promoting organic management in schools to an analysis of the effects of organic management on student achievement. Here, we conceptualize organic management as an independent variable, and we investigate the extent to which variation among schools in patterns of organic management predicts patterns of student achievement in these schools.

Throughout, we take an explicitly comparative approach to the analysis of organic management in schools. In particular, we focus on differences in organic management that arise at different levels of the school system (i.e., in elementary versus secondary schools), and on whether organic management at these different levels has positive effects on student achievement in different academic subjects (i.e., reading versus mathematics). This comparative work is made possible by the inclusion of identical survey measures of organic management in three large-scale education surveys conducted by the U.S. Department of Education during the 1990s. In this chapter, we use survey data collected from the 1993–1994 Schools and Staffing Survey (SASS) to examine why different kinds of schools develop organic patterns of management. To study the effects of organic management on student achievement in reading and mathematics, we use data on elementary schools collected from Prospects: The Congressionally-Mandated Study of Educational Opportunity and data on secondary schools collected as part of the National Educational Longitudinal Study of 1988 (NELS: 88). Because each of these studies included the *same* questionnaire items, we were able to perform a comparative analysis examining (a) patterns of organic management in elementary versus secondary schools, and (b) the effects of organic management on student achievement in reading and mathematics at these different levels of schooling.

The analyses presented here are part of a larger body of work conducted by Rowan and colleagues and rooted in a theoretical perspective on organizations known as contingency theory (for a review of this analytic perspective as it applies to educational organizations, see Rowan, 1990, 2002a, 2002b). As a theory of organizational design, contingency theory revolves around two basic assumptions: (1) the assumption that organizations develop managerial configurations in response to the technical and environmental circumstances they face; and (2) the assumption that specific managerial configurations are effective only to the extent that they are appropriately "matched" to these technical and environmental circumstances. In particular, contingency theory suggests that "organic" patterns of management (i.e., participatory forms of decision making, supportive forms of leadership, and network forms of control) are more likely to emerge within, and be effective for, organizations that operate uncertain technologies in dynamic environments, while "mechanistic" patterns of management (i.e., centralized forms of management, directive forms of leadership, and hierarchical forms of control) are more likely to emerge within, and be effective for, organizations operating more routine technologies in stable environments (Burns & Stalker, 1961; Lawrence & Lorsch, 1967; Perrow, 1965).

For over a decade, Rowan and colleagues have been investigating these ideas. The initial impetus for this work was the assumption—widespread in educational research—that teaching is a complex and nonroutine task best managed through organic forms of management. To investigate this idea, Rowan and colleagues conducted a series of studies in secondary schools. In all of these studies, the researchers used a set of survey items identical to the ones used here to measure the presence of organic management in schools. These measures assessed the strength of teachers' participation in school decision making, the extent of staff collegiality and collaboration in schools, and the presence of supportive leadership by school administrators. In an initial study, Rowan, Raudenbush, and Kang (1991) studied differences among secondary schools in the presence of organic management, producing two main findings. One was that smaller, private secondary schools showed stronger patterns of organic management than did larger, public secondary schools. A second was that teachers *within* secondary schools varied in their perceptions of organic management, largely as a result of their locations within the school's academic division of labor. In a related study, Raudenbush, Rowan, and Kang (1991) repeated this analysis, examining whether the three dimensions of organic management measured in the earlier study could be treated as a single organizational configuration. The basic findings of this study were that the three, separate measures were strongly intercorrelated and that, for most purposes, the separate measures could be treated as a single organizational configuration.

In subsequent studies, Rowan and colleagues elaborated on these early findings, explicitly testing hypotheses drawn from contingency theory. One goal of the later studies was to measure the extent to which teaching was a routine or nonroutine task. Another was to test a basic argument from contingency theory—that the extent of task routinization experienced by teachers would vary across the different academic subjects and tracks within secondary schools and affects the extent to which teachers participated in or experienced "organic" forms of management. These later studies yielded two important findings. First, it was found that many different instructional conditions—including teachers' disciplinary specializations and track assignments—affected teachers' perceptions of task routinization. And second, these studies supported a central hypothesis from contingency theory—that teachers who faced less routine instructional task environments were more likely than teachers who faced more routine task environments to report the presence of organic management in schools (Rowan, 1998, 2002a; Rowan, Raudenbush, & Cheong, 1993).

In related work, Rowan and colleagues examined the relationship of organic management to indicators of school effectiveness. In one set of studies, it was found that teachers who worked in schools characterized by stronger patterns of organic management were more likely than other teachers to report a higher sense of teaching efficacy, higher levels of workplace commitment, and greater professional learning (Raudenbush, Rowan, & Cheong, 1992; Rowan, 1998, 2002b; Rowan, Raudenbush, & Cheong, 1993). In another study, Rowan, Chiang, and Miller (1997) investigated the effects of organic patterns of management on the mathematics achievement of high school students, using NELS:88 data. The results of this study suggested that teacher participation in decision making had small, positive effects on students' 10th-grade mathematics achievement, but that other elements of organic management (i.e., teacher collaboration/collegiality, supportive principal leadership) had no effects on this measure of student learning.

Taken as a whole, the body of work just discussed suggests that contingency theory has at least some promise as a theory of organizational design for schools. For example, it allows researchers to develop a unified set of hypotheses, not only about conditions shaping the organizational design of schools, but also about the effects of organizational design on teacher *and* student outcomes. However, as developed to date, the empirical work by Rowan and colleagues has two shortcomings. First, the work just reviewed has been focused exclusively on secondary schools. As we shall see, however, there is strong reason to believe that the organizational design features associated with organic management might vary in important ways across elementary *versus* secondary schools, a problem not yet investigated by Rowan and colleagues. In addition, the body of research just discussed strongly suggests that managerial arrangements governing teachers' work, as well as the consequences of these arrangements for student outcomes, can differ across academic subjects. In particular, research by Rowan (2002a) showed that teachers working in different academic areas developed different perceptions of teaching as a routine (versus nonroutine) task, with math and science teachers tending to see teaching as a routine task, and English and social studies teachers tending to view teaching as a nonroutine task. On the basis of these results, we might expect (from contingency theory) that the effectiveness of patterns of organic management would vary across different academic areas, with organic management being *less* effective for academic subjects that are more routine, and *more* effective in subject areas perceived as nonroutine.

HYPOTHESES

The major goal of this chapter is to develop these insights further. In the first part of this chapter, we do this by investigating the extent to which elementary and secondary schools are characterized by organic patterns of management. In the second part of the chapter, we analyze the effects of organic management on students' achievement in reading and mathematics in both elementary and secondary schools. In both sections of the chapter, we see ourselves as testing propositions drawn directly from contingency theory.

Organic Management in Elementary and Secondary Schools

Our initial ideas about organic management in elementary and secondary schools are influenced by the work of Firestone and colleagues (Firestone,

Herriot, & Wilson, 1984; Herriot & Firestone, 1984), who argued that schools at different levels of the educational system take on different managerial configurations as a result of structural contingencies, individual differences in personnel composition, and institutional factors. Building on these ideas, we argue that a variety of factors combine to make elementary schools more likely than secondary schools to be characterized by patterns of organic management.

One reason to expect this is that elementary and secondary schools generally differ along two important dimensions of organizational structure that previous research has found affect the emergence of organic forms of management. Many organizational theorists have noted, for example, that bureaucratic and hierarchical forms of management are most likely to be found in larger, and more structurally complex, organizational forms, whereas organic forms of management are more likely to develop in smaller organizations, where employees are relatively undifferentiated in status and responsibilities (Scott, 1981). Of course, in American education, the organizational size and structural complexity of schools varies systematically across levels of schooling. Secondary schools tend to be larger than elementary schools, and they tend to have a more complex and differentiated (i.e., departmentalized) structure than do elementary schools. So, one reason that elementary and secondary schools might develop different levels of organic management is that they differ in organizational context, with the larger and more structurally complex secondary schools showing lower levels of organic management than smaller, and less differentiated, elementary schools.

However, there is a great deal of variation in these structural features among schools at the *same* level of schooling. As a result, we formulate hypotheses about the effects of larger size and greater structural complexity on organic management so that they apply to schools at any level—that is, to both elementary and secondary schools. This leads to our first set of hypotheses:

H_1: In both elementary and secondary schools, the smaller a school's size, the more likely it is to be characterized by organic forms of management.

H_2: In both elementary and secondary schools, departmentalization and other forms of structural differentiation reduce the likelihood of organic management.

Obviously, the hypotheses just presented explain variation *among* schools in organizational form. However, organization theory also suggests that differences in organizational design can exist *within* schools. Consider, for example, the academic specialization that exists within both elementary and secondary schools. In secondary schools, teachers are grouped into academic departments by subject matter specialization. As Rowan and colleagues (1991) found, this academic division of labor creates "micro-climates" within secondary schools, that is, differences in organizational design that develop at the department level in response to the different task contingencies faced by individuals working in these different units. In particular, the findings reported in Rowan and colleagues and Rowan (2002a) suggest that departments like mathematics and science (which have more routine instructional technologies) will show lower levels of organic management than departments like English and social studies (which operate less routine technologies of instruction). It is also the case that elementary schools contain a certain amount of academic specialization. There are, for example, a host of specialist teachers in elementary schools, including not only art, music, and physical education teachers (who sometimes work as itinerant teachers), but also remedial math and reading teachers supported by specialized funding sources. Because these teachers often work in task environments that are less heavily inspected and regulated, and because they also tend to be more isolated from existing patterns of instructional coordination such as grade-level teaching groups, we predict that such teachers will report more autonomy (and therefore control over school decisions affecting them), but less cooperation and collegiality than do regular classroom teachers. All of this leads to two more hypotheses:

H_3: In both elementary and secondary schools, math and science teachers should report lower levels of organic management than English and social studies teachers.

H_4: In both elementary and secondary schools, teachers who work in specialized areas outside the mainstream academic subjects (i.e., arts, music, physical education, and remedial specialists) will report higher levels of control over work, but lower levels of staff cooperation and administrative support.

Teachers' personal characteristics also can be expected to create "micro-climates" within schools, as Rowan and colleagues (1991) demonstrated. This can be illustrated, for example, in a finding of gender differences among teachers in reports about levels of organic management in schools. Of course, the elementary school teaching force has more females than does the secondary teaching force, but holding constant the level of schooling, previous research by Rowan and colleagues suggests that females will be more likely than males to report that their immediate school environments are characterized by cooperation and support. This general tendency, however, might be moderated when a school is headed by a male principal, especially if patriarchal traditions and direct forms of control function to deny females a certain amount of control over their work. Teachers also differ in their levels of educational attainment. Here too, there are compositional differences in the labor force at different levels of the school system, with high school teachers being more likely than elementary school teachers to have advanced degrees and academic specialties. However, controlling for level of schooling, we argue that teachers with higher levels of professional certification will be more likely to make claims for autonomy and self-direction, thus decreasing the likelihood that they will participate in organic forms of management within schools. This leads to the further hypotheses:

H_5: Within both elementary and secondary schools, female teachers should be more likely than male teachers to report school environments characterized by high levels of organic management.

H_6: Within both elementary and secondary schools, teachers with higher levels of advanced professional certification should seek greater personal autonomy and therefore report lower levels of organic management in their schools.

Finally, following Firestone and colleagues (Firestone et al., 1984; Herriot & Firestone, 1984), we argue that after controlling for the structural and compositional differences among elementary and secondary schools, important differences in organizational form will remain across schools operating at different levels of the education system. This, we argue, is due in large part to differences in the nature of the task environments in which teachers at different levels of the education system operate, differences that result from deeply institutionalized expectations about educational goals for younger versus older children and the associated task arrangements that emerge at different levels of schooling. In elementary schools, for example, teachers are expected to socialize students for diverse purposes, including both development of students' social skills and development of basic academic skills. Moreover, students at this level are typically grouped into age-graded classrooms, but within these classrooms, it is widely understood that students' academic and social needs vary widely, creating a set of structural contingencies that (we assume) act to heighten both the task complexity and task uncertainty of teaching in elementary schools. By contrast, high school teachers are expected to pursue a narrower set of goals with students, goals that revolve mainly around the attainment of advanced, and specialized, academic training. Here, students are grouped more narrowly in terms of ability and interest, creating a set of structural contingencies that (we assume) should act to reduce task complexity and task uncertainty. In this sense, we assume that the "core technology" of elementary and secondary schools differ in fairly profound ways, with the task environment of elementary school teaching being more child centered and nonroutine than the task environment faced by high school teachers. This leads to the following hypothesis, which is central to contingency theory:

H_7: Controlling for school size, departmentalization, and personnel composition, elementary schools should show higher levels of organic management than secondary schools due to the higher levels of task complexity and task uncertainty existing in the technical core of elementary schools.

Effects of Organic Management

The arguments just presented are intended to explain differences in the extent of organic management occurring across educational organizations as a result of various structural contingencies, as well as to explain the emergence of "micro-climates" within schools that result from the different status characteristics of individual teachers and their different locations within the academic division of labor in schools. In general, the hypotheses just presented lead us to predict that elementary schools should be more likely than secondary schools to be characterized by organic patterns of management, but they also suggest that this pattern will be moderated by differences in size and structural complexity that exist among schools at the same level, and by differences in the structural locations of individual teachers within schools at a given level.

Having formulated these ideas, we turn now to hypotheses about the consequences of organic management for student achievement. We begin by stating what might be called the "naive assumption" about the effects of organic management on patterns of student achievement in schools. As discuss earlier, many educational researchers assume that *all* teaching is complex and nonroutine and that, as a result, organic forms of management should have generally positive effects on student achievement, no matter what the subject being taught, in both elementary and secondary schools. This leads to the hypothesis that:

H_8: All else equal, the effects of organic management on student achievement will be positive at all levels of schooling and in all academic subjects.

Although this hypothesis is consistent with a great deal of thinking in research on schools, we believe it is not especially faithful to the logic of contingency theory. Instead, we argue that the "core technology" of schools differs in fundamental ways across elementary and secondary schools, and that within schools, the "core technology" differs across the academic subjects of reading/language arts and mathematics. For example, the arguments just presented suggest that elementary school teachers face higher levels of task complexity and task uncertainty than do secondary school teachers. Moreover, based on previous research conducted by Rowan (2002a), we expect that mathematics teaching will be more routinized than teaching of the English language arts (e.g., reading and writing). This leads us to modify the naive hypothesis in the following ways:

H_9: All else equal, the effects of organic management on student achievement should be greater in elementary schools than in secondary schools.

H_{10}: All else equal, the effects of organic management on student achievement should be greater in reading (where the task is nonroutine) than in mathematics (where the task is more routine).

In fact, based on these hypotheses, we predict that organic management will have the following effects (in order of magnitude) on achievement. The largest positive effects on achievement will be found for elementary school reading (the subject that we assume is the most nonroutine), and the effects on achievement will become progressively smaller for elementary school mathematics, then high school reading, and then high school mathematics. Such a prediction, we argue, is consistent with the general thrust of contingency theory, which argues that the effects of organic forms of management are highest when tasks are complex and uncertain (i.e., nonroutine) and become much smaller as tasks become more routine.

STUDY #1: ORGANIC MANAGEMENT IN ELEMENTARY AND SECONDARY SCHOOLS

We tested the hypotheses in two separate studies. In the first study, we examined hypotheses 1–7, which presented ideas about the conditions under which schools (or personnel within them) report higher levels of organic management.

Data Source

To test hypotheses about the extent of organic management in elementary and secondary schools, we used data from the 1993–1994 Schools and

Staffing Survey (SASS), which involved administration of multipurpose questionnaires to a large and nationally representative sample of teachers. In this chapter, we analyze these data in two ways. First, we examine differences in organic management occurring across elementary and secondary schools using a sample consisting of *all* teachers in *all* schools. Then, we turn to separate analyses, one of teachers in elementary schools and another consisting of teachers in secondary schools. We arrived at the final samples for each of these analyses by applying a number of data filters. First, we selected only those teachers who provided complete responses to SASS questions about organic management in their schools, since these are the outcome measures in our analyses. Then, we dropped teachers who worked in schools where sufficient school-level data were unavailable, including schools with fewer than three sampled teachers. This resulted in an *all* teachers/*all* schools sample of 44,657 teachers (22,850 secondary teachers, 17,466 elementary teachers, and 4,341 combined-/unidentified-level teachers) in 8,248 schools (3,375 secondary schools, 3,955 elementary schools, and 918 combined-/unidentified-level schools). The sample of secondary teachers included 22,850 teachers in 3,375 schools, a sample that includes not only secondary schools but also middle junior high schools. The elementary sample is composed of 17,466 elementary teachers working in 3,955 schools.

Analytic Strategy

As our hypotheses indicate, we are interested in differences in organic management that occur at two levels of analysis—those occurring among schools and those occurring within schools. We look at variation among schools in order to test the assumption that larger schools, those that are more structurally complex, and those that are located at different levels of the education system develop different patterns of organic management. We also are interested in variations in organic management that occur within schools, variations that we earlier argued result because teachers are located in different sectors of the academic division of labor within schools and/or differ in terms of status characteristics such as gender and educational attainment. To simultaneously investigate hypotheses at both these levels of analysis, we developed a set of two-level hierarchical-linear regression models using the computing program HLM/2L (Bryk, Raudenbush, & Congdon, 1994). We then estimated these models to assess the extent of organic management across schools with different global and aggregate characteristics, and within schools, across teachers with different individual characteristics.

Measures

Dependent variables.

In the analyses, organic management was measured by three multi-item scales taken from teacher responses to the SASS teacher questionnaire. These multi-item scales included most of the same items originally used by Rowanand colleagues (1991) and in subsequent research on organic management in secondary schools conducted by Rowan and colleagues. The three scales used here measure (1) teachers' perceived control over school decision making; (2) teachers' perceptions about levels of staff collegiality and cooperation in their schools; and (3) teachers' perceptions of the degree of supportive leadership exercised by the administrators in their schools. The scales have good reliability (in both the elementary and secondary school samples) and, on the basis of previous research, appear also to have strong construct validity. The items for each of the scales and their internal consistencies are available from the authors.[2]

The supportive leadership scale consists of 10 items measuring teachers' perceptions of a principal's capacity to set goals, share decision making, lead instruction, evaluate staff, acquire resources, and support the staff (α = .87). The staff cooperation scale consists of four items measuring teachers' perceptions of collegiality, a shared sense of mission, and the extent of coordinated efforts among teachers (α = .65). The teacher control scale consists of 12 items intended to measure teachers' perceived control and influence over issues critical to their work. The items assess the extent of teacher control in the areas of curriculum, student discipline, in-service training, day-to-day-operations, and evaluation (α = .81). Each of the three outcome measures has been standardized in this analysis to have a mean of zero and a standard deviation of one.

Independent variables.

As discussed, we are interested in predicting variations in the three dependent variables at two levels of analysis—variation occurring among schools and variation occurring within schools. At the school level, we included the following as independent variables in our HLM/2L regression analyses: school enrollment size; percent minority enrollment in a school; percent of students receiving free/reduced-price school lunches; school sector (public, Catholic, other private); school urbanicity; principal's gender; and level of schooling (elementary versus secondary). The measures of school size, percent minority enrollment, percent free/reduced-price lunch, and teacher's experience are standardized to have mean zero and standard deviation one in the analyses. Urbanicity is represented by a dummy coding scheme where rural and urban areas are compared to suburban locations. School sector is also represented by a dummy coding scheme where public schools and other private schools are compared to Catholic schools. Principal's gender is a dichotomous variable where female principal = 0, male principal = 1. As seen, our theoretical interest lies mainly in examining the effects of school level (elementary versus secondary) on patterns of organic management, but previous research suggests that the other variables listed above should be entered into our analyses in order to avoid specification error.

As discussed, we are also interested in explaining within-school variance in teachers' reports of organic management, variance that we assume results from social differences among teachers and/or from teachers' differential location in the academic division of labor. In the within-school portions of our two-level HLM analyses, we included the following independent variables as measures of status differences among teachers: teacher's highest degree held, total years of experience, race, and gender. Highest degree held is a dichotomous variable representing teachers who possess a master's degree or higher versus those with less education. Race has been simplified into minority status = 1, else = 0.

We also included several measures of a teacher's location in the academic division of labor in schools. In the elementary sample, a dummy coding scheme is used to indicate whether teachers are working in departmentalized units, in other instructional arrangement (i.e., enrichment class, pull-out, or team teaching), or in the contrast category, which is teachers working in self-contained classrooms. Another dummy coding scheme is used to indicate whether elementary teachers are assigned to teach a single subject such as English, math, science, social studies, other subject, or special education compared to the contrast category, which is teachers assigned to general elementary classrooms. In the secondary sample, teachers assigned to self-contained classrooms or other instructional arrangement are compared to the bulk of teachers assigned departmentalized units using the same type of dummy-coding scheme used in the elementary sample. Finally, secondary teachers assigned to teach the core subjects of English, math, science, and social studies are compared to teachers assigned to all other high school subjects. Descriptive statistics for these variables can be obtained from the authors.[3] In the analyses presented below, all variables except those that are dummy-coded have been standardized to have a mean of zero and a standard deviation of one.

Results

The results of the first study are presented in Tables 3.1a–3.1c, 3.2a–3.2c, and 3.3a–3.3c. Each dependent variable examined in this research required a separate data analysis. Throughout the series of analyses, administrative support as a dependent outcome is designated by the letter *a* (Tables 3.1a, 3.2a, and 3.3a); staff cooperation is designated by the letter *b* (Tables 3.1b, 3.2b, and 3.3b); and teacher control is designated by the letter *c* (Tables 3.1c, 3.2c, and 3.3c). Tables 3.1a–3.1c show the results of the HLM/2L regression analysis of data from the *all* schools and *all* teachers sample. This table can be used to assess most of the hypotheses we developed about sources of within- and between-school variance in organic management, but its main role here is to show the specific effect of level of schooling (elementary versus secondary) on the three measures of organic management included in the analyses. Tables 3.2a through 3.3c, by contrast, are provided mainly to examine patterns of within-school variation in teachers' reports about organic management. Tables 3.2a–3.2c represent the series of analyses performed for the elementary school level, while Tables 3.3a–3.3c show the results for the secondary school level. In what follows, we summarize results from all three tables at once rather than discussing the tables individually.

The effects of level of schooling on organic management.

The most important finding for this study is shown in Table 3.1a–3.1c, where the effects of level of schooling on patterns of organic management is estimated controlling for other factors, such as the public/private control of schools, the geographic location of schools, school enrollment size, and staff and student composition variables. Tables 3.1a–3.1c show that elementary and secondary schools do indeed differ in patterns of organic management, but not in precisely the ways predicted in hypothesis 8 above. For example, while elementary schools are generally characterized by more supportive administrative leadership than secondary schools (the effect size [e.s.] here being +.21 standard deviation units), and while elementary schools also show higher levels of staff cooperation (e.s. = +.37), it appears that teachers in elementary schools experience less control over decision making than do their secondary school counterparts (e.s. = –.08).

Note the parallel results shown in Tables 3.2a through 3.3c. In Tables 3.2a–3.2c, for example, we find that elementary school teachers working in departmentalized settings, which typify secondary school organization but are occasionally also found in elementary schools, tend to report lower levels of administrative support (e.s. = –.08), lower levels of staff cooperation (e.s. = –.08), and less control over school decision making (e.s. = –.08) than do teachers working in nondepartmentalized settings. Moreover, in Tables 3.3a–3.3c, the findings suggest that secondary school teachers working in self-contained classrooms, a pattern more typical of elementary schooling, tend to report higher levels of administrative support (e.s. = +.05), higher levels of staff cooperation (e.s. = .19), and higher levels of control over school decision making (e.s. = .08).

**Table 3.1a.   Two-Level HLM Regression Analyses:
All School Levels with Administrative Support as the Dependent
Variables (N = 8,248 schools, 44,657 teachers)**

Independent Variable	Regression Coefficient	SE	t-ratio	p-value
School-level model				
Public school	−0.31	0.03	−10.35	0.00
Other private school	0.11	0.03	3.08	0.00
Rural	−0.01	0.02	−0.77	0.44
Urban	−0.03	0.02	−1.75	0.08
Elementary	0.21	0.02	12.69	0.00
Combined/unidentified	0.11	0.02	4.65	0.00
Male principal	−0.07	0.02	−4.40	0.00
% Free lunch	−0.01	0.01	−1.35	0.18
% Minority	−0.06	0.01	−6.64	0.00
School enrollment	−0.03	0.01	−3.31	0.00
Teacher-level model				
Yrs. teaching exp.	0.00	0.00	−0.96	0.34
Master's degree	−0.09	0.01	−9.33	0.00
Female	−0.03	0.01	−2.73	0.01
Minority	0.15	0.01	10.29	0.00

Between-school variance = 25%; within-school variance = 75%. Proportion of variance explained = 19%; proportion of variance explained = 1%.

**Table 3.1b.   Two-Level HLM Regression Analyses:
All School Levels with Staff Cooperation as the Dependent Variables
(N = 8,248 schools, 44,657 teachers)**

Independent Variable	Regression Coefficient	SE	t-ratio	p-value
School-level model				
Public school	−0.38	0.03	−14.36	0.00
Other private school	0.12	0.03	3.96	0.00
Rural	−0.03	0.02	−1.66	0.10
Urban	−0.05	0.02	−2.85	0.01
Elementary	0.37	0.01	26.20	0.00
Combined/unidentified	0.19	0.02	9.20	0.00
Male principal	−0.05	0.01	−3.36	0.00
% Free lunch	0.01	0.01	1.72	0.09

**Table 3.1b.   Two-Level HLM Regression Analyses:
All School Levels with Staff Cooperation as the Dependent Variables
(N = 8,248 schools, 44,657 teachers) (Cont.)**

Independent Variable	Regression Coefficient	SE	t-ratio	p-value
% Minority	−0.07	0.01	−8.47	0.00
School enrollment	−0.07	0.01	−10.66	0.00
Teacher-level model				
Yrs. teaching exp.	0.08	0.00	16.48	0.00
Master's degree	−0.09	0.01	−9.77	0.00
Female	0.12	0.01	12.77	0.00
Minority	0.15	0.01	9.98	0.00

Between-school variance = 22%; within-school variance = 78%. Proportion of variance explained = 48%; proportion of variance explained = 1%.

**Table 3.1c.   Two-Level HLM Regression Analyses:
All School Levels with Teacher Control as the Dependent Variables
(N = 8,248 schools, 44,657 teachers)**

Independent Variable	Regression Coefficient	SE	t-ratio	p-value
School-level model				
Public school	−0.14	0.03	−5.01	0.00
Other private school	0.28	0.03	8.43	0.00
Rural	0.04	0.02	2.43	0.02
Urban	−0.02	0.02	−0.90	0.37
Elementary	−0.08	0.02	−5.12	0.00
Combined/unidentified	−0.04	0.02	−1.74	0.08
Male principal	−0.01	0.02	−0.55	0.58
% Free lunch	−0.05	0.01	−6.05	0.00
% Minority	−0.08	0.01	−9.86	0.00
School enrollment	−0.08	0.01	−10.68	0.00
Teacher-level model				
Yrs. teaching exp.	−0.02	0.00	−4.81	0.00
Master's degree	−0.02	0.01	−1.75	0.08
Female	−0.01	0.01	−0.94	0.35
Minority	0.14	0.02	9.63	0.00

Between-school variance = 22%; within-school variance = 78%. Proportion of variance explained = 18%; proportion of variance explained = 1%.

Table 3.2a.   Two-Level HLM Regression Analyses: Elementary School Level with Administrative Support as the Dependent Variable (N = 3,955 schools, 17,466 teachers)

Independent Variable	Regression Coefficient	SE	t-ratio	p-value
School-level model				
Public school	−0.26	0.04	−6.31	0.00
Other private school	0.11	0.05	2.36	0.02
Rural	−0.02	0.03	−0.69	0.49
Urban	−0.04	0.03	−1.63	0.10
Male principal	−0.10	0.02	−4.77	0.00
% Free lunch	−0.03	0.01	−1.85	0.06
% Minority	−0.06	0.01	−3.95	0.00
School enrollment	−0.02	0.01	−1.30	0.20
Teacher-level model				
Yrs. teaching exp.	0.01	0.01	0.89	0.38
Master's degree	−0.07	0.02	−4.38	0.00
Female	−0.03	0.02	−1.70	0.09
Minority	0.14	0.02	6.09	0.00
Special ed.	−0.02	0.03	−0.77	0.44
Specialize other elem.	0.05	0.02	1.94	0.05
English	−0.05	0.05	−1.17	0.24
Math	−0.09	0.05	−1.93	0.05
Science	−0.08	0.05	−1.62	0.11
Social studies	−0.10	0.05	−1.92	0.05
Other subject	−0.04	0.03	−1.26	0.21
Departmentalized	−0.08	0.02	−3.11	0.00
Other instructional arr	0.00	0.02	0.23	0.82

Between-school variance = 26%; within-school variance = 74%. Proportion of variance explained = 19%; proportion of variance explained = 1%.

Together, these findings provide modest support for our supposition that the task environments typical of elementary schooling generally give rise to organic forms of management, while the task environments typical of secondary schooling work against the emergence of this form of management. Note, however, that the effect sizes here are not particularly large, and that our predictions were not completely confirmed. All of this

Table 3.2b. Two-Level HLM Regression Analyses: Elementary School Level with Staff Cooperation as the Dependent Variable (N = 3,955 schools, 17,466 teachers)

Independent Variable	Regression Coefficient	SE	t-ratio	p-value
School-level model				
Public school	−0.32	0.04	−8.82	0.00
Other private school	0.10	0.04	2.53	0.01
Rural	−0.02	0.02	−0.91	0.37
Urban	−0.07	0.02	−2.89	0.00
Male principal	−0.07	0.02	−3.89	0.00
% Free lunch	−0.02	0.01	−1.47	0.14
% Minority	−0.07	0.01	−5.95	0.00
School enrollment	−0.07	0.01	−6.82	0.00
Teacher-level model				
Yrs. teaching exp.	0.08	0.01	11.54	0.00
Master's degree	−0.07	0.02	−4.95	0.00
Female	0.15	0.02	7.91	0.00
Minority	0.15	0.02	6.63	0.00
Special ed.	−0.10	0.03	−3.33	0.00
Specialize other elem.	−0.04	0.02	−1.75	0.08
English	−0.15	0.04	−3.43	0.00
Math	−0.21	0.05	−4.44	0.00
Science	−0.14	0.05	−2.71	0.01
Social studies	−0.24	0.05	−4.71	0.00
Other subject	−0.17	0.03	−6.06	0.00
Departmentalized	−0.08	0.02	−3.18	0.00
Other instructional arr	0.05	0.02	2.35	0.02

Between-school variance = 20%; within-school variance = 80%. Proportion of variance explained = 37%; Proportion of variance explained = 1%.

suggests that the task environment in which teachers work, while exercising at least some effect, might not be an especially powerful predictor of variation in the organizational design of schools (for a similar conclusion, see Rowan, 2002b).

**Table 3.2c.   Two-Level HLM Regression Analyses:
Elementary School Level with Teacher Control as the Dependent
Variable (N = 3,955 schools, 17,466 teachers)**

Independent Variable	Regression Coefficient	SE	t-ratio	p-value
School-level model				
Public school	–0.02	0.04	–0.43	0.67
Other private school	0.35	0.05	7.50	0.00
Rural	0.08	0.03	2.95	0.00
Urban	–0.01	0.03	–0.50	0.62
Male principal	0.03	0.02	1.16	0.25
% Free lunch	–0.08	0.02	–5.57	0.00
% Minority	–0.04	0.01	–3.12	0.00
School enrollment	–0.07	0.01	–5.89	0.00
Teacher-level model				
Yrs. teaching exp.	–0.04	0.01	–4.58	0.00
Master's degree	–0.05	0.02	–3.08	0.00
Female	–0.01	0.02	–0.59	0.56
Minority	0.19	0.03	7.33	0.00
Special ed.	0.14	0.03	4.35	0.00
Specialize other elem.	0.18	0.03	6.89	0.00
English	0.15	0.05	3.22	0.00
Math	0.00	0.05	–0.01	0.99
Science	0.16	0.05	3.05	0.00
Social studies	0.10	0.06	1.77	0.08
Other subject	0.25	0.03	7.94	0.00
Departmentalized	–0.08	0.03	–2.91	0.00
Other instructional arr	0.09	0.02	3.79	0.00

Between-school variance = 22%; within-school variance = 78%. Proportion of variance explained = 17%; proportion of variance explained = 1%.

Effects of other school-level variables on organic management.

Tables 3.1a–3.1c demonstrate this point, showing that level of schooling is neither the most powerful nor the most uniform predictor of the emergence of organic management in schools. Instead, the most powerful predictor, by far, measures an important property of the institutional environment of schools—the public/private status of schools (for a discussion of institutional controls as predictors of organizational design in schools, see Rowan & Miskel, 1999). The data in Tables 3.1a–3.1c, for example, show that after controlling for level of schooling and all of the other variables in our analysis, public schools are much less likely than Catholic schools to be characterized by supportive forms of administrative leadership (e.s. = −.31), staff cooperation (e.s. = −.38), and teacher control over school decisions (e.s. = −.14). Moreover, the differences in organic management are even larger when public schools are compared to other (non-Catholic) private schools. Here, Tables 3.1a–3.1c show effect sizes of −.41 for administrative support, −.50 for staff cooperation, and −.42 for teacher control over school decisions. These results, it should be noted, are duplicated in Tables 3.2a through 3.3c, the separate data on elementary and secondary schools. Clearly, then, patterns of institutional control over schools are key predictors of organic management in schools, and more powerful in their effects than are differences in level of schooling.

Table 3.3a. Two-Level HLM Regression Analyses: Secondary School Level with Administrative Support as the Dependent Variable (N = 3,375 schools, 22,850 teachers)

Independent Variable	Regression Coefficient	SE	t-ratio	p-value
School-level model				
Public school	−0.41	0.05	−8.49	0.00
Other private school	0.09	0.07	1.36	0.17
Rural	0.01	0.03	0.47	0.64
Urban	−0.06	0.03	−1.94	0.05
Male principal	−0.01	0.03	−0.38	0.70
% Free lunch	0.00	0.01	−0.32	0.75
% Minority	−0.05	0.01	−3.94	0.00
School enrollment	−0.02	0.01	−1.37	0.17
Teacher-level model				
Yrs. teaching exp.	−0.01	0.01	−2.07	0.04
Master's degree	−0.09	0.01	−6.34	0.00
Female	−0.04	0.01	−3.25	0.00
Minority	0.15	0.02	6.91	0.00
English	−0.07	0.02	−3.67	0.00
Math	−0.07	0.02	−3.77	0.00
Science	−0.09	0.02	−4.52	0.00
Social studies	−0.07	0.02	−3.29	0.00
Self-contained	0.05	0.03	1.92	0.05
Other instructional arr	0.02	0.03	0.80	0.42

Between-school variance = 22%; within-school variance = 78%. Proportion of variance explained = 5%; proportion of variance explained = 1%.

**Table 3.3b. Two-Level HLM Regression Analyses:
Secondary School Level with Staff Cooperation as the Dependent
Variable (N = 3,375 schools, 22,850 teachers)**

Independent Variable	Regression Coefficient	SE	t-ratio	p-value
School-level model				
Public school	−0.50	0.04	−11.43	0.00
Other private school	0.09	0.06	1.50	0.13
Rural	−0.01	0.02	−0.49	0.63
Urban	−0.06	0.03	−2.30	0.02
Male principal	0.03	0.02	1.06	0.29
% Free lunch	−0.04	0.01	−3.77	0.00
% Minority	−0.05	0.01	−4.69	0.00
School enrollment	−0.06	0.01	−4.92	0.00
Teacher-level model				
Yrs. teaching exp.	0.08	0.01	11.15	0.00
Master's degree	−0.10	0.01	−7.07	0.00
Female	0.08	0.01	5.99	0.00
Minority	0.15	0.02	6.47	0.00
English	−0.03	0.02	−1.52	0.13
Math	−0.01	0.02	−0.37	0.71
Science	0.00	0.02	−0.18	0.86
Social studies	−0.06	0.02	−2.73	0.01
Self-contained	0.19	0.03	6.83	0.00
Other instructional arr	0.16	0.03	6.03	0.00

Between-school variance = 14%; within-school variance = 86%. Proportion of variance explained = 14%; proportion of variance explained = 1%.

Other school-level variables show generally small effects on the emergence of organic management in schools. For example, school size has the expected negative effects on the emergence of organic management, although the standardized regression coefficients in Tables 3.1a–3.3c show that these effects are very small. In Tables 3.1a–3.1c, for example, the standardized β for the effect of school size is −.03 for administrative support, −.07 for staff cooperation, and −.08 for teacher control over decisions. The effects of school enrollment size on these same variables in Tables 3.2a through 3.3c are roughly similar, suggesting that while school size is a consistent and negative predictor of patterns of organic management in schools, it exercises only a very small effect on this organizational design

**Table 3.4. Two-Level HLM Regression Analyses:
Secondary School Level with Teacher Control as the Dependent
Variable (N = 3,375 schools, 22,850 teachers)**

Independent Variable	Regression Coefficient	SE	t-ratio	p-value
School-level model				
Public school	−0.39	0.04	−8.62	0.00
Other private school	0.32	0.06	5.19	0.00
Rural	0.06	0.02	2.60	0.01
Urban	−0.08	0.03	−3.00	0.00
Male principal	−0.08	0.03	−3.07	0.00
% Free lunch	−0.03	0.01	−2.71	0.01
% Minority	−0.12	0.01	−10.24	0.00
School enrollment	−0.06	0.01	−5.37	0.00
Teacher-level model				
Yrs. teaching exp.	0.00	0.01	0.36	0.72
Master's degree	−0.02	0.01	−1.69	0.09
Female	0.00	0.01	0.19	0.85
Minority	0.09	0.02	4.04	0.00
English	−0.15	0.02	−8.21	0.00
Math	−0.27	0.02	−14.02	0.00
Science	−0.11	0.02	−5.56	0.00
Social studies	−0.16	0.02	−7.68	0.00
Self-contained	0.08	0.03	3.10	0.00
Other instructional arr	0.00	0.03	−0.03	0.97

Between-school variance = 20%; within-school variance = 80%. Proportion of variance explained = 25%; proportion of variance explained = 3%.

configuration. Similarly, school composition and geographic location variables associated with larger schools (e.g., urban location, percentage of students on free/reduced lunch, percentage of minority students) also show only very small, negative effects on the development of organic patterns of management in Tables 3.1a–3.3c.

Perhaps the most intriguing findings in Tables 3.1a–3.3c concern the effects of principals' gender on the emergence of organic management in schools. Tables 3.1a–3.1c, for example, show that schools headed by male principals are characterized by less administrative support (e.s. = −.07) and less staff cooperation (e.s. = −.05), but equal levels of teacher control over school decision making compared to schools headed by female principals. However, Tables 3.2a through 3.3c show that these effects vary across levels of schooling. In elementary schools, the same pattern persists, although the negative effects of a male principal on administrative support and staff cooperation are slightly larger, while the data in Tables 3.3a–3.3c show that secondary schools headed by male principals do not differ from those headed by female principals on administrative support and staff cooperation but do show lower levels of teacher control over decision making (e.s. = –.08).

Within-school variation organic management.

Another interesting set of findings in Tables 3.1a–3.3c concern the extent to which teachers in the same school vary in the extent to which they report the presence of organic forms of management in their schools. As the tables show, only about 15–25% of the variance in the three measures of organic management used in this study lies among schools, with the remaining 75–85% lying within schools. Of course, some of this within-school variance reflects unreliability of measurement of the dependent variables, but even after correcting for unreliability, it appears that 70–80% of the reliable variance in measures of organic management lies among teachers in the same school (these results are virtually identical to those reported in Rowan and colleagues [1991]).

As hypotheses 3–6 above suggested, contingency theory points to a variety of factors that might account for this within-school variance. The most important factor from the perspective of this chapter is the disciplinary specialization of teachers. Recall from our discussion of hypotheses 3 and 10 that we expect teachers of English/language arts (ELA) and social studies to work in task environments that are less routine than those of mathematics and science teachers, and that on this basis, we expect ELA and social studies teachers to report higher levels of organic management in their environments than do mathematics and science teachers in the same school. The data in Tables 3.2a through 3.3c give only the most modest support to this idea. For example, in elementary schools, Tables 3.2a–3.2c confirm that teachers specializing in ELA report higher levels of organic management than do teachers of mathematics and science, but these differences are quite tiny. Moreover, in elementary schools, the very few social studies specialists in the survey reported lower levels of organic management than did math and science specialists in the same school. The results in the data on secondary schools (shown in Tables 3.3a–3.3c) provide equally limited support for the idea that task routinization plays a large role in the emergence of organic forms of management within schools. For example, while ELA teachers generally reported higher levels of administrative support and control over school decision making than did math and science teachers in secondary schools, they reported less staff cooperation.

Moreover, these differences were tiny. Comparisons of social studies teachers to others also produced tiny, and very inconsistent, effects.

In secondary schools, the most important factor explaining the emergence of organic management within schools appears to be whether an individual is an academic teacher (i.e., a teacher of ELA, social studies, mathematics, and science) versus all other types of teachers (e.g., art, music, physical education, foreign languages, and so on). Here, we find that teachers of the mainstream academic disciplines—which are increasingly the targets of institutionalized inspection and control—uniformly report lower levels of administrative support, staff collaboration, and control over school decision making. In fact, as Tables 3.3a–3.3c show, the effect sizes here can be quite striking, especially in the area of teacher control over decision making, where effect sizes vary between –.10 to –.27 depending on the academic discipline being compared to nonacademic teachers.

In elementary schools, the most important contrast explaining within-school differences in organic management appears to be across regular classroom teachers versus specialist teachers generally. As in the secondary school data, these effects occur largely along a single dimension—the extent to which specialist teachers report a heightened sense of control over school decision making compared to regular classroom teachers. For example, as Tables 3.2a–3.2c show, specialist teachers—no matter whether they teach special education, ELA, social studies, science, or another specialized subject—report a higher sense of control over school decision making than do regular classroom teachers in the same school. In fact, the effect sizes here are striking, ranging from .10 to .25. The explanation for these findings could again be that regular classroom teachers are under more bureaucratic pressures for accountability and thus feel less in control of organizational decisions than their specialist colleagues, but the findings could also be explained by the relative isolation—and therefore personal autonomy—of specialist teachers in elementary schools.

A final set of findings in Table 3.2a through Table 3.3c concern the effects of teachers' degree status on patterns of organic management in schools. Looking at the data on elementary schools shown in Tables 3.2a–3.2c, we see that elementary school teachers earning graduate degrees report lower levels of administrative support (e.s. = –.07), lower levels of staff cooperation (e.s. = –.07), and lower levels of control over school decisions (e.s. = –.05) than do teachers without graduate degrees. The results are roughly similar for teachers with graduate degrees working in high schools. As Tables 3.3a–3.3c show, in comparison to secondary school teachers without graduate degrees, teachers with graduate degrees report lower levels of administrative support (e.s. = –.08), lower levels of staff cooperation (e.s. = –.10), but roughly similar levels of control over school decisions (e.s. = –.05). Having controlled for teacher experience, we do not believe these effects can be dismissed as older employees resisting change to organic management forms. Instead, we attribute these results to the enhanced drive for autonomy that comes from obtaining advanced professional certification, a process that in American schools at least, appears to isolate teachers with advanced degrees from collegial support.

STUDY #2: THE EFFECTS OF ORGANIC MANAGEMENT ON STUDENT ACHIEVEMENT

Having reviewed the evidence on factors affecting patterns of organic management in elementary and secondary schools, we turn now to a study of the effects of organic management on student achievement. Recall that this study is designed to test hypotheses 7–10 above, which assert that organic management will have generally positive effects on patterns of student achievement in schools, but that these effects will be more positive in elementary than in secondary schools, and more positive in the curricular domain of reading than in mathematics.

Data and Analytic Approach

In order to test hypotheses 7–10, we drew on two large-scale data sets that allowed us to assess the effects of *exactly* parallel measures of organic management on student achievement in elementary and secondary schools. The two data sets used were (1) Prospects: The Congressionally-Mandated Study of Educational Opportunity, a large-scale survey of student achievement in elementary schools; and (2) NELS: 88, a large-scale study of student achievement in American high schools. Both data sets contain information on student achievement at multiple years in a student's academic career, and both contained the items we needed to construct measures of organic management consistent with our previous research.

In the analyses presented below, we estimated a series of two-level hierarchical-linear models using the statistical computing package HLM/2L (Bryk et al., 1994). These models were used to estimate the effects of organic management and other variables on student achievement in reading and math, controlling for students' prior achievement in these subjects. In the Prospects data set, we examined student achievement in reading and math over the one-year interval from spring of third grade to spring of fourth grade. In the NELS: 88 data, we examined student achievement in reading and math over the two-year interval from spring of eighth grade to spring of tenth grade. While the length of time between achievement assessments is not exactly parallel in the two data sets, other analyses (not reported here) suggest that this has little effect on our results.

In each data set, we developed a set of indicators of organic management using *exactly* the same items. The items are among those that Rowan and colleagues used in their previous studies, except that measures of the central features of organic management in the current analysis generally contain fewer items than in these previous studies. The three measures of organic management used here were (1) a measure of supportive leadership by school administrators; (2) a measure of teachers' control over key instructional decisions; and (3) a measure of the amount of staff collaboration present in the school. The exact items used to develop these scales and their internal consistencies can be obtained from the authors.[4] In all analyses, the measures are based on teacher reports, which are formed into individual-level scales and then aggregated to the school level. These school-level measures are then entered into the regression models. In the analyses presented below, the effects on student achievement of these aggregate measures of supportive leadership, teacher control over school decisions, and staff collaboration are of central interest.

In order to control for possible specification error in estimating the effects of organic management on student achievement, we attempted to include measures of the *same* set of control measures in regression analyses conducted in both the elementary and secondary data sets. This was not always possible, however, although we did find roughly parallel items for a surprising number of constructs. In general, in estimating the effects of organic management on student achievement, we controlled for the following variables: (1) school socioeconomic composition (measured in both data sets as the percentage of students in the school receiving free or reduced-price lunches; (2) student gender (male or female); (3) student ethnicity (coded as 0 = white; 1 = minority in both data sets); (4) student socioeconomic status (measured by an SES composite in the NELS data and as 1 = student receives free or reduced-price lunch, 0 = else in Prospects); (5) ability group placement of student (in NELS, a series of dummy-coded variables that indexed placement in the honors and college prep tracks versus all other tracks; in Prospects, a series of dummy-coded variables that indexed placement in a gifted and talented program or in the Chapter 1 program versus no special placement); (6) a series of parallel scales measuring student motivation (in both data sets, a measure of locus of control and measures of subject matter efficacy); (7) other measures of student motivation based on student and/or teacher reports (in NELS, two dummy-coded variables of the student's expectation that he or she will go to college and the student's subject area teacher's expectation that the student will go to college; in Prospects, a multi-item assessment by a student's teacher of the student's general attitudes and motivation toward school as well as the student's general ability to do school work); and (8) a measure of teacher qualifications (measured by whether or not the student's teacher has an undergraduate or graduate degree in the subject being taught, i.e., English for the reading tests and mathematics for the math tests). The items used to construct the scales just mentioned, and the internal consistencies of these scales, are available from the authors.[5]

In the analyses presented below, the sample sizes vary depending on the data set and analysis. After applying data filters of the sort described in study #1, the 10th grade reading sample includes 6,065 students, taught by 1,972 teachers, in 466 schools. For 10th grade math, the sample includes 4,744 students, taught by 1,853 teachers, in 354 schools. For fourth grade reading, the sample includes data on 6,120 students, taught by 506 teachers, in 148 schools. For fourth grade mathematics, the sample includes data on 6,149 students, taught by 526 teachers, in 148 schools. Descriptive statistics for each of the samples on the relevant variables included in the analysis are available from the authors.[6]

Results

Tables 3.4–3.7 present the results of these analyses. Each table reports the standardized regression coefficients from a two-level HLM analysis conducted using the computer program HLM/2L (Bryk et al., 1994). The independent and dependent variables were transformed into standardized scores prior to entry into the regression equations, and each regression model is a random intercepts, fixed slope model that assumes that the effects of all independent variables on student achievement are the same across schools in the sample.

Effects of student characteristics on achievement.

In both the high school and elementary school regression analyses, and for both reading and math, the variables measuring student characteristics had generally strong and consistent affects. In the elementary school data, Tables 3.4 and 3.5 show that after controlling for prior achievement in third grade, male and minority students show lower reading and mathematics achievement than do female and white students (the effects of SES, as measured by eligibility for free/reduced-price lunch are statistically insignificant). Students' placement in different instructional groups also affects student achievement after controlling for prior achievement, with students in gifted and talented programs showing higher achievement, and those in Chapter 1 groups showing lower achievement. Finally, the measures of student motivation included here all had statistically significant, positive effects on student achievement.

In the high school analyses, these same variables are related to patterns of student achievement, but often in ways that differ from the elementary school data. For example, by high school, males are outperforming females in mathematics, and have achieved equal levels of achievement in reading. Minority students still achieve at lower levels in reading and mathematics than do white students, and, in the high school data, SES also begins to exercise an affect on achievement, with higher SES students outperforming lower SES in both reading and math. Once again, variables measuring students' group placement also are related to patterns of student achievement in schools, with students in advanced and academic tracks outperforming students in other tracks in both reading and mathematics. Finally, there are once again statistically significant relationships of student motivation to achievement, with more motivated students outperforming less motivated students in both reading and mathematics.

Effects of organic management on student achievement.
The main purpose of study #2, of course, was not to replicate prior research on the effects of student characteristics on achievement but rather to examine the effects of organic management on patterns of achievement across schools. Looking at the data in Tables 3.4–3.7 as a set, we see that our study includes 12 different (but not always independent) tests of the effects of properties of organic management on student achievement—three measures, by two subjects, at two levels of schooling. As we shall see, across these 12 tests, we found only three statistically significant effects of a measure of organic management on student achievement, leading to the conclusion that this form of management is *not* a particularly powerful determinant of patterns of student achievement across schools.

Consider the data on patterns of achievement in elementary schools presented in Tables 3.4 and 3.5. Looking at the tables together, it appears that in elementary schools, the most important element of organic management affecting student achievement is supportive leadership by school administrators. Our measure of this factor, for example, had a statistically significant and positive effect on fourth grade students' mathematics achievement (standardized $\beta = .07$), and a smaller (and nearly significant effect, standardized $\beta = .04$) on reading achievement. Other dimensions of organic management in elementary schools, however, had either *no* effect on achievement (i.e., teacher control), or effects on achievement that tended toward negative (i.e., staff cooperation). Data on achievement in secondary schools, presented in Tables 3.6 and 3.7 shows similarly small and inconsistent effects of organic management on patterns of student achievement in schools. Here, teacher control over school decisions has a

Table 3.4.   HLM Regression Analysis of Fourth Grade Math Achievement

Independent Variable	Regression Coefficient	SE	t-ratio	p-value
School-level model				
% Free/rdcd. lunch	–0.16	0.03	–5.69	0.00
Administrative support	0.07	0.03	2.44	0.02
Teacher control	0.00	0.03	0.17	0.87
Staff cooperation	–0.05	0.03	–1.91	0.06
Student-level model				
3rd gr. math score	0.30	0.01	28.63	0.00
Male	–0.03	0.01	–2.49	0.01
Minority	–0.08	0.02	–3.96	0.00
Missing minority	0.02	0.05	0.37	0.72
Free/rdcd. lunch	0.01	0.02	0.69	0.49
Missing free/rdcd. lunch	0.09	0.05	1.75	0.08
Taking chp. 1 math	–0.22	0.04	–5.89	0.00
Gifted/talented prgrm.	0.03	0.04	1.21	0.23
Missing gifted/tal prgrm.	–0.13	0.06	–2.13	0.03
Student locus of control	0.03	0.01	3.59	0.00
Subject area efficacy	0.02	0.01	2.21	0.03
Motivation/abil (tchr rpt.)	0.07	0.01	7.91	0.00
Degree in ,ath	0.02	0.04	0.34	0.73

Table 3.5.   HLM Regression Analysis of Fourth Grade Reading Achievement

Independent Variable	Regression Coefficient	SE	t-ratio	p-value
School-level model				
% Free/rdcd. lunch	–0.18	0.02	–8.55	0.00
Administrative support	0.04	0.02	1.79	0.07
Teacher control	–0.01	0.02	–0.25	0.80
Staff cooperation	–0.01	0.02	–0.59	0.56
Student-level model				
3rd gr. math score	0.33	0.01	33.31	0.00
Male	–0.05	0.01	–3.45	0.00
Minority	–0.06	0.02	–3.07	0.00

Table 3.5. HLM Regression Analysis of Fourth Grade Reading Achievement (Cont.)

Independent Variable	Regression Coefficient	SE	t-ratio	p-value
Missing minority	0.04	0.04	0.84	0.40
Free/rdcd. lunch	−0.02	0.02	−0.78	0.44
Missing free/rdcd. Lunch	0.13	0.04	3.23	0.00
Taking chp. 1 math	−0.25	0.03	−8.63	0.00
Gifted/talented prgrm.	0.07	0.02	2.76	0.01
Missing gifted/tal prgrm.	−0.13	0.06	−2.31	0.02
Student locus of control	0.02	0.01	2.76	0.01
Subject area efficacy	0.02	0.01	2.93	0.00
Motivation/abil (tchr rpt.)	0.07	0.01	7.79	0.00
Degree in math	0.00	0.02	−0.06	0.95

Table 3.6. HLM Regression Analysis of 10th Grade Math Achievement

Independent Variable	Regression Coefficient	SE	t-ratio	p-value
School-level model				
% Free/rdcd. lunch	−0.02	0.01	−2.19	0.03
Administrative support	−0.01	0.01	−0.47	0.64
Teacher control	0.03	0.01	2.87	0.01
Staff cooperation	0.00	0.01	0.37	0.71
Student-level model				
8th gr. math score	0.61	0.01	59.91	0.00
Male	0.05	0.01	3.11	0.00
Minority	−0.07	0.02	−3.18	0.00
SES composite	0.03	0.01	3.11	0.00
Advanced track	0.25	0.03	7.81	0.00
Academic track	0.23	0.02	11.99	0.00
Missing track	0.21	0.04	5.19	0.00
Other track	−0.17	0.05	−3.23	0.00
Student locus of control	0.02	0.01	2.03	0.04
Subject area efficacy	0.05	0.01	6.39	0.00
Student expectation	0.07	0.02	3.62	0.00
Teacher expectation	0.19	0.02	10.16	0.00
Degree in math	0.06	0.02	3.73	0.00

Table 3.7.   HLM Regression Analysis of 10th Grade Reading Achievement

Independent Variable	Regression Coefficient	SE	t-ratio	p-value
School-level model				
% Free/rdcd. lunch	–0.01	0.01	–1.09	0.28
Administrative support	0.00	0.01	–0.33	0.74
Teacher control	0.01	0.01	0.86	0.39
Staff cooperation	–0.01	0.01	–0.57	0.57
Student-level model				
8th gr. reading score	0.61	0.01	63.73	0.00
Male	0.01	0.02	0.76	0.45
Minority	–0.09	0.02	–3.98	0.00
SES composite	0.05	0.01	5.19	0.00
Advanced track	0.14	0.03	5.35	0.00
Academic track	0.06	0.02	3.05	0.00
Missing track	0.00	0.04	–0.01	0.99
Other track	–0.15	0.04	–4.01	0.00
Student locus of control	0.05	0.01	6.67	0.00
Subject area efficacy	0.04	0.01	4.66	0.00
Student expectation	0.04	0.02	2.00	0.05
Teacher expectation	0.14	0.02	–0.01	0.00
Degree in math	–0.01	0.02	7.48	0.58

positive effect on 10th grade students' mathematics achievement (standardized β = .03), but not on reading achievement. Moreover, none of the other measures of organic management had effects (either positive or negative) on achievement (in either reading or math).

Discussion

Having discussed the findings from our two studies in some detail, the time has come to step back and revisit the major goals of this chapter. The chapter presented here is part of a continuing program of research by Rowan and colleagues exploring the promise of contingency theory as an analytic perspective on the organizational design and instructional effectiveness of American schools. Throughout this work, it should be noted, Rowan and colleagues have emphasized a particular theme in contingency theory—one that some analysts have called the "technical imperative" in organizational design. The idea has been that task environments in educational organizations exercise a particularly important influence on the organizational design of schools and that schools are effective only to the extent that they develop an appropriate "match" between their task environments and managerial forms (Rowan, 1990). In particular, Rowan and colleagues have examined what is perhaps contingency theorist's best known general assertion—that "organic" forms of management arise in and enhance the performance of organizations operating nonroutine technologies, and that "mechanistic" forms of management arise in and enhance the performance of organizations operating routine technologies. Following this logic, we argued in this chapter (and on the basis of some previous research) that the core technology of instruction in elementary schools is probably more complex and uncertain (i.e., nonroutine) than the core technology of instruction in secondary schools, and that at each level of the school system, the core technology associated with teaching reading/English/language arts is more nonroutine than the core technology associated with teaching mathematics. Based on these assumptions (and the logic of contingency theory), we then argued that (a) elementary schools should show higher levels of "organic" management than secondary schools; and that (b) organic forms of management should have their most positive effects on student achievement in elementary (versus secondary) schools and in the area of reading (as opposed to mathematics) achievement.

The data presented in this chapter only partially confirmed these ideas, however. For example, we found that patterns of organic management did vary across elementary and secondary schools, but *not* in the precise manner predicted by our hypotheses. For example, we found that elementary schools tended to have higher levels of supportive leadership and staff collaboration than did secondary schools, but that secondary schools had higher levels of teacher control over decision making than did elementary schools. These findings are not completely consistent with the "technical imperative" in contingency theory, or with our previous findings (Raudenbush et al., 1992) that the three indicators of organic management used in this chapter covary uniformly in response to various structural or task contingencies.

The data presented here also suggest that variations in task environments, both within and across schools, are not especially powerful predictors of variation in patterns of organic management in schools. For example, assuming that our assumptions about elementary schools operating a more "nonroutine" technology of instruction than secondary schools are true, the data analyses presented in this chapter show that the contrast between elementary and secondary schools is not the most powerful predictor of variations in organic management across schools. Instead, a variable measuring the type of institutional sector in which schools function—that is, whether schools are public or private—has a far more powerful effect on the emergence of organic management in schools.

Similarly, in making an argument about variations in organic management occurring within schools, we argued that the instructional technologies associated with teaching reading/English/language arts and social studies were more nonroutine than those associated with teaching mathematics and science, and that we therefore should expect reading/English/language arts and social studies teachers to report higher levels of organic management than math or science teachers. In fact, however, we found little evidence of such an effect. This does not mean that teachers' locations within the academic division of labor in schools are unimportant to the emergence of organic forms of management. In fact, our results confirm this point. But the most important contrast here—at both the elementary and secondary levels—was whether a teacher was assigned to teach a mainstream academic subject or to another type of assignment—in elementary schools, to a role as a teaching specialist, and in secondary schools, to a role as a teacher of one of the many nonacademic or support areas in the high school curriculum.

The overall point, then, is that the data presented in this chapter do not provide either strong or consistent support for the analytic power of explanations based on a "technical imperative" version of contingency theory—at least not in the data on American schools. Instead, the findings presented here suggest that many factors *other than* differences in task environments contribute to variations in patterns of organic management—both across schools, and in different sectors of the academic division of labor within schools.

Further evidence of the relative weakness of contingency theory as an analytic perspective on educational organizations comes from our analyses of achievement data. Here, we derived several hypotheses about the differential effects of organic management on student achievement from contingency theory, hypotheses that predicted different effects across elementary and secondary schools, and across the subject areas of reading and mathematics. Moreover, we conducted 12 (not completely independent) tests of these hypotheses. Overall, however, we found little support for the hypotheses, with only three of our 12 tests showing statistically significant effects of organic management on student achievement, and only two of these effects being positive in direction.

If the analyses of achievement data presented in this chapter tell us anything about the effects of management configurations in schools on student achievement, it is that supportive leadership by elementary school principles has a (small, positive) relationship to variations in student achievement (see Tables 3.4 and 3.5). But one needn't appeal to the elaborate theoretical apparatus of contingency theory to make this argument. Indeed, leadership effects on student achievement are more easily—and more elegantly—explained by reference to the voluminous literature on school leadership, especially the effective schools literature (see, e.g., Hallinger & Heck, 1996). Moreover, the lack of leadership effects on achievement in secondary schools (shown in Tables 3.6 and 3.7) can be explained largely by reference to the structural constraints on leadership that arise in the larger and more differentiated organizational settings of high schools rather than by the nature of the core technology of instruction in these schools.

It is possible, of course, to argue that we have not found much empirical support for contingency theory because we developed very weak measures of organic management in our empirical work. We have some sympathy with this point of view, but we are nevertheless unwilling to dismiss our findings on this basis. Instead, we see our findings as consistent with a great deal of prior research. We have, for example, confirmed that differences in managerial configurations exist across elementary and secondary schools, and across public and private schools, in ways that make sense and are consistent with other research and theory (e.g., Chubb & Moe, 1990; Herriot & Firestone, 1984). But such differences, as we have seen, do not appear entirely consistent with the predictions of contingency theory. Moreover, we have confirmed the effects of principal leadership on student achievement in elementary schools, a major finding from the effective schools literature, but did not find that leadership effects generalize to secondary schools, as a naive version of contingency theory might suppose. Nor is our failure to find effects on student achievement of factors such as teachers' control over school decisions or staff collaboration necessarily a sign that our measures of these constructs are weak. Recent research on teacher empowerment and staff collegiality, for example, have begun to suggest that these dimensions of organic management have effects on student achievement *only* when many other conditions are present (see, e.g., Marks & Louis, 1997; Newmann, 1996; Robertson, Wohlstetter, & Mohrman, 1995). This, of course, is tantamount to saying that there are few main or direct effects of these dimensions of organic management on student achievement, which is precisely what we found in this chapter.

CONCLUSION

What, then, do we conclude about the continuing role of contingency theory in research on the organizational design and effectiveness of schools? Looking back at over 10 years of research conducted by Rowan and colleagues on this topic, we see many important contributions to research on schooling. Rowan's (1990) original application of contingency theory to the study of organizational design in schools provided researchers with a clear statement of the assumptions that often underlie arguments about school reform. Moreover, in empirical work on organic management, Rowan and colleagues have presented a variety of explanations for why schools differ in patterns of organic management (see, e.g., Rowan et al., 1991, 1993; Rowan, 2002a; and this chapter). Their research also demonstrates the effects of organic patterns of management on teacher commitment and professional development (Raudenbush et al., 1992; Rowan, 2002b), and the (general lack of) effects of organic management on student achievement (Rowan et al., 1997, and this chapter). Clearly, much has been learned from this work about how and why patterns of organic management arise in different kinds of schools, and with what consequences for teachers and students.

But this body of work also calls attention to the limitations, both of contingency theory as an analytic perspective in research on schools, and about the power of organic forms of management to fundamentally improve instructional outcomes in education. As a theoretical perspective, it appears that contingency theory—and especially contingency theory built largely around the "technical imperative" argument—calls attention to a set of explanatory variables (such as task routinization) that have only very small effects on the organizational design of schools, and from that perspective, contingency theory therefore fails as a kind of "grand" theory in educational administration. It is better, we think, to view contingency theory as one of many theoretical perspectives available to analysts in the field, and to always emphasize that task environments are but one of many factors producing variation in the organizational design of schools.

A decade of work by Rowan and colleagues also suggests that the implementation of "organic" forms of management in schools is *not* the magic bullet that many school reformers think it is. As in studies conducted by other researchers, the data presented in this chapter suggest that organic forms of management have only the most limited effects on student achievement, effects that appear to be dependent on a number of other circumstances that make the efficacy of this pattern of management far more complex than the naive theory discussed in this chapter would have it. This does not mean that we should abandon our efforts to study elements of organic management in schools, or to search for evidence of their effectiveness. But if such evidence is to be found, we suspect that it will arise only in studies that deliberately search for the conditions under which such effects occur, rather than searching for universally (and unconditionally) strong main effects of organic management on achievement.

NOTES

1. This is a revised version of papers read at the annual meetings of the American Educational Research Association in April 1998 and April 1999. Work on the papers was supported by Grant R308A6003 from the U.S. Department of Education, Office of Educational Research and Improvement to the Consortium for Policy Research in Education.

2. The measures and their psychometric properties can be obtained by contacting either Robert Miller or Brian Rowan at the University of Michigan, School of Education, 610 East University, Ann Arbor, MI 48109-1259.

3. See note 2 above.

4. See note 2 above.

5. See note 2 above.

6. See note 2 above.

REFERENCES

Bird, T., & Little, J. W. (1986). How schools organize the teaching occupation. *Elementary School Journal, 86,* 493–511.

Blase, J. (1993). The micro-politics of effective school-based leadership: Teachers' perspectives. *Educational Administration Quarterly, 29,* 142–163.

Blase, J., & Blase, J. (2002). The micro-politics of instructional supervision: A call for research. *Educational Administration Quarterly, 38,* 6–44.

Bossert, S., Dwyer, D., Rowan, B., & Lee, G. (1982). The instructional management role of the principal. *Educational Administration Quarterly, 18,* 34–64.

Bryk, A. S., Camburn, E., & Louis, K. S. (1996). Professional community in Chicago elementary schools: Facilitating factors and organizational consequences. *Educational Administration Quarterly, 35,* 751–781.

Bryk, A. S., Raudenbush, S. W., & Congdon, R. T. (1994). *HLM: Hierarchical linear modeling with the HLM/2L and HLM/2L programs.* Chicago: Scientific Software.

Burns, T., & Stalker, G. M. (1961). *The management of innovation.* London: Tavistock.

Chubb, J. E., & Moe, T. E. (1990). *Politics, markets, and America's schools.* Washington, DC: Brookings Institute.

Conley, S. (1991). Review of research on teacher participation in school decision making. In C. Grant (Ed.), *Review of research in education* (Vol. 17). Washington, DC: American Educational Research Association.

Conway, J. M. (1984). The myth, mystery, and mastery of participative decision making in education. *Educational Administration Quarterly, 20,* 21–53.

Duke, D. L., Showers, B. K., & Imber, M. (1981). Studying shared decision making in schools. In S. B. Bacharach (Ed.), *Organizational behavior in schools and school districts.* New York: Praeger.

Firestone, W. A., Herriott, R. E., & Wilson, B. L. (1984). *Explaining differences in between elementary and secondary schools: Individual, organizational, and institutional perspectives.* Philadelphia: Research for Better Schools, Inc. (ERIC Document Reproduction Service No. ED 342 054)

Grossman, P., Wineburg, S., & Woolworth, S. (2001). Toward a theory of teacher community. *Teachers College Record, 103,* 942–1012.

Hallinger, P., & Heck, R. H. (1996). Reassessing the principal's role in school effectiveness: A review of empirical research, 1980–1995. *Educational Administration Quarterly, 32,* 40–80.

Herriot, R. E., & Firestone, W. A. (1984). Two images of schools as organizations: A refinement and elaboration. *Educational Administration Quarterly, 20,* 41–57.

Lawrence, P., & Lorsch, J. (1967). *Organization and environment.* Cambridge, MA: Harvard University Press.

Little, J. W., & McLaughlin, M.W. (1993). *Teachers' work: Individuals, colleagues, and contexts.* New York: Teachers College Press.

Louis, K. S., Marks, H. M., & Kruse, S. D. (1996). Teachers' professional community in restructuring schools. *American Journal of Education, 33,* 757–798.

Malen, B., Ogawa, R. T., & Kranz, J. (1990). What do we know about school-based management? A case study of the literature—A call for research. In W. H. Clune & J. F. Witte (Eds.), *Choice and control in American education. Vol. 2: The practice of choice, decentralization, and school restructuring.* New York: Falmer.

Marks, H. M., & Louis, K. S. (1997). Does teacher empowerment affect the classroom? The implications of teacher empowerment for instructional practice and student academic performance. *Educational Evaluation and Policy Analysis, 19,* 245–275.

Marks, H. M., & Louis, K. S. (1999). Teacher empowerment and the capacity for organizational learning. *Educational Administration Quarterly, 35,* 707–750.

McLaughlin, M. W., & Talbert, J. (2001). *Secondary school teaching in context.* Chicago: University of Chicago Press.

Newmann, F. M. (1996). *Authentic achievement: Restructuring schools for intellectual quality.* San Francisco: Jossey-Bass.

Perrow, C. (1965). A framework for the comparative analysis of organizations. *American Sociological Review, 32,* 194–208.

Raudenbush, S. W., Rowan, B., & Cheong, Y. F. (1992). Contextual effects on the self-perceived efficacy of high school teachers. *Sociology of Education, 65,* 150–167.

Raudenbush, S. W., Rowan, B., & Kang, S. J. (1991). A multilevel, multivariate model for studying school climate with estimation via the EM algorithm and application to U.S. high school data. *Journal of Educational Statistics, 16,* 295–330.

Robertson, P. J., Wohlstetter, P., & Mohrman, S. A. (1995). Generating curriculum and instructional innovations through school-based management. *Educational Administration Quarterly, 31,* 375–404.

Rosenholz, S. J. (1985). Effective schools: Interpreting the evidence. *American Journal of Education, 93,* 352–388.

Rowan, B. (1990). Commitment and control: Alternative strategies for the organizational design of schools. In C. Cazden (Ed.), *Review of research in education* (Vol. 16). Washington, DC: American Educational Research Association.

Rowan, B. (1998). The task characteristics of teaching: Implications for the organizational design of schools. In R. Bernhardt, C. N. Hedley, G. Cattaro, & V. Svolopoulos (Eds.), *Curriculum leadership: Rethinking schools for the 21st century.* Cresskill, NJ: Hampton.

Rowan, B. (2002a). Teachers' work and instructional management, part I: Alternative views of the task of teaching. In W. K. Hoy & C. G. Miskel (Eds.), *Theory and research in educational administration* (Vol. 1, pp. 129–149). Greenwich, CT: Information Age.

Rowan, B. (2002b). Teachers' work and instructional management, part II: Does organic management promote expert teaching? In W. K. Hoy & C. G. Miskel (Eds.), *Theory and research in educational administration* (Vol. 1, pp. 151–168). Greenwich, CT: Information Age.

Rowan, B., Chiang, F. S., & Miller, R. J. (1997). Using research on employees' performance to study the effects of teachers on students' achievement. *Sociology of Education, 70,* 256–284.

Rowan, B., & Miskel, C. G. (1999). Institutional theory and the study of educational organizations. In J. Murphy & K. S. Lewis (Eds.), *Handbook of research on educational administration.* San Francisco: Jossey-Bass.

Rowan, B., Raudenbush, S. W., & Cheong, Y. F. (1993). Teaching as a non-routine task: Implications for the management of schools. *Educational Administration Quarterly, 29,* 479–500.

Rowan, B., Raudenbush, S. W., & Kang, K. J. (1991). Organizational design in high schools: A multilevel analysis. *American Journal of Education, 99,* 238–266.

Scott, W. R. (1981). *Organizations: Rational, natural, and open systems.* New York: Prentice Hall.

Smylie, M. A. (1994). Redesigning teachers' work: Connections to the classroom. In L. Darling-Hammonds (Ed.), *Review of research in education* (Vol. 20). Washington, DC: American Educational Research Association.

Smylie, M. A., Lazarus, V., & Brownless-Conyers, J. (1996). Instructional outcomes of school-based participative decision making. *Educational Evaluation and Policy Analysis, 18,* 181–198.

Taylor, D. L., & Bogotch, I. E. (1994). School-level effects of teachers' participation in decision making. *Educational Evaluation and Policy Analysis, 16,* 302–319.

Weiss, C. H., & Cambone, J. (1994). Principals, shared decision making, and school reform. *Educational Evaluation and Policy Analysis, 16,* 287–301.

CHAPTER 4

PRINCIPALS RESPOND TO THE SCHOOL ENVIRONMENT WITH FLUIDITY, ALIGNMENT, VIGILANCE, AND FEAR

Janice R Fauske and Bob L. Johnson, Jr.

ABSTRACT

This chapter examines the cognitive processes guiding principals' responses to the environment of their schools. The focus is on *what principals act upon, how they explain their actions,* and *what underlying mental models guide their actions.* Data include multiple in-depth interviews of 18 principals. Principals fluidly directed their attention among factors in an uncertain environment with constant vigilance based on perceptions of vulnerability and fear of diminishing their schools' and own legitimacy and resources. Mental models were similar across principals regardless of gender, race, or longevity in the role, but longevity enabled principals to immediately consider more alternative responses.

Studies in Leading and Organizing Schools, pages 91–119

91

ENVIRONMENTAL ENACTMENT

Effective organizations act on their environments in strategic ways. This relationship between the environment and organizations has been described as creating bridges and buffers between organizations and the environment (Aldrich, 1979; Thompson, 1967). Similarly, organizational leaders often actively develop bridging or buffering structures to mitigate environmental effects on the organization (Scott, 1998; Thompson, 1967; Weick, 1979). The nature of those bridging and buffering structures found in the public school organizational context has been described in some detail (Corwin & Wagenaar, 1976; Ogawa, 1996; Rowan, Raudenbush & Cheong, 1993). These studies emphasize the importance of a leader's interaction with the school environment in order to ensure organizational efficacy.

Weick (1979, 1995) refers to this process of the leader's interaction with the environment as environmental enactment. For Weick, the concept of enactment explains how leaders select, construct, rearrange, and dissolve many features of their environments. It is this act of selecting and attending to these features of an organization's environment and the information gleaned from these interactions that comprise school leaders' responses (Johnson & Fauske, 2000). Schein (1992) characterizes these processes of environmental response as those guided by shared individual beliefs and individual action leading to a collective organizational response. Furthermore, these enactment processes have been described as making sense of the environment (Fauske & Ogawa, 1987; Weick, 1979, 1995). Other researchers (Hallinger, Leithwood, & Murphy, 1993) emphasize the importance of understanding cognition as it guides the thinking and behavior of educational leaders. The acknowledgment of individual beliefs and actions in the environmental enactment process is of critical importance to studying the responses of principals to the environments of their schools.

MENTAL MODELS

The cognitive processes of individuals making sense of entities and events in the environment are called mental models (Jih & Reeves, 1992; Johnson-Laird, 1983; Kim, 1993; Senge, 1990). Individuals make sense of the world through mental models that are contextually activated. Mental models function by activating a collection of schema previously developed to solve earlier (sometimes similar) problems or to respond to previous incidents. They allow one to interpret new events and give them meaning (Kim, 1993). They also allow one to receive new information and to develop new schema or modify existing schema through assimilation and accommodation of that information (Piaget, 1977). Mental models, as collections of schema, are continually developed or modified. Thus, mental models are defined as individual cognitive structures invoked to make sense of and to guide action toward an environmental event or series of events. Elements of mental models are identified as knowledge, assumptions, beliefs, values, and norms for action that guide the behaviors and actions emerging from those elements (DiBella & Nevis, 1998; Jih & Neeves, 1992; Johnson-Laird, 1981; Raybould, 2000).

Kim (1993) describes mental models as having two dimensions: *routines*, reflecting the operational components of the mental model, and *frameworks*, reflecting the conceptual knowledge and components of the mental model. *Routines* involve the procedural steps taken in action and *frameworks* reflect the reasons for taking such action. Because we are often not explicitly aware of our mental models, they are rarely tested or examined (Senge et al., 2000). Yet being aware of our own and others' mental models can lend clarity to our professional roles and can help avoid pitfalls brought on by limitations inherent in our thinking processes:

> The core task of the discipline of mental models is bringing tacit assumptions and attitudes to the surface so people can explore and talk about their differences and misunderstandings with minimal defensiveness. This process is crucial for people who want to understand their world, or their school, more completely—because like a pane of glass framing and subtly distorting our vision, our mental models determine what we see. In any new experience, most people are drawn to take in and remember only the information that reinforces their existing mental models. (Senge et al., 2000, p. 67)

Mental models, whether accurate or not, are embedded in the thinking of educators and have real effects on their actions.

Furthermore, elements of mental models can be similar, or shared, across groups of individuals and can inform collective as well as individual action (Schein, 1992; Weick, 1995). The notion of shared or similar elements of mental models in the thinking of principals as they enact the school environment is central to theory development explaining such actions. The aim of this chapter is to identify the shared mental model *routines* (what they do) and *frameworks* (why they act) of principals as they respond to, or *enact*, the environment. Exploring the guiding beliefs and assumptions embedded in principals' thinking can help us understand how principals' make sense of the school environment and conceive their responses to it.

Principals are not equally effective in responding to entities and events in the school environment. There are those who prove adept at mapping, managing, and adapting to a variety of constraints and demands. Likewise, there are those who prove equally inept. Many known and unknown factors account for these differences—intelligence, years of experience, socialization, the richness of one's past experiences, and context (Greenfield, 1995; Parkay, Currie, & Rhodes, 1992; Weick, 1978). These and other factors are explored in relation to principals' shared mental models activated to guide their interaction with the school environment.

A STUDY OF PRINCIPALS' ENVIRONMENTAL ENACTMENT

The study on which this chapter is based used a research design that allowed researchers to (a) explore the environmental entities, events, and activities that capture principals' attention for environmental enactment; (b) identify *routines* and *frameworks* of mental models guiding this enactment that include an explanation of how and why principals explain leadership behavior; (c) compare and contrast the information given by each principal with other principals to identify those elements of the mental models that are shared across principals; and (d) move toward developing a theory of principals' interaction with the school environment (Johnson & Fauske, 2000). Toward these ends, a modified form of the critical incident technique (Flanagan, 1954) was used for data collection.

The critical-incident technique (CIT) is a qualitative-research method used to generate descriptive data on a variety of human activities and behaviors. While the critical-incident technique has its origins in industrial psychology (Flanagan, 1954; Stano, 1983; Woolsey, 1986), it has since been utilized in a number of disciplines and settings (Fivars, 1980). The method consists of soliciting incidents of a given activity or behavior from individuals involved in those incidents and exploring the meaning of these incidents with participants. CIT represents a structured yet flexible data collection method for producing a thematic or categorical representation of a given behavior and its components.

Because mental models are defined as knowledge, assumptions, beliefs, values, and norms that guide behavior, their description requires self-reporting from research subjects, yet directly asking subjects to describe their mental models can yield untrustworthy data. Responses to such direct questions are shaped by additional mental models, such as those of second guessing the research agenda, that may not be articulated or explored in the study. Similarly, relying solely on data collection through observing principals in action may yield untrustworthy data because researchers must interpret observed behaviors through their own mental models. Thus, mental models are difficult to assess. The CIT method allowed researchers to solicit and clarify narratives of actual events or incidents. Once rich accounts of these events or incidents had been recorded and categorized, researchers returned to the subjects to explore the cognition behind the responses to events or incidents. In that way, researchers have been able to first identify the principals' *routines* (what they did) and, second, to have them explain their *frameworks* (why they acted in that way).

Principals' Critical Incidents

Critical incidents for this study were reported in a series of in-depth, semi-structured interviews (Spradley, 1979) over a 12-month period. A purposive qualitative sampling strategy was used to identify principals as interviewees who could provide "information-rich" critical incidents of specific interactions between themselves and the environment of the school. Principals perceived as "successful" were identified by colleagues and educators in educational administration and were targeted for study. Selection criteria included seeking representatives from both genders and from varying races. Sampling strategy of this sort is not designed to maximize external validity (Campbell & Stanley, 1981), but provides substantial data for concept or theory development purposes as well as for analytical generalizations (Miles & Huberman, 1994; Patton, 1990; Yin, 1994).

Of the 18 principals interviewed, five were elementary principals, eight held positions at high schools, and five served at middle or junior high schools (Table 4.1). Interview participants ranged in age from 37 to 62. The mean in years of administrative experience for the interview pool was 8.8 years; the range of experience varied from 2 to 23 years. The majority of interviewees were white male. Among the six females interviewed, two were African American and one Hispanic American. The majority of schools from which the principals came were located in urban and suburban settings in various regions of the United States. The average number of students was 609 at the elementary schools, 895 at the middle or junior high schools, and 1,450 at the high schools.

Interviews were conducted in three phases: semistructured interviews, focused interviews, and selected interviews for member checking. All interviews (46) were recorded and transcribed verbatim for analysis. Critical incidents were recorded in the first round of interviews. Information gaps found in the initial round of data collection were addressed through developing additional questions for each of the 18 principals. In the second phase of data collection, focused interviews (Spradley, 1979) elicited any more information needed on the specific incidents that emerged from the initial interviews and then solicited principals' reflections on reasons for their responses in the critical incidents. The tentative interpretations and conclusions reached at this stage were then shared in a third round of selected interviews with study participants for member checking (Spradley, 1979).

Table 4.1.   Demographic Profile of Principals Interviewed in Study (n = 18)

Age Range	Race/Gender	School Setting	Enrollment	Years as Administrator
Elementary level				
35–40	White-Male	Urban, Northeast	600	3
50–55	Black-Female	Urban, South	525	10
35–40	White-Male	Suburban, West	580	3
35–40	White-Male	Suburban, West	660	4
40–45	White-Female	Urban, West	680	8
Middle/junior high level				
50–55	Black-Female	Urban, South	675	7
45–50	White-Male	Urban, South	1250	9
40–45	Black-Male	Suburban, South	1150	10
50–55	White-Male	Suburban, West	850	8
40–45	White-Male	Rural, Northeast	550	6
High school level				
45–50	White-Male	Suburban, Northeast	800	5
45–50	White Male	Urban, Northeast	1900	8
45–50	White-Male	Urban, Northwest	1250	2
50–55	White-Female	Suburban, Midwest	1900	14
60–65	White-Male	Suburban, Midwest	2200	23
45–50	White-Female	Suburban, Northwest	1100	6
45–50	Hispanic-Female	Suburban, West	650	10
40–45	White-Male	Suburban, West	2000	12

Steps for Analyzing Mental Models

In addition to categorizing the incidents according to community type (Step 1), the text of each principal's set of interviews was analyzed for stated assumptions, beliefs, and values (elements of mental models) that supported and explained each principal's responses to the school environment (Step 2). In the third step of analysis, these elements were compared to identify elements of mental models that were shared across principals. In the next step of analysis, researchers categorized the shared elements of principals' mental models into four major emergent themes. Identification of similar elements and themes in the principals' shared mental models allowed researchers to begin theory building from the data in the final phase of data analysis and interpretation.

In analyzing these interview data, researchers moved inductively from the raw data to higher levels of categorization that resulted in correspondingly higher levels of abstraction. Rigorous analysis techniques called for revisiting the data and ultimately reducing the data before achieving a level of abstraction and synthesis that could lead to theory building. Table 4.2 is included here to illustrate the steps in data analysis, reduction, and interpretation of principals' mental models.

Table 4.2.   Steps in Analysis of Principals' Mental Models

1. Categorizing critical incidents into community types

2. Isolating beliefs, assumptions, and value statements by principal

3. Identifying shared elements in mental models across principals in each community category

4. Categorizing shared elements of mental models into major emergent explanatory themes

5. Interpreting findings for theory development

PRINCIPALS' CONCEPTUALIZATION
OF THE SCHOOL ENVIRONMENT

Before describing the principals' *routines* for enacting the school environment, it is important to describe the principals' shared mental model *framework* for conceptualizing the school environment that emerged during data analysis. Though researchers initially solicited critical incidents using the terms internal and external environment, many principals had difficulty defining where the school itself ended and the external environment began in answer to specific questions and descriptions of critical incidents. The boundary between the two was blurred by the principals. As one principal noted, "Though we talk about it this way, I have a hard time separating and distinguishing my school from the community,...what's happening here...[from] what's happening there." When asked specifically about this distinction, another principal remarked, "I don't see a difference between the external and internal environment of my school."

This ambiguity did not prove to be a stumbling block for principals. When asked to describe their own school and offer specific incidents of interaction with the internal and external school environment, these principals proceeded with little hesitation (Johnson & Fauske, 2000). In responding to questions, principals conceptualized the internal and external school environment as a *school community that is integrated, without distinct boundaries.* The voice of one principal represents the collective view that the school environment "is every event, entity, and person that I encounter in the performance of my role as principal, whether inside or outside of the school building." This conceptualization of the school environment exemplifies Scott's (1998) theory of organizations as open systems for which boundaries are fluid and amorphous. To more accurately capture the principals' own conceptualization of the school environment, the term *extended school community* is used throughout this chapter when discussing the findings from principals' interview data.

PRINCIPALS' MENTAL MODELS
FOR ENVIRONMENTAL ENACTMENT

To explore principals' mental model *routines* and *frameworks* for attending to and acting upon incidents in the extended school community, researchers analyzed and coded the interview data around the specific incidents that principals named. Seventy-seven incidents were described by the 18 principals, who offered between two and seven incidents for an average of four each. These have been organized into three larger categories locating the sources of the incidents: the immediate school community, the school-governance community, and the broader noneducational community. A further subdivision has been made of the locations of the incidents into those more proximal or distal to the school. Within the school-governance community, for example, the school district office and the city government are governing units that are both physically and relationally closer to study participants than the more distal state department of education. It is incidents with these proximal entities that were identified most frequently (Johnson & Fauske, 2000). This suggests that study participants attended more to the immediate as opposed to the more distal entities in the extended school community (Bowditch & Bruno, 1985).

The incidents were quite varied and included such events as parents' complaints over restricting sophomore enrollment in a chemistry class, a student-generated attempt to impose a 24 hour cigarette and alcohol sales ban, and state legislator mandates for Outcomes-Based Education. A list and a frequency count of those incidents appear in Table 4.3. The incidents within each community category were clustered into subgroups and the number of principals who mentioned incidents in each subgroup is also outlined in Table 4.3. An overview of six incidents is offered in Table 4.4 to give the reader an enriched sense of the kinds of incidents that were described by principals.

Table 4.3.   Critical Incidents and Entities Identified by Occurrence

Category of Incident	Principals Reporting (N)
Immediate School Community	
Proximal	
Parents	18
School neighborhood	18
Teacher unions	5
Distal	
Other schools	8
Other school districts	8
School-Governance Community	
Proximal	
School district office	15
City/county government	11
Distal	
State department of education	9
State legislature	8
State health & human services	2
Broader Noneducational Community	
Distal	
Local businesses/corporations	14
Law enforcement	12
Media	9
Religious leaders	7
Service organization leaders	7
Gangs/community gang activity	7
Organized special interests	6
State colleges/universities	5
Chambers of commerce	4
Financial elite	3
Local health clinics/hospital	1
Community think tanks	1
Military base/installation	1

Table 4.4.   Representative Critical Incidents by Community Level

School Community—Student Protest

This first incident involved a student walkout and the principal's attempts to deal with the media coverage that ensued. In a move to show support for an earlier walkout by teachers, a small group of vocal students organized and threatened school officials to "walk" if teachers' demands were not met. After numerous attempts by the principal to persuade otherwise, 25 students chose to participate in the protest. The incident generated more publicity in the community than expected. Reporters from the local media (newspaper and television) descended on the scene, generating a substantial amount of negative publicity for both principal and school.

School Community—Neighborhood Parents' Petition

A petition was gathered and signed by a group of neighborhood residents regarding the after-school use of the school's playground facilities. The concern expressed by leaders of the petition was the congregation of gang members on the basketball court after school hours and the potential threat to neighborhood safety. Complaints and concerns over the incident had reached the mayor's office. Parents circulated a petition requesting that the principal have the goal posts removed. The principal promptly communicated the nature of the incident to the central office and then organized a meeting of all concerned parents to seek a solution to the problem. Representatives from the district office and the city's parks and recreation division were also invited.

Governance Community—Visit from District Representative

This incident involves a series of interactions between the principal and the district office. These interactions culminated with a visit of the assistant superintendent to the school. At issue was the lack of district "support" perceived by teachers to exist for the school. Given the consistently high standardized test scores produced by the school, the principal reported that teachers felt as if the school was not getting the recognition from the district that it deserved. This perception was affecting teacher morale, so the principal initiated a series of formal and informal contacts with the associate superintendent. As described by the principal, the strategic intent of this initiative was to "highlight and communicate over the positive things happening at the school."

Governance Community—State-Level Curriculum Mandates

Curriculum mandates came down from the State Department of Education and the principal did not believe that they fit the needs of the school. Although the principal didn't agree with certain aspects and philosophy of the curriculum being mandated by the SDE, district personnel felt strongly about complying with the state curriculum core. This put some pressure on the principal. The district's desire to comply with state mandates meant that the principal had to communicate compliance to them while adapting the curriculum in an acceptable way for the school.

Table 4.4. Representative Critical Incidents by Community Level (Cont.)

Governance Community—School Recognition Grant

To encourage innovation at the local school level, the newly elected governor proposed a
school reform program and persuaded the state's legislature to appropriate the funds
needed to implement it. Administered by the state department of education, the program
was touted by the governor and media as the key to much-needed change and progress in
the state's public education system. To ensure that the program would achieve the desired
effect, participation was made competitive. Although the program offered prestige that was
important to the school's parent community, the principal and teachers decided not to
spend time and resources applying because it would detract from the "rhythm" of the
school.

Noneducational Community—Student Recognition Program

The "Champions for Life" Program was created in the school for monthly recognition of
outstanding students. The principal was looking for ways to generate good will in the school
community. Businesses were looking for ways of displaying their corporate citizenship. The
incident centers on the principal looking for finances to support the program. Thus, an
exchange relationship provided a program to generate excitement in school by rewarding
students for high achievement. The principal hoped to generate goodwill among local businesses for possible future support by publicly acknowledging support from these businesses
to the community.

Immediate School Community

Principals consistently attended to the community in which the school was
situated. They viewed parents of students as well as the surrounding neighborhood as both resources, or opportunities, and potential threats.

Parents: Individual and collective

As would be expected, parents were identified as capturing the attention of all principals. Whether identified individually or corporately, that is,
organized groups and coalitions, or as disruptive or supportive, parents
were seen as entities upon which the principal depends heavily for school
success. Though success was defined rather ambiguously, the principal's
and the school's success were seen as closely linked.

Various labels or metaphors were used to describe parents and the role
they play: taxpayer, patron, customer, and client. In such roles, parents
were viewed as potential and legitimate sources of demands, supports, and
opposition, "Parents are my client; they're the taxpayer," described a sea-
soned principal. "I need to be responsive to their concerns and their
desires. They can make my life great or they can make my life miserable.
They represent a very powerful coalition."

Acknowledging the need to respond to parental needs, a middle school
principal remarked, "If I'm not responsive to the realistic and important

needs of these patrons, then I think I'm not very credible with them as a parent, and I think they'll tell their neighbors. I have my agenda; they have their agenda [and] the more points of convergence, the easier it's going to be for us to make changes in this school." However, not all parents were seen as equal in their ability to mobilize and influence. For this reason, most principals noted that certain parents and parental groups captured their attention with greater frequency and intensity than others.

Neighborhood

Various features of the school neighborhood were identified in incidents by the entire sample of principals. The dynamics, values, stability, demographic character, and socioeconomic conditions of the neighborhood were specifically mentioned as capturing the attention of principals. The information cues embedded in neighborhood characteristics provide these principals with a means for assessing the nature of community needs, demands, and support. "It's where the kids come from," observes a high school principal. "For our school to be out of touch with or somehow ignore what our neighborhood is, is a big mistake." Principals reported that knowing the neighborhood functions to (a) reduce the level of unpredictability presented by the school community; and (2) increase principals' belief in their ability to control and anticipate demands or opportunities.

For many, the quality of the school neighborhood and the ability of the principal and school to succeed were assumed to be directly related. Principals assess the neighborhood along the following dimensions: mid to high SES, cultural homogeneity, minimal number of at-risk students, and minimal number of dysfunctional families. According to these principals, in quality neighborhoods, parents support the school. Study participants characterized neighborhood support in the following ways: (a) a willingness to help when called upon, (b) a willingness to come to the principal and discuss problems, (c) standing behind and supporting the principal when tough decisions are made, (d) minimizing opposition to the school and principal, and (e) active help in making the needs of the school known to the governing boards and electorate.

As noted earlier, both principal and school depend on neighborhood support for success. Yet to garner this support, principals described the importance of responding to neighborhood and community values and incorporating these values into the character and structure of the school. As one high school principal remarked concerning the school's dress code policy, "As principal, it's important to make sure that the policies such as the school dress code are in line with the values of the community. When the school reflects the values of the community, it gains support, trust, and credibility."

Governance Community

The school-governance community represents those governing entities that directly or indirectly exercise authority over the school. In response to interview questions or in describing critical incidents, five specific entities from the government community were identified and discussed by study participants. The three most prevalent subgroups of entities and incidents are described for illustration.

District office

Although recognized as a source of support, the district office captured the attention of principals because of the dependence it creates for and the mandates it makes on both principal and school. "They [the central office] have the power to help or hinder us," commented an experienced elementary principal. "They are a source of information. ... They provide us with technical assistance. More importantly, they control the resources on which I depend."

To the extent that both the mandates and the assistance offered by the district office proved consistent with the vision and direction these principals had for their school, the district office was believed to be a "supporting" entity. In terms of information and technical support, principals described the district as supportive in dealing with special needs students, larger curricular issues, and situations involving potential litigation. Two principals reported specific incidents of "standing behind" a district policy (i.e., using a district policy as a point of leverage when convenient), one in dealing with disgruntled parents and the other in selling a curriculum idea to teachers.

However, where demands and assistance proved inconsistent with the vision principals had for their school, the district was seen as interfering. Three specific concerns were voiced by principals in such cases: (a) complying with these demands (or at least creating the appearance of compliance) so as to maintain the legitimacy of one's own leadership and school with the district office; (b) minimizing the potential disruptive effects of the demand on school operations; and (c) creatively adapting the demand in such a way as to meet the needs of the school. Remarks by a high school principal reflect these concerns, "As a designated authority, the district office is my boss. They represent a threat in the sense that I am responsible to them. You want to cooperate with them, so you respond when they make demands.... [Yet,] I attempt to adapt their demands and mandates to the needs of my school."

As a part of the district office, the superintendent and local board were specifically singled out by more than half of the principals in this study. Discussions surrounding both entities emphasized the demands and expectations rather than the supports emanating from each. As one middle-school principal cynically noted, "The superintendent and school board have things they expect your school to do, and part of it is listening to what it is they expect from you."

City government

City government, particularly the mayor and city council, was likewise identified as an important community entity by a majority of study participants. Given the political influence of individuals who hold these offices and realizing the effect decisions made at city hall could have on their school, principals expressed an eagerness to influence and cooperate with city government. "Decisions they make [city government], particularly annexation and school boundary realignment decisions, have an enormous impact on my school," noted one elementary school principal who had experienced the effects of a realignment decision. One middle school principal observed:

> I'm always looking for opportunities to get the mayor's attention for my school....When someone comes in from the mayor's office and says, "Do any of your teachers and students want to participate in such and such an activity?" I'd be foolish not to say yes!... Not being cooperative could jeopardize the next bond election. So to me, it's an economic issue. It's also a goodwill issue. It's a matter of, "Hey, we want to be good neighbors with the police, with the fire department, with the mayor's office," because I might have a favor...someday...in the future I'm going to need that cooperation. It's a you-scratch-my-back, I'll-scratch-your-back kind of thing.

These observations suggest a relationship based on a recognized interdependence. As such, principals believed that the relationship was open to some negotiation. Principals recognized the impact of annexation, boundary realignment, bond and tax referenda decisions—decisions made by city government—on their own lives and school. Further, principals recognized their dependence on the services that city governments provide. City governments were reciprocally dependent on schools to provide services acceptable to the public and those that might attract new residents. The positive images of the schools contributed to the overall efficacy of the community as overseen by city government.

State department of education (SDE)

As a recognized entity with legislative and executive authority in educational matters, the state department of education was identified as a distant, out-of-touch entity often imposing unworkable, disruptive mandates on the local school. The imposition of certain mandates inconsistent with local agendas was a concern voiced by almost half of the principals. Dealing with curriculum mandates coming from the SDE, one frustrated elementary school principal remarked, "The state office has power over us, particularly in the area of curriculum. They control the curriculum!... [And yet], they don't know diddly! They sit up there and...they keep dumping all of this stupid curriculum on us!... They're removed and out of touch...[and] what they're asking us to do reflects that!"

In light of these voiced concerns, the challenge and resulting action for these principals focused on adapting mandates to local needs, even to the point of substantially watering down, reworking, or ignoring the policy in question. "They [the SDE] seem very far removed from what I'm doing.... I regard them more as a foe than a friend...an imposing force, you know, being far removed from what's actually happening. ... We kind of do our own thing. We figure out what we think is state-of-the-art, what we think is the most effective approach, and then we do that and kind of ignore the state office."

Broader Community

More different kinds of incidents (11) in the broader noneducational community were identified by principals than in the other two categories. Only the three kinds of incidents mentioned by at least half of the principals are discussed here.

Local businesses and corporations

The most frequently cited cluster of entities in the broader noneducational community was specific businesses or corporations (14). These businesses and corporations were primarily seen as potential sources of financial support for the school. Most principals viewed them as the means through which desired and needed special programs beyond the school's financial reach could be realized. An elementary school principal, who with the help of a local business was able to initiate a program recognizing student achievement, was quite aware of this, "By providing financial support and services, businesses help my school do things that it could otherwise not afford to do."

Not all principals, however, shared this view. One middle-school principal viewed the business community as an intrusion. Leaders of the local Junior Achievement (JA) chapter initiated a program for schools in the district and proved heavy-handed in insisting (to the point of demanding) that the program be incorporated into the principal's school. Not fully convinced of the academic contributions of the program and seeing its potentially disruptive effects on the school's established rhythm, the principal was hesitant to accept the JA offer. In spite of these concerns, and given the fact that the local superintendent was on the JA Board of Directors, the principal was eventually pressured into accepting the invitation.

Law enforcement

Local law enforcement was identified by 12 principals (nine secondary, three elementary). Though perceived primarily as a supportive entity, police were also seen on occasion as being intrusive, particularly regarding issues of student protection and privacy. Nevertheless, the need for the principals to develop and maintain a cooperative working relationship with police was evident in the data. "Police help us deal with student disruptions," exclaimed a high school principal. "They're also helpful [to us] in dealing with things like traffic safety, athletic events, student discipline problems, shoplifting, threats, and fights. We have a need for them and they have a need for us, so we try to maintain a cooperative relationship with them."

As with other community entities, principals expressed the need to establish and build "goodwill credit" with the police so as to ensure continued cooperation. Realizing their dependence on the police to maintain a safe and orderly school and given the unpredictability of knowing when their services might be needed, principals often cooperated with the police even when such cooperation proved inconvenient for the school. Such cooperation often involved the gathering and collecting of information on students suspected of being involved in criminal activity away from the school. An experienced middle-school principal of a school in a neighborhood described as low in socioeconomic status observed, "There are times when I need the police to help with problems at the school, but there are times when the police need me to help. I try to maintain a cooperative relationship with them. It's a matter of being "good neighbors" with the police.... I've had to use [my cooperation with them in the past] as...leverage." These comments capture the ideas of exchange, negotiation, interdependence, and maintaining goodwill capital.

Media

The media was also identified as capturing the attention of principals. Of particular concern was the media's role in defining the image of the school to the public and principals' inability at times to influence the creation of this image. "Reporters create images of your school for the public. Many times their work and the images they create of your school are out of your control," observed a principal who had a difficult time with the media during a teacher walkout and subsequent student sit-in.

Though the media did report positive, human interest–type stories of schools in the district, principals likewise recognized the volatility and problems created by the media in their coverage of unexpected, traumatic school events. To counteract this, one principal described "working" newspaper reporters covering education in that school's area, "You've got to get to know these people and develop a positive relationship with them. You want them to have a positive view of you, because down the line something negative is going to happen and they're going to report it. There's going to be a negative issue that's going to affect your school, and you want to be able to come out and point to all of these positive things before the negative one ever hits."

Echoing this vulnerability and recognizing dependence, an elementary principal describes why the media captured attention, "You need to be equipped to deal with the media ... because they have a job to do.... [That] job is to let the public know what's going on in the schools. It doesn't matter to them that it's detrimental to the school's image. What they're interested in is selling news....You have to take the opportunity to communicate [with the media] those things that you and your community think are important."

THEMES IN PRINCIPALS' MENTAL MODELS
FOR ENVIRONMENTAL ENACTMENT

As principals reflected on the incidents reported in the first round of interviews, each offered reasons (*frameworks*) for their courses of action. A summary of the mental model *frameworks* (beliefs, assumptions, and values) identified in the critical incident data is offered in Table 4.5 for each community category mentioned by at least half the principals.

Further reduction of the data allowed researchers to make some preliminary theoretical generalizations (Yin, 1994) about the nature and characteristics of these principals' mental models for scanning the extended school community. Analysis of principals' reflections on why they chose their responses to the incidents revealed four themes in the mental models that guide administrative action that are shared across both principals and categories of community.

Fluidity of Attention Directing

The principals under study viewed school environment boundaries as ambiguous and amorphous. Such fluid boundaries are described by Scott (1998) as characterizing open systems. Study findings show that the principals' process of responding to the extended school community defied categorization into internal and external entities. Principals responded to that extended school community in a seamless and fluid manner, shifting their attention readily from proximal to distal entities and events. While principals' resistance to classifying incidents as internal or external to the school was initially puzzling, researchers found that the fluidity of this pro-

Table 4.5. Summary of Mental Model *Frameworks* in Community Categories Reported by at Least 50% of the Principals

Community Categories	Element 1	Element 2	Element 3	Element 4
		Framework		
Parents individual and collective	Parents have numerous roles as individuals and in groups.	Parents influence school and principal success.	Parents can be sources of opposition or support.	Certain parents are more powerful than others.
Neighborhood	Neighborhoods have distinctive features (SES, culture, etc.).	Knowing the neighborhood increases predictability.	"Quality" neighborhoods support the principal and school.	Schools must reflect neighborhood values.
District office	District offices create demands for the principal and school.	District offices can offer resources and assistance.	District offices can interfere with the school's vision.	
City government	City governments have political and economic power to impact schools.	Principals are eager to cooperate in return for services and attention.		
State Department of Education (SDE)	SDEs are out of touch with the work of schools.	SDEs impose unworkable mandates on schools.	SDEs have control over curriculum in particular.	SDE mandates can be adjusted to local needs or ignored.
Law enforcement	Schools need to maintain a positive relationship to receive prompt services.	Law enforcement is mostly supportive of the school and principal.	Law enforcement is sometimes intrusive in student privacy area.	
Local businesses and corporations	Businesses are providers of financial support and services not available through state funding.	Businesses can be prescriptive about use of funds or implementation of sponsored programs.		
Media	Schools are unable to control or influence the media.	Some media reporting positive and beneficial to schools.	The media seems interested in "selling" news not in the welfare of the school.	The media is something that principals must deal with.

cess enabled principals to make decisions more readily in the face of uncertainty. Indeed, these principals often were forced to make decisions without full knowledge of alternatives and consequences, and they were able to focus on that information most relevant to the decision at hand without the unnecessary filter of proximal or distal location in relation to the school.

Necessary Alignment

Principals responded to events in the extended school community on a personal level that reflected immersion in and commitment to the success of the school. The principals clearly assumed that their public persona must be congruent with the values of the culture and community in which the school was situated. Principals' *routines* also reflected a belief that their professional identity largely coincided with the school's identity; the school's success or legitimacy was viewed as one and the same with their own (Johnson & Fauske, 2000).

Principals' mental models for enacting the school environment reveal a belief that they must protect the reputation and resources of their school. Scott (1998) describes this concept as seeking *legitimacy* from constituencies. Such legitimacy may be defined as something given by others to the school and the principal:

> Legitimacy is granted by one's audience. The metaphor is that of the theater with accompanying drama. As the primary actor, the leader plays out a role that evokes approval or disapproval from the audience. Sensitive actors committed to their craft seek to portray a character in a credible fashion to various audiences including fellow actors, patrons, directors, spectators, and others. Without a critical level of approval from these audiences, the credibility of their role and skills are unsubstantiated. (Johnson & Fauske, 2000)

Retention and enhancement of the school's and their own legitimacy and resources in the face of uncertainty and ambiguity were paramount concerns to the principals under study.

Another form of resources, social capital, also relies on relationships to others in the environment (Coleman, 1988; Garner & Sisk, 2000; Neilson, 1997; Smylie & Hart, 1999). School leadership is conducted in a social environment that includes a number of coalitions and community groups. Developing social capital includes leaders' behaviors that (a) set shared norms, expectations, and sanctions; (b) build information networks; and (c) nurture trust (Coleman, 1988; Smylie & Hart, 1999). In addition to legitimacy and fiscal resources, principals in the study hoped to gain social capital from various community coalitions and groups. To do so, principals described the need for alignment with the values and expectations of the various community groups; "knowing" the community was a consistently dominant element emerging from the critical incidents. The data clearly indicate a continued effort on the part of principals to align with community standards and values as well as with perceived standards of excellence in the school's instructional program. These principals felt compelled to communicate compliance to a number of groups at a number of levels, including compliance to state level–mandated standards even when such compliance was largely symbolic. The perceived pressure to comply with standards was seen in many of the principals' responses; examples of articulating norms, expectations, and possible sanctions for noncompliance were threaded throughout the data. The shared value that emerged from analysis of the pervasive efforts to "please" various community groups was the perceived importance of compliance in order to retain or enhance legitimacy and resources, including social capital, for the school and principal.

Constant Vigilance

In addition, principals' actions reflected constant vigilance directed toward protecting the school and themselves from threats in the community. The extended school community, therefore, was represented in the interview data as continually uncertain and unpredictable; it was viewed as most often presenting threats rather than opportunities. Both schools and principals were perceived as vulnerable to the environment (Johnson & Fauske, 2000). Information needed to make decisions was incomplete, and often the stakeholders could not be represented in the decision-making process because of logistical or time constraints. When the principal's communication with stakeholders had been regular and ongoing, the principal could anticipate community reactions more accurately. Thus, uncertainty was reduced and potential threats avoided. Belief in the importance of ongoing communication networks for gathering and disseminating information was manifest as principals vigilantly responded to the perpetual uncertainty within the extended school community.

It makes sense that principals' responses to the extended school community were embedded in a network of social connections through which they attempted to protect and develop legitimacy and resources, including social capital. An examination of communication through networks rather than through the organizational hierarchy is important to the discussion of developing social capital in the form of information flow. A great cause of fear and frustration for principals was their frequent inability to reduce the uncertainty and ambiguity that accompanied making response decisions. More complete and timely information would have reduced this frustrating "muddiness" of the process (March, 1991). In a perfect system, that information might have flowed logically and sequentially through the organizational hierarchy. In an "imperfect" system, that information flows unevenly along loose networks among those involved (Galvin & Fauske, 2000), and urgency to act may force a decision before sufficient information can be shared. In this view of communication flow, information exchange is a weighty element of social capital and becomes a resource that can be exchanged for other resources (Ring, 1996). Principals reported many incidents related to receiving or sharing information in the process of protecting the school and themselves. Exchange of student information for continued support from law enforcement is one example.

Frustration and Fear

Principals often expressed frustration at not getting information sooner and, thus, were fearful of not being able to "head off" incidents. They were continually apprehensive about incidents that were unpredictable or unexpected. The temporal nature of their responses was potent; timing in many critical incidents proved critical. Timely, often immediate, responses were typically required. Frustration and the related fear of potential loss of legitimacy and a potential loss of resources were evident throughout the interview data. Theorists have consistently linked legitimacy to critical resources that flow from this legitimacy such as money, personnel, time, or cooperation (DiMaggio & Powell, 1991; Johnson & Fauske, 2000; Meyer & Scott, 1992; Scott, 1998). For the principals under study, protecting their own and the school's legitimacy was integral to securing multiple forms of resources.

One means of reducing fear that emerged in data analysis was building trust within the extended school community. Ring (1996) and others (Jones, Hesterly, & Borgatti, 1997; Pearce, 1997; Williamson & Masten, 1995) describe the exchange relationship that exists among successful for-profit ventures, and Ring further defines the nature or trust building among organizations where information is the primary resource as repetition of exchanges that reduce uncertainty and ambiguity over time. Such repetition acts as a safeguard for protecting resources and legitimacy (Galvin & Fauske, 2000). Given the limited resources available to principals in an exchange relationship with the extended school community, repeated interactions with numerous publics can begin to build predictability and to nurture trust that can, in turn, protect and enhance the legitimacy, resources, and specifically social capital, for both principals and their schools.

Summary of Frameworks

Principals' *frameworks* for enacting the school environment reflect ongoing scanning for the potential threat or opportunity that each incident represented. Principals interpret their responses to the extended school community as a process of constant scanning and negotiation for securing resources, including social capital, and for seeking legitimacy to protect the school's image as well as their own professional reputation. Both their *routines* and their *frameworks* reflect an implicit belief that the school environment is characterized by three interrelated challenges that principals continually monitor and react to: *dependence, uncertainty,* and, consequently, their own *vulnerability* (Johnson & Fauske, 2000. These principals and their schools are *dependent* on the extended school community for both legitimacy and resources that are *uncertain* and unpredictable, and, in the context of dependence and subsequent uncertainty, both principals and school were *vulnerable.*

Greenfield (1995) characterizes the school environment as a *demand environment* in which threats to legitimacy and resources capture the attention of principals. A majority of the 77 incidents reported (54) were indeed categorized as threats by the principals. However, the remaining incidents (23) were categorized by principals as opportunities. Thus, the school environment is also an *opportunity environment* that can offer possibilities to enhance both legitimacy and resources (Johnson & Fauske, 2000). Principals' mental models for environmental enactment include *routines* for scanning the environment for both threats and opportunities because their *frameworks* reflect the recognition of an exchange relationship between themselves and the school environment. This exchange relationship has been described by public choice theorists (Arrow, 1951; Buchanan & Tullock, 1962; Downs, 1957; Niskanen, 1971; Olson, 1965), in resource dependence theories (Benson, 1975; Pfeffer & Salancik, 1978), and in several studies of school administration and governance (Boyd, 1982; Mahlios & Carpenter, 1982; Michaelsen, 1981; Galvin & Fauske, 2000; Johnson & Fauske, 2000; Johnson & Galvin, 1996). Some researchers describe this exchange relationship in terms of the "rational pursuit of self-interest" (Becker, 1976; Johnson & Fauske, 2000). As applied to the principalship, these theories portray principals as "utility maximizers who seek to benefit from exchanges in a variety of settings within and across social systems" (Johnson & Fauske, 2000, p. 181). The authors go on to say that "given conditions of scarcity and uncertainty, few individuals have the resources to maximize all interest [and] must choose the best way possible to use or allocate the resources available to them through exchange relationships" (p. 181). Consequently, principals vigilantly scan the environment for threats and opportunities but cannot attend to them all. Principals choose those that they believe will best protect or enhance their own and their school's legitimacy and resources.

In Table 4.6, the principals' mental models for characterizing and negotiating challenges in the extended school community are summarized along with the themes, or patterns, of principals' responses.

Table 4.6. Summary of Principals' Mental Models for Enacting the School Environment

Environmental Challenges	Principal Responses	Response Patterns
• Dependency • Uncertainty • Vulnerability (Johnson & Fauske, 2000)	• Scanning for threats to the school's and their own legitimacy and resources • Scanning for opportunities for legitimacy and resources (Johnson & Fauske, 2000)	• Fluidity • Constant vigilance • Seeking legitimacy through alignment • Frustration and fear

SIMILARITY OF PRINCIPALS' ENVIRONMENTAL ENACTMENT

Influence of Principal Longevity

Elements of mental models are similar across all the principals regardless of gender, race, or longevity in the role. However, longevity gives some principals the advantage of a richer and more extensive mental model that could be made immediately active in their responses to the environment (Greenfield, 1995; Johnson & Fauske, 2000). According to their own assessment, principals with greater longevity are able to more readily anticipate problems or events and to consider a wider range of potential actions. Thus, principals with more experience exhibit the same *routines* and *frameworks* but are more facile in their response decision making. Nevertheless, all principals, regardless of longevity, report that they and their schools are compelled to continually attend and respond to entities and incidents in the extended school community and are moved to retain and protect the social capital of their schools (Johnson & Fauske, 2000). This continual concern for monitoring and quickly respond to the environment does not diminish with longevity as some theorists suggest (see Parkay et al., 1992).

Similar Responses across Unique Contexts

The interview data show that principals view their own school's extended community as unique. They emphasize the singularity of their role as "protector" of the school and describe the urgency of getting to know the players particular to the community in which the school is situated. Analysis reveals, however, that many elements of mental models are more similar than different across principals, as is reflected in the four shared elements of mental models for responding to the extended school community. While researchers note that school and community context does indeed inform the responses of the principals, it did not entirely capture and define their responses. In other words, though the principals themselves assumed a certain "aloneness" in their role, researchers found several indicators of similarity in professional behavior across principals that lead to a few generalizations about these principals' mental models for enactment.

Weick (1995) described the collective mind that can emerge from similar selection, meaning making, and action taking over time. The alikeness of principals, the similarity of their mental models for responding to the extended school community, suggested applying the concepts of collective mind to a loosely connected but nevertheless likeminded group of individuals. If principals share a professional orientation (mental model) for enacting the extended school community, then examining their similar ways of knowing (*frameworks*) and doing (*routines*) can extend the body of knowledge that grounds educational leadership. Identifying that shared orientation toward the extended school community can also inform administrative practice as well as the preparation and professional development of principals. This, making explicit the mental models of principals in their responses to the extended school community, can inform the work of prospective and beginning administrators; likewise, making these shared norms for action explicit can also stimulate reflection among experienced principals.

Lack of Perceived Reciprocal Influence

Remarkably lacking in the interviews of the principals under study was a reported belief that they could influence the school environment. These principals scanned for and recognized opportunities in the school environment (Johnson & Fauske, 2000), but did not describe proactively creating such opportunities. None of the principals under study explicitly described, or even alluded to, an understanding of the reciprocal nature of their role as one who not only is shaped by the environment but as one who can in turn shape the environment. They see themselves almost exclusively responding to the school environment but not as shaping the school environment. They do acknowledge some exchange of resources and mutual goodwill, but it is framed as a necessary exchange rather than an intentional effort to influence entities in the school environment. Even in taking advantage of opportunities, these principals revealed *frameworks* of responding to opportunities in the school environment rather than actively and intentionally creating those opportunities.

Some attempt to influence the school environment is evident in an incident where the principal solicited a district visit to gain recognition for the school (even this visit was in reaction to perceived lack of recognition) and in an incident where the principal sought to convince the community that the school should not participate in the state recognition program (this incident, too, was primarily a response action). Even in these examples, the principals recognized opportunities but did not articulate or recognize their potential for influencing the school environment, for creating opportunities, or for shaping community values rather than merely aligning with them. The belief that principals can shape as well as respond to the school environment is not a shared element in the principals' mental models. The absence of conscious and intentional influence of the school environment among the principals under study is intriguing and worthy of further exploration.

CONCLUSIONS

The study of these principals' mental models reveals a number of shared assumptions, beliefs, and values that characterize their enactment of the extended school community. Principals' actions are guided by the mental models activated during responses to potential threats or opportunities for enhancing resources and the community's perceptions of legitimacy for both the school and themselves. The comments of an elementary principal in a suburban community reflect this conclusion: "I find I'm excessively dependent on a host of environmental forces and demands in fulfilling my role. I can't really do this job without the cooperation and help from other people. To get the help and support I need, they must believe in me and what I'm trying to do here." Principals conceive the extended school community most often as a *demand environment* characterized by three interrelated threats: *dependency, uncertainty,* and *vulnerability.* Less often, they recognize certain incidents as representing an *opportunity environment* that is equally uncertain and also creates vulnerability and dependence. Their responses (*routines*) to both environmental threats and opportunities are reflected in the four themes of the shared mental model *frameworks* for principals' environmental enactment: *fluidity* of attention directing, seeking legitimacy and resources through *alignment* with community values and expectations, constant *vigilance* needed, and frustration and *fear* at loss of control. The preponderance of principal responses to incidents and reflections on those responses were focused on eliminating or reducing threats rather than on actively developing opportunities. That principals tend to focus on protecting or enhancing resources and legitimacy for themselves and the school while responding to incidents rather than on proactively developing influence within the community is an important finding in the study.

Though stage theorists suggest that continual concern for survival will usually diminish as a principal becomes more socialized to the role (Parkay et al., 1992), that generalization was not supported in this study. The data in this study show that principals, with varying longevity in the position, all react passionately to those incidents that threaten themselves or their school. Established mental models refined over time may give some principals a rich repertoire of skills for responding to entities and incidents, but fear and constant vigilance remain intense even among principals with substantial experience.

Incidents demand critical responses from principals and those responses emanate through the extended school community. Depending on how the incident is dealt with and its outcomes, the perceived success of the principal and the school may increase or diminish (Johnson & Fauske, 2000). Greenfield (1995) attributes this action-oriented, reactive nature of an administrator's work to the *demand environment* that is called here the extended school community. Others extend that notion to acknowledge the existence of an *opportunity environment* that is equally demanding of principals (Johnson & Fauske, 2000). The principal and the school encounter multiple, often unpredictable threats or opportunities daily; mental models offer a "map" for responding with greater predictability. If the principals' mental models enable successful responses to threats and opportunities, the principal and the school are perceived as successful. The incidents analyzed in this study highlight the principals' shared mental model *routines* and *frameworks* for responding to an *extended school community* characterized by *dependence, uncertainty,* and *vulnerability.* They enact this environment with *fluidity, vigilance,* and *fear* shaped by the perceived need for *alignment* with community values and expectations.

REFERENCES

Aldrich, H. E. (1979). *Organizations and environments.* Englewood Cliffs, NJ: Prentice-Hall.

Arrow, K. (1951). *Social choice and individual values.* New Haven, CT: Yale University Press.

Becker, G. (1976). *The economic approach to human behavior.* Chicago: University of Chicago Press.

Benson, K. J. (1975). The interlocking network as a political economy. *Administrative Science Quarterly, 20,* 229–249.

Bowditch, J. L., & Bruno, A. (1985). *A primer on organizational behavior.* New York: Wiley.

Boyd, W. L. (1982). The political economy of public schools. *Educational Administration Quarterly, 18*(3), 111–130.

Buchanan, J., & Tullock. G. (1962). *The calculus of consent.* Ann Arbor: University of Michigan Press.

Campbell, D. T., & Stanley, J. C. (1981). *Experimental and quasi-experimental designs for research.* Boston: Houghton Mifflin.

Coleman, J. (1988). Social capital in the creation of human capital. *American Journal of Sociology, 94,* 95–120.

Corwin, R. G., & Wagenaar, T. C. (1976). Boundary interaction between service organization and their publics: A study of teacher–parent relationships. *Social Forces, 55,* 471–492.

DiBella, A., & Nevis, E. (1998). *How organizations learn: An integrated strategy for building learning capacity.* San Francisco: Jossey-Bass.

DiMaggio, P. J., & Powell, W. W. (1991). The iron cage revisited: Institutional isomorphism and collective rationality in organizational fields. In W. W. Powell & P. J. DiMaggio (Eds.), *The new institutionalism in organizational analysis* (pp. 63–82). Chicago: University of Chicago Press.

Downs, A. (1957). *An economic theory of democracy.* New York: Harper and Row.

Fauske, J. R., & Ogawa, R. T. (1987) Detachment, fear, and expectation: Faculty's response to the impending succession of its principal. *Educational Administration Quarterly, 23*(2), 23–44.

Fivars, G. (1980). *The critical incident technique: A bibliography* (2nd ed.). Palo Alto, CA: American Institute for Research.

Flanagan, J. C. (1954). The critical incident technique. *Psychological Bulletin, 51*(4), 327–358.

Galvin, P. F., & Fauske, J. R. (2000). Transaction costs and the structure of interagency collaboration: Bridging theory and practice. In B. Jones (Ed.), *Educational leadership: Policy dimensions in the 21st century* (pp. 41–67). Stamford, CT: Ablex.

Garner, R., & Sisk, J. (2000). *Report on the development and delivery of learning in electronic environments.* Paper presented in the Teaching Online in Higher Education Cyberconference.

Greenfield, W. D., Jr. (1995). Toward a theory of school administration: The centrality of leadership. *Educational Administration Quarterly, 31*(1), 61–85.

Hallinger, P., Leithwood, K., & Murphy, J. (Eds.). (1993). *Cognitive perspectives on educational leadership.* New York: Teachers College Press.

Jih, H. J., & Reeves, T. C. (1992). Mental models: A research focus for interactive learning systems. *Educational Technology Research and Development, 40*(3), 39–53.

Johnson, B. J., & Fauske, J. R. (2000). Principals and the political economy of environmental enactment. *Educational Administration Quarterly, 36*(2), 159–185.

Johnson, Jr., B. L., & Galvin, P. (1996). Understanding the organizational dynamics of collaborative partnerships: Two frameworks. In P. A. Cordeiro (Ed.), *Boundary crossings: Educational partnerships and school leadership* (pp. 99–114). San Francisco: Jossey-Bass.

Johnson-Laird, P. N. (1983). *Mental models: Toward a cognitive science of language, inference, and consciousness.* Cambridge, UK: Cambridge University Press.

Jones, C., Hesterly, W. S., & Borgatti, S. P. (1997). A general theory of network governance: Exchange conditions and social mechanisms. *Academy of Management Review, 22*(4), 911–945.

Kim, D. H. (1993). *A framework and methodology for linking individual and organizational learning: Applications in TQM and product development.* Unpublished doctoral dissertation, Massachusetts Institute of Technology.

Mahlios, M. C., & Carpenter, R. L. (1982). Political economy as a conceptual framework for the analysis of school–university cooperation. *Education, 103*(1), 15–21.

March, J. (1991). How decisions happen in organizations. *Human Computer Interaction, 6,* 95–117.

Meyer, J. W., & Scott, W. R. (1992). *Organizational environments: Ritual and rationality.* Newbury Park, CA: Sage.

Michaelsen, J. B. (1981). The political economy of school district administration. *Educational Administration Quarterly, 17*(3), 98–113.

Miles, M. B., & Huberman, A. M. (1994). *Qualitative data analysis* (2nd ed.). Thousand Oaks, CA: Sage.

Neilson, R. (1997). *Collaborative technologies and organisational learning.* London: Idea Group.

Niskanen, W. A. (1971). *Bureaucracy and representative government.* Chicago: Aldine-Atherton.

Ogawa, R. T. (1996). Bridging and buffering relations between parents and schools. *UCEA Review, 37,* 1–3.

Olson, M. (1965). *The logic of collective action.* Cambridge, MA: Harvard University Press.

Parkay, F. W., Currie, G. D., & Rhodes, J. W. (1992). Professional socialization: A longitudinal study of first-time high school principals. *Educational Administration Quarterly, 28*(1), 43–75.

Patton, M. Q. (1990). *Qualitative evaluation and research methods* (2nd ed.). Newbury Park, CA: Sage.

Pearce, R. J. (1997). Toward understanding joint venture performance and survival: A bargaining and influence approach to transaction costs theory. *Academy of Management Review, 22*(1), 203–225.

Pfeffer, J., & Salancik, G. R. (1978). *The external control of organizations.* New York: Harper and Row.

Piaget, J. (1977). *The development of thought: Equilibrium of cognitive structures.* New York: Viking.

Raybould, R. (2000). *Mental models: A key for understanding individual, collective, and organizational learning.* Unpublished doctoral dissertation, University of Utah.

Ring, P. S. (1996). Networked organization: A resource based perspective. *Studia Oeconomiae Negotiorum, 39*, 6–52.

Rowan, B., Raudenbush, S. W., & Cheong, Y. K. (1993). Teaching as a non-routine task: Implications for the management of schools. *Educational Administration Quarterly, 29*, 479–500.

Schein, E. H. (1992). *Organizational culture and leadership* (2nd ed.). San Francisco: Jossey-Bass.

Scott, W. R. (1998). *Organizations: Rational, natural, and open systems* (4th ed.). Englewood Cliffs, NJ: Prentice-Hall.

Senge, P. M. (1990). *The fifth discipline: The art and practice of the learning organization.* New York: Doubleday Dell.

Senge, P. M., Cambron-McCabe, N., Lucas, T., Smith, B., Dutton, J., & Kleiner, A. (2000). *Schools that learn: A fifth discipline fieldbook for educators, parents, and everyone who cares about education.* New York: Doubleday Dell.

Smylie, M., & Hart, A. (1999). School leadership for teacher learning and change: A human capital and social capital development perspective. In J. Murphy & K. S. Louis (Eds.), *Handbook of research on educational administration* (2nd ed.). American Educational Research Association.

Spradley, J. (1979). *The ethnographic interview.* New York: Holt, Rinehart.

Stano, M. (1983, April). *The critical incident technique: A description of the method.* Paper presented at the annual meeting of the Southern Speech Communication Association, Lincoln, NE.

Thompson, J. D. (1967). *Organizations in action.* New York: McGraw-Hill.

Weick, K. E. (1978). The spines of leadership. In M.W. McCall, Jr., & M. M. Lombardo (Eds.), *Leadership: Where else can we go?* (pp. 37–61). Durham, NC: Duke University Press.

Weick, K. E. (1979). *The social psychology of organizing* (2nd ed.). New York: McGraw-Hill.

Weick, K. E. (1995). *Sensemaking in organizations.* Newbury Park, CA: Sage.

Williamson, O. E., & Masten, S. E. (1995). *Transaction cost economics: Policy and applications* (Vol. II). London: Edward Elgar.

Woolsey, L. K. (1986). The critical incident technique: An innovative qualitative method of research. *Canadian Journal of Counseling, 20*, 242–254.

Yin, R. K. (1994). *Case study research: Design and methods* (2nd ed.). Thousand Oaks, CA: Sage.

CHAPTER 5

A RIVER RUNS THROUGH IT

Tacit Knowledge in Educational Administration

Nancy S. Nestor-Baker

ABSTRACT

Tacit knowledge is informal, action-oriented knowledge garnered with little external support. The study of tacit knowledge seeks to understand the role of embedded, implicit knowledge in our everyday actions, successes, and failures. While tacit knowledge has been examined in other fields, with a particular emphasis in business management, it has not been widely considered in educational administration. This chapter seeks to shed light on tacit knowledge, paying particular attention to tacit knowledge conceptualizations, the use of tacit knowledge in managerial and administrative contexts, the role of tacit knowledge in organizations and socialization, the development and transfer of tacit knowledge, and the use of tacit knowledge in the preparation of educational administrators.

All there is to thinking is seeing something noticeable which makes you see something you weren't noticing which makes you see something that isn't even visible.

—Norman Maclean (1976)

Studies in Leading and Organizing Schools, pages 121–155
Copyright © 2003 by Information Age Publishing

When we think of educational administration, we may think of leadership or vision or mission. We may think of accountability or student achievement or finance. We do not usually think of rivers. But there are rivers of knowledge flowing through the work of educational administrators; big, wide Mississippis, muddy Ohios, mysterious Pee Dees, flowing in and through our practice and theories, cutting new channels of thought and deepening old ones in ways we may not knowingly comprehend and may be unable to explain. As we figuratively fish and swim in these rivers of tacit knowledge that run through and around our endeavors, our decisions are made and our actions take shape.

Rich with experiential meaning, tacit knowledge helps us develop solutions to the complex, poorly defined problems encountered in our daily lives. Like those daily problems, tacit knowledge is multifaceted and difficult to define. It is also coming to be seen as an important component of our successes and failures.

Much of the systematic study of tacit knowledge has occurred in the military (Sternberg, Wagner, Williams, & Horvath, 1995), in sales (Wagner, Sujan, Sujan, Rashotte, & Sternberg, 1999), in law (Marchant & Robinson, 1999), and in medicine (Patel, Arocha, & Kaufmann, 1999). Recent years have seen a significant upsurge in tacit knowledge research in the management arena, particularly in the areas of knowledge management and organizational processes, as business strives to understand the hidden currents that affect such issues as competitive edge and employee development (e.g., Ambrosini & Bowman, 2001; Augier & Vendelo, 1999; Grant, 1991; Nonaka, 1994; Nonaka & Takauchi, 1995; Spender, 1993). However, the systematic investigation of the tacit knowledge of American educational administrators has been ignored in spite of the fact that experience and practical intelligence have long been held to be critical for effective school administration examination (see, however, Nestor-Baker, 2002; Nestor-Baker & Hoy, 2001; Nestor-Baker & Tschannen-Moran, 2001).

WHAT IS TACIT KNOWLEDGE?

A river, though, has so many things to say that it is hard to know
what it says to each of us.
I don't know what it is or where, because sometimes it is in my arms and sometimes in
my throat and sometimes nowhere in particular except somewhere deep.

—Norman Maclean (1976)

Tacit knowledge is personal knowledge so thoroughly grounded in experience that it cannot be fully expressed (Horvath et al., 1999). It allows a person to know when to adapt to the environment, when to shape the environment, and when to select a new one. Generally perceived as action oriented, it is relevant to goal attainment and is acquired with minimal help from others (Horvath et al., 1994). Tacit knowledge is not delivered through school curricula or found in textbooks, though such offerings can assist in its development. Rather, tacit knowledge can be considered as "educated common sense" (Bereiter & Scardamalia, 1993, p. 51).

Polanyi's (1966) philosophical treatise on personal knowledge laid the theoretical foundation for studies of tacit knowledge. Building on his widely quoted statement, "we can know more than we can tell" (p. 6), Polanyi argued that tacit knowing accounts "for a valid knowledge of the problem, for the individual's capacity to pursue it, guided by his sense of approaching its solution, and for a valid anticipation of the yet indeterminate implications of the discovery arrived at in the end" (p. 24). In his view, all knowledge has tacit dimensions. Perhaps in part for theoretical ease, some theorists place tacit and explicit knowledge in discrete categories (Leonard & Sensiper, 1998). Polanyi, however, subscribed to a messier view of knowledge, wherein knowledge exists on a continuum from utterly tacit and inaccessible to totally explicit and accessible.

Wagner and Sternberg (1985, 1986) suggest that tacit knowledge is a manifestation of practical intelligence. Practical intelligence is the underlying ability governing the capacity to gain tacit knowledge and solve practical problems (Sternberg, 1985). It has been called "common sense" (Sternberg, 1985), "street smarts" (Horvath et al., 1994), and "the mind in action" (Scribner, 1986). The practical abilities are used to navigate successfully through everyday life. They include interpersonal and supervisory skills, self knowledge, insight into the actions and behaviors that lead to goal achievement, and the ability to solve practical problems and to shape environments that impede success (Sternberg, 1985). In short, "Practical intelligence ... involves the ability to grasp, understand, and solve real life problems in the everyday jungle of life ... you can't be successful if you lack practical intelligence" (Sternberg, quoted in Miele, 1995). Tacit knowledge, then, points to the presence of practical intelligence.

Practical intelligence can be considered as "thinking that is embedded in the larger purposive activities of daily life and that functions to achieve the goals of those activities" (Scribner, 1986, p. 15). This involves reflective adaptation of one's behaviors and thought processes to the realities of life. It involves responding to novelty in ways that allow maximum benefit. The purposive activities that lead to goal achievement regularly place the practically intelligent individual in novel situations that require action, adaptation, and mastery. The practically intelligent individual is skilled at identifying relationships, whether they are verbal, spatial, interpersonal, or otherwise, and acting upon those identifications to achieve desired goals.

Sternberg (1981, 1985) believes that primary keys to intellectual gifted-ness lie not in IQ-like academic abilities but in an individual's insight abili-ties and abilities to do nonentrenched thinking. If it is accepted that dealing with non-entrenchment is an important aspect of practical intelli-gence, then this idea is important to an understanding of what separates the highly practically intelligent from the individual of moderate or lower practical intelligence.

In Bereiter and Scardamalia's (1993) discussion of tacit knowledge and expertise, they categorize tacit knowledge as:

- Informal knowledge—the common sense procedures of everyday life;
- Impressionistic knowledge—feelings that are an essential part of knowledge;
- Self-regulatory knowledge—the regulation of self and the under-standing of what leads to effective performance for oneself.

Impressionistic knowledge supports the acquisition of formal knowl-edge (Minsky, 1980) and provides important connections for formal knowledge. According to Minsky (1980), knowledge is recalled and recon-structed based on the impressions that originally accompanied the process-ing of that knowledge. The ill-defined aspects of impressions, coupled with the sensory-based nature of impressionistic acquisition, suggest agreement with tacitness as defined by Wagner and Sternberg (1985) and intimated by Polanyi (1966).

"Self-regulatory knowledge may be thought of as knowledge that con-trols the application of other knowledge...it is often referred to as meta-knowledge or metacognition" (Bereiter & Scardamalia, 1993, p. 60). The seemingly instinctive choice of learning strategies and the self-knowledge of one's rhythms and needs can be attributed to tacit knowledge of the self-regulatory kind.

The categories of impressionistic and self-regulatory knowledge suggest ties to the concepts of social and emotional intelligence as discussed by Salovey and Mayer (1990) and to the inter- and intrapersonal categories of tacit knowledge as discussed by Gardner (1993), Wagner and Sternberg (1985), and Sternberg (1985).

The context of tacit knowledge is also an important consideration for real-world accomplishment (Wagner, 1987). Context can be considered as local, referring to a focus on short-term, more immediate goals, or as glo-bal, referring to long-term goals and focusing on how the current situation fits into a larger framework. These delineations of context are a reminder of Neisser's (1976) statements that intelligent performance consists of "responding appropriately in terms of one's long-range and short-range goals, given the actual facts of the situation as one discovers them" (p. 137).

However, in considering tacit knowledge, and, more specifically, considering its role in accomplishment, we should remember that contexts are emergent phenomena (Augier, Shariq, &Vendelo, 2001), shifting in nuance and interpretation in the environment and in the minds of individuals. "Context is determined by the questions which people ask of events...many questions can be asked of events, so there will be many contexts...." (Rapport, 1999, p. 190). The formation and usage of tacit knowledge will be heavily influenced by our understanding and interpretation of context—which is, in turn, influenced by our tacit knowledge.

While tacit knowledge is often considered to be action oriented and linked to procedural competencies or "know how," there is also a broader view of tacit knowledge (Haldin-Herrgard, 2000; Nonaka, 1994). This broader view acknowledges the technical aspects of tacit knowledge but suggests that tacit knowledge also has elements of declarative knowledge. The broader view assumes not only that tacit knowledge includes "knowing how"—the technical dimension—but also includes "knowing that"—the cognitive dimension (Gore & Gore, 1999). The cognitive dimension provides additional theoretical room for our values, perceptions, and the mental models arising from those. However, it also muddies the water in an area that is murky even with the narrower, more widely accepted "know how" definition.

Weick's (1993) concept of bricolage provides yet another view of tacit knowledge. A "bricoleur" is one who relies on deep-seated, unarticulated forms of knowing and understanding that lie dormant until needed to accomplish a particular purpose. The idea of bricolage is also seen in the work of Berry and Irvine (1986) who present the idea that practical know-how is adaptive, cross-cultural, and a necessity for group survival.

Like Berry and Irvine, Shaw and Hazelett (1986) draw attention to the aspects of active adaptation utilized for survival. They suggest that knowing *how* requires different schemas than knowing *that,* though the necessities of survival require a close relationship between schemas.

Castillo (2002) attempts to synthesize various definitions and categories of tacit knowledge by suggesting we look at tacit knowledge as a four-part typology. He theorizes that tacit knowledge can be classified as:

1. Nonepistle, or unarticulated and perhaps unarticulatable tacit knowledge;
2. Sociocultural, or collective, culturally embedded tacit knowledge;
3. Semantic, or tacit knowledge that is verbalizable but is so widely accepted because of symbolism or other distinction that it becomes tacit; and
4. Sagacious tacit knowledge, which is related to expertise and which grows from the ability to synthesize and combine relevant information in appropriate and novel ways.

In fact, the concept of tacit knowledge suffers from a multitude of definitions. A natural concept like furniture or, perhaps, love, at times it seems to fall into that muddy we-know-it-when-we-see-it category. The ill-defined nature of impressionistic knowledge and the seeming instinctiveness of tacit knowledge development and utilization are fascinating to consider but present problems in testing.

Those who approach tacit knowledge from a psychological viewpoint have achieved some success in mapping and measuring tacit knowledge (e.g., Horvath et al., 1994; Nestor-Baker & Hoy, 2001; Sternberg et al., 1995; Wagner, 1987) in part because of a focus on practical intelligence; however, measurement success in business has failed repeatedly (e.g., Hennart, 1992), perhaps due to definitional issues.

Horvath and colleagues (1994, 1999) believe aspects of practical intelligence, particularly tacit knowledge, help account for successful performance. Wagner and Sternberg (1993) found that tacit knowledge scores are better predictors of job performance than personality or cognitive styles and suggest that an overreliance on the general cognitive factor of IQ tests is probably short-sighted when considering real-world performance, or potential for performance. Sternberg contends (1996; see also Wigdor & Garner, 1982) that the average validity coefficient between cognitive ability tests and job performance measures is approximately .2, meaning that only about 4% of the variance among people in their job performance is accounted for by IQ tests, leaving a vast amount of variance in performance unexplained by cognitive ability tests. However, Schmidt and Hunter (1981) believe that the variance is higher, perhaps as high as 25%. Even if the higher validity coefficient average is accepted, roughly 75% of the variance in real-world performance still remains to be explained. Practical intelligence, manifested as tacit knowledge, accounts for a portion of that variance.

Practical intelligence is recognized primarily through behavior, or perceptions of behavior. However, real-world performance is not necessarily a component of a number of the studies conducted on practical intelligence and tacit knowledge. Patel and colleagues (1999) state that the typical methodology for examining tacit knowledge consists of providing subjects with problems that require the subject to determine the implicit rules necessary for problem solution. While such studies point to implicitly developed understandings, they may lack connection to real-world events that have relevance to the subject. In effect, the individual faced with the constructed problem or scenario improvises, "reworking precomposed material and designs in relation to unanticipated ideas conceived, shaped, and transformed under the special circumstances of performance...." (Berliner, 1994, in Weick, 1998, p. 547) Given the highly contextualized nature of tacit knowledge, this suggests caution in interpreting results, not only those results arising from research but also those achieved as part of licensure testing (e.g., PRAXIS examinations).

The validity of studies that ask subjects to respond to simulations not based on actual purposive situations should be examined closely, in that the eduction occurring in real-life situations, affecting real-life goals of the subject, may not be effectively measured by tests that are disconnected to the lives of the subjects. Real-life problems are distorted by paper-and-pencil tests. Even open-ended questions such as "What would you do?" fail to capture the complex relations that occur in real-life situations; multiple-choice questions may limit the amount of obtainable information available to the tester and the breadth of options available to the test taker that are necessary to truly illuminate practical intelligence (see Levine, McGuire, & Nattress, 1970; Ward, Frederiksen, & Carlson, 1980); and the limitations of paper-and-pencil instruments cannot capture the multitude of stimuli that enter into real-world interactions.

Klemp and McClelland (1986) voiced concerns that behavioral lists and descriptions do not provide sufficient validation, and ethnographic studies are too limiting because of the time and expense necessary to attain a statistically significant sample. Therefore, they chose to use a behaviorally based job competence assessment methodology. They observed "intellectual competencies in action and as operants ... rather than as responses to controlled situations or stimuli" (p. 47). The significance of the Klemp and McClelland approach is that overall quality of performance and the situational context are taken as givens, out of which come dimensions of difference in performance levels. This contrasts with approaches that begin with specific assumptions, such as particular constitutionalizations of practical intelligence, and tests those assumptions in experimental situations.

Wagner and Sternberg's *Tacit Knowledge Inventory for Managers* (1991) combines aspects of those measurements. This management inventory was developed to provide a tool for discerning the level of tacit knowledge agreement between an individual respondent and an organization's expert managers. Using general management scenarios, respondents choose how likely they would be to select various responses. By aggregating the responses of organizationally determined experts, a firm- or field-specific tacit knowledge profile is developed. This profile is then used as a touchstone for considering the goodness of fit between individual and group.

Generally, tacit knowledge tests have been scored in one of three ways: subject responses have been correlated with a group membership index; the difference between subject responses and a prototype have been computed; or the degree to which subjects' responses conform to experts' rules of thumb (Horvath et al., 1994; Sternberg, 1985).

Horvath and colleagues (1994) chose an ideographic approach and a qualitative method to conduct their research on tacit knowledge for the

United States Army. Officers were interviewed, and the interviews were coded and analyzed in order to develop a clearer understanding of the content and structure of tacit knowledge within the officer ranks of the U.S. Army. Their approach allowed for greater exposure to, and thus, increased opportunities to understand, the multidimensionality of the participants' experiences. Building on the Horvath and colleagues study, Nestor-Baker and Hoy (2001) used a combination of critical-incident technique (Flanagan, 1954) and sense-making interview methodology (Dervin, 1983) to elicit data that was then cluster-analyzed to map superintendent tacit knowledge.

When studying practical intelligence and tacit knowledge, the investigator should seek out a methodology that permits a balancing of implicitness and explicitness. The complex, interwoven variables of practical intelligence, coupled with the socially constructed aspects of tacit knowledge, make accurate measurement difficult to perform and difficult to defend due to extensive validity errors. On the other hand, an overreliance on interviews and personal events reduces the study of practical intelligence to the level of a human interest story—interesting to read, but of little consequence.

And tacit knowledge is of consequence. Tacit knowledge is not just a bunch of random pieces of information. Rather, it is highly contextualized, informal, experientially based knowledge that takes the form of a laddered production system (Sternberg, 1998). This production system can be thought of as a sequence of if–then statements that the individual moves through as he or she pursues goal achievement; "if" a particular condition exists, "then" a particular step is taken (Horvath et al., 1994). Though it may sound simplistic and linear, in execution there can be multiple series of ifs and multiple series of thens, each acting upon the others, and each having a contextual relationship with the pursued goal(s).

Based on the previous discussion, it might be easy to leap to the conclusion that tacit knowledge is merely a synonym for expertise. That, however, would be an error. Though related, and possessed of some overlap, tacit knowledge and expertise are not equivalent, as can be seen in the following portion of this chapter.

TACIT KNOWLEDGE AND EXPERTISE

I thought that I had fished the hole just the way my brother had taught me, except that he hadn't told me what to do when a fish goes up a tree. That's one trouble wit hanging around a master—you pick up some of his stuff, like how to cast into a bush, but you use it just when the master is doing the opposite.

—Norman Maclean (1976)

If you can learn to do it correctly, to read the river and the fish and yourself,
and to do what needs to be done without one wasted motion, you will have attained
some of the grace and economy needed to live a good life. If you can do it and under-
stand that the river, the fish and the whole world are God's gifts to use wisely,
you will have gone the rest of the way.

—Roger Ebert, review of *A River Runs Through It, Chicago Sun-Times,*
October 9, 1992

Tacit knowledge and expertise are not interchangeable. If expertise is conceived as the possession of complex skills and knowledge, reliable application in actions intended to accomplish generally endorsed goal states, and a record of goal accomplishment (Leithwood & Steinbach, 1995), then tacit knowledge may be seen as an important thread woven through the development of expertise: a portion of the accumulation of domain-specific knowledge, coupled with understandings of how to apply that knowledge in order to reach desired end states. This view is in line with Chi, Glaser, and Farr's (1988) indications that experts have many domain-specific concepts, procedures, and strategies. The experiential, action-oriented orientation of tacit knowledge thus may be a vital component of the development of expertise, as expertise appears to be similarly vital to the expansion of tacit knowledge.

Leithwood and Steinbach (1995) argue that experts and nonexperts differ in whether they have sufficient domain knowledge to respond effectively to problems encountered within the domain. The interplay of context-specific knowledge, and practical adaptation and application of that knowledge in the development of expertise, is illuminated by Patel and colleagues' (1999) analysis of the development of expertise in medical professionals. They note that the acquisition of tacit knowledge occurs in real-world environments, involves decision making under time pressure and conditional constraints, and is characterized by the interplay of multiple factors. Furthermore, they argue that tacit knowledge is vital to the development of professional expertise, acting as a pivotal link in the reification of domain knowledge in practice. The implicit knowledge garnered in practice and the explicit knowledge attained in formal training are key to understanding the complex role of implicit and explicit knowledge in experts. This underscores the work of Allison and Allison (1993), in which the effect of expertise in principals was shown to be highly complex. Quoting Kennedy (1987, p. 148), Allison and Allison point out that time-in-role will not necessarily produce experts, for "experience can only contribute to expertise if practitioners are capable of learning from it." Or, in other words, "explicit knowledge is for everyone to use, but tacit knowledge separates the masters from the common" (Haldin-Herrgard, 2000, p. 359).

Though tacit knowledge and expertise are not interchangeable, there are strong conceptual connections between the development and application of expertise and tacit knowledge, particularly when that expertise is related to goal-oriented problem solving. Bereiter and Scardamalia (1993) posit that tacit knowledge—the invisible knowledge hidden behind intelligent action—is highly developed in experts. However, while tacit knowledge increases with job experience, it is not a direct function of that experience. In other words, the amount of experience one has is less important than what is done with that experience to acquire knowledge, solve the complex problems of practice, and achieve goals (Leithwood & Steinbach, 1995; Wagner, 1987). There are those with long years of service who do not evidence high levels of expertise, and those with shorter tenure who clearly have gleaned more from their experiences. To illustrate, a principal once aired his frustration with a veteran teacher who was having difficulties in the classroom. Throwing his hands in the air, he said, "She's been a first year teacher for 10 years in a row."

Expert performance depends in large part on a large, accumulated knowledge base, which allows intuitive perceptual orientation to the task at hand (Perkins, 1996). In addition to a stored accumulation of facts, the knowledge base contains remembered impressions, emotions, and mental pictures, all of which are part of knowledge structures and may be utilized in decision-making processes (Leithwood & Steinbach, 1995). This "accumulated knowledge base," however, is only important insofar as it is relevant to achieving the goals and desires of the individual.

Impressionistic knowledge in expertise may be a matter of degree of development. Non-experts "have impressions but they do not have much impressionistic knowledge. Their impressions are not stable or clear enough or consistently enough related to actual instances that they can play a useful role in communication or judgment" (Bereiter & Scardamalia, 1993, p. 55). Support for this statement comes from Wagner and colleagues' (1999) discussion of the effect of tacit knowledge differences on effective salesmanship. The authors conclude that salespeople who continue to improve their performance levels are those who continue to search for abstract, underlying principles related to customer classification. Conversely, the salespeople who do not seek to strengthen or extend their command of sales-related abstract, impressionistic knowledge do not improve in expertise.

Scribner (1984) suggests that "expertise in practical problem solving frequently hinges on an apt formulation or redefinition of the initial problem. ... One artful aspect of practical thinking is to construct or redefine a problem that experience or a hunch suggests will facilitate a solution" (p. 21). Flexibility, schematic chunking, and utilization of the environment in solution generation differentiate expert workers from novices. Problems cannot be solved simply by automatized retrieval of previously acquired information. Rather, using complex forms and combinations of relationships, variables in the task must be identified and an appropriate strategy for solving the problem must be selected.

Having given consideration to the relationship between expertise and tacit knowledge, I now turn to a consideration of tacit knowledge at the managerial or administrative level.

MANAGERIAL AND ADMINISTRATIVE TACIT KNOWLEDGE

Sometimes a thing in front of you is so big you don't know whether to comprehend it by first getting a dim sense of the whole and then fitting in the pieces or by adding up the pieces until something calls out what it is.

—Norman Maclean (1976)

Argyris (1999) claims that tacit knowledge is the primary basis for effective management, arguing that effective management requires the definition and transformation of behaviors essential to turning organizational objectives into routines that work. Routines are implemented through skillful actions, and skillful actions are based largely on tacit knowledge. Of course, tacit knowledge can have negative as well as positive consequences, especially when such action becomes self-reinforcing of the status quo and prevents inquiry into inconsistencies.

Sternberg (1998) and Wagner and Sternberg (1985, 1986) argue that much of the learning contributing to real-world success happens without formal instruction, and often without open expression or acknowledgment. In other words, it happens through the development of tacit knowledge. Often unspoken or poorly articulated, tacit knowledge is not generally shared among individuals because the rules on which it is based often belong to complex groupings of highly abstract, automatized procedures. However, automatization is not the only reason tacit knowledge is not shared professionally. For example, sharing tacit knowledge may appear oppositional to goals for personal success held by the individual with the tacit knowledge. The holder of the knowledge may be led by that tacit knowledge to believe that providing informal knowledge to colleagues or to the organization may remove a personal benefit; knowing the ins and outs of an occupation or situation gives a comparative advantage to the holder of that information (Sternberg, 1985). Think of the successful building level administrator who chooses not to mentor her colleagues or the superintendent who will not open up to other superintendents for fear of losing his "edge."

There are far less Machiavellian reasons that tacit knowledge is not shared easily (Leonard & Sensiper, 1998; Nonaka & Takauchi, 1995). Verbalizing automatized knowledge is difficult; because of the unconscious nature of the knowledge, individuals do not realize the depth and breadth of the knowledge they hold. Additionally, high levels of expertise may get in the way of tacit knowledge articulation. As a person develops higher levels and additional layers of experience and knowledge, the tacitness of those layers increases (Cooke & MacDonald, 1987; Haldin-Herrgard, 2000). In our river metaphor, these layers are like the sediment that builds on the river bed, covering over items within it, hiding from view that which it is built upon.

Time is also a factor in the difficulty of sharing professional tacit knowledge. Reflection on the implicit knowledge is essential for embedding it. However, reflection is a scarce commodity in today's organizations, including schools. Schön's (1983) "reflection in action" quickly becomes Weick's (1998) improvisation. In schools, changes in necessary knowledge come rapidly as new information and new requirements are added by external and internal constituencies; the knowledge once relied upon may no longer be effective and the opportunities to develop new schemas may be limited. Fiscal restraints erode the amount of individual and shared planning time for teachers and administrators; our efforts to be efficient with our limited time and dollars may actually result in less ability to develop tacit knowledge that can lead to better system efficiencies.

Rapid turnover in certain administrative positions, particularly those in urban settings, suggests that the tacit knowledge generated may be more closely related to short-term goal achievement and personal career survival skills, leaving gaps in other potentially important areas such as the culture, rituals, and values of the specific school system and its community. In the life of schools, it sometimes seems that there is a belief—or perhaps a hope—that educational cultures across schools and districts are so similar that revolving superintendents and principal shuffling do not create challenges for the individual and the organization. However, "perhaps the biggest roadblock to effective assimilation, or at least absorption into a culture, is the existence of hidden differences across cultures in what it means to be competent" (Sternberg, 1998, p. 712). Our expectations often do not permit the time for knowledge generation needed to meet them.

The discussion above suggests that degree of importance, or value, is an important aspect in the development and sharing of tacit knowledge. We are more likely to develop tacit knowledge if it, or the goals that it can help us reach, are valuable to us (Haldin-Herrgard, 2000; Sternberg, 1998). The organization and the individuals who comprise the organization value particular types of knowledge and pursue certain types of goals. There are implicit expectations that suggest what knowledge is valued. These expectations are hinted at in the support of various persons and activities and in the resistance to other persons and activities.

Implicit expectations do not necessarily conform to the explicit expectations received by administrators. To illustrate, Glass and colleagues (1992; Glass, Bjork, & Brunner, 2000) found that boards of education engaged in evaluating superintendents do not rely heavily on the formal job description that might be argued to be the technical baseline for success or failure in the superintendency. While boards may utilize explicit performance indicators such as test scores, they are also likely to evaluate based on other, more implicitly oriented aspects of the superintendent's job, such as superintendent relations with the board and community, superintendent effectiveness in policy, and the remarkably nebulous "general effectiveness."

Although boards of education have superintendent evaluation policies and are encouraged by their state and national associations to evaluate against stated criteria, the evaluative criteria tend to be based on the tacit knowledge of both the board and the superintendent. Thus, evaluation of success in the superintendency appears to be predicated on how well the superintendent has understood and acted upon the tacit expectations of the board and the community. The implicit expectations of a superintendent will differ in each district, though the job descriptions may be similar. Value systems, vision, relationships, and even ethics are affected by local context. The superintendent's responses to the varying implicit expectations of a local board and community will be affected by his or her accumulated experiences.

The works of Johnson (1996), Glass (1992), and Glass and colleagues (2000) provide evidence that superintendent success may be linked to the effective acquisition and use of tacit knowledge. Their work illustrates Patel and colleagues' (1999) remark that "probably nowhere is the study of implicit knowledge more important than in the professions, where a large part of learning occurs in practice, after formal training has been completed" (p. 77). It is interesting to note that only 48% of the superintendents of large districts believe that their board's primary expectation is that they will be educational leaders. While academic preparation stresses educational leadership, day-to-day practice of the superintendency requires considerable levels of other knowledge for successful performance.

Sternberg and Horvath (1999) maintain that "successful performance is the only true test of successful intelligence" (p. 251). Thus, successful administrators can be considered in part as those who have been able to go beyond the explicitly stated requirements of their educational training and job descriptions to meet implicitly held expectations. If that is the case, tacit knowledge (Sternberg, 1985; Wagner & Sternberg, 1986) appears to play a significant role in successful performance.

In looking at the tacit knowledge of highly successful superintendents, Nestor-Baker and Hoy (2001) considered the differences in tacit knowledge quantity and content between a group of superintendents reputed to be highly successful and a group not reputed to be so. There is a significant difference in the amount of tacit knowledge evinced by highly successful super-intendents and their typical counterparts. There are also differences in tacit knowledge content between the two groups. The categories are described in Table 5.1 and their distribution by category is found in Figure 5.1.

Table 5.1.   Superintendent Tacit Knowledge Categories as Derived from Hierarchical Agglomerative Cluster Analysis (Nestor-Baker & Hoy, 2001)

Cluster Categories	Interpretation
Behaving Consistently	Maintaining specific behaviors to achieve consistent employee behavior
Building and Sustaining Board Relations	Dealings with the board, including communications, elections, personal relationships
Building Credibility	Building trust and belief in the superintendent in order to increase organizational confidence
Building Personal Performance Capacities	Efforts to encourage higher levels of emotional and practical performance in self and others
Developing Administrators	Encouraging administrators' professional development
Encouraging External Outreach	Connecting the system to outside constituencies
Fostering Organizational Stability	Maintaining smooth operations (includes fiscal and political)
Handling Public Relations	Strategies to create/maintain a positive school system image
Involving Subordinates	Management preferences
Maintaining Board Unity	Keeping board members unified during controversy
Managing Problem Administrators	Strategies to remove poor administrators
Managing Organizational Goal Achievement	Strategic planning and behaviors used to focus the system on organizational goals
Meshing Staff and Organization	Using hiring and evaluation to align employees with the organizational culture and goals
Negotiating	Unions and contracts, including personal and employee
Reducing Conflict and Alienation	Processes and behaviors to calm agitated or disenfranchised constituencies
Responding to Perception	Reacting to perceptions held of self and system
Sharing Mission and Goals	Efforts to create/maintain a clear, specific focus with the board regarding the district
Strengthening the Role/ Image of the Superintendent	Strategies and behaviors used to solidify formal and informal power
Supporting Board Decisions	Public support of the board
Upholding Personnel Standards	Achieve/maintain a high-character, quality staff
Using Inter- and Intrapersonal Knowledge	Utilization of knowledge of self and others to maintain focus or achieve goals

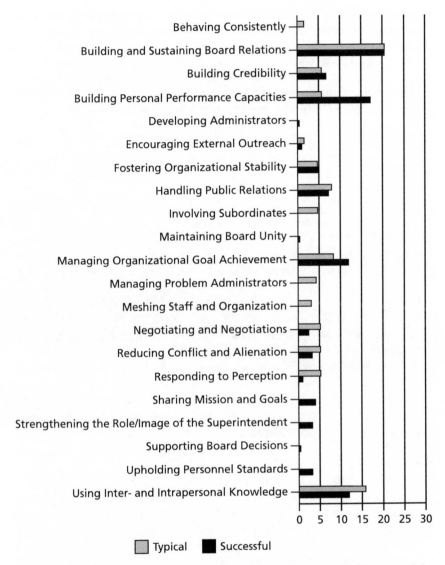

Figure 5.1.   Distribution of superintendent tacit knowledge for highly successful and typical superintendents (Nestor-Baker & Hoy, 2001)

Though sometimes bearing different names, the three areas found most commonly in the extant research on tacit knowledge at the managerial level are interpersonal tacit knowledge, intrapersonal tacit knowledge, and organizational tacit knowledge.

Interpersonal tacit knowledge exerts a consistent presence in the work of Ford (1986), Klemp and McClelland (1986), Horvath and colleagues

(1994), Sternberg (1985), and Wagner and Sternberg (1985). This knowledge includes influencing, controlling, and managing others; establishing trust; supporting, understanding, and cooperating with others; communicating with others; learning from others; and handling social relationships. Sternberg (1985) and Wagner and Sternberg (1985) are emphatic in saying that interpersonal tacit knowledge is important to managerial success. In examining the tacit knowledge of superintendents, Nestor-Baker and Hoy (2001) found that superintendents focus extensively on the interpersonal aspects of educational management; of the 21 tacit knowledge categories derived via cluster analysis and illustrated in Figure 5.1, 11 were based all or in part on tacit knowledge concerning relationships with others.

In tandem with tacit knowledge related to interpersonal relationships, there is a clear strand in the tacit knowledge literature dealing with self-knowledge and self-regulation, called "intrapersonal" by Gardner (1993), Sternberg (1985), and Wagner and Sternberg (1985). This is supported by Nestor-Baker and colleagues (Nestor-Baker, 2002; Nestor-Baker & Hoy, 2001; Nestor-Baker & Tschannen-Moran, 2001), who found strands of interpersonal knowledge woven through the tacit knowledge categories of superintendents. It is entwined with interpersonal tacit knowledge, illustrating the tightly woven contextual interplay of self and others discussed by Gardner (1993).

Inter- and intrapersonal aspects of tacit knowledge are especially important in school administration given the contextual nature of tacit knowledge and the fact that an administrator's realm of work is highly people-intensive, requiring formation and utilization of relationships to achieve organizational and personal goals.

Sternberg (1985) and Wagner and Sternberg (1985) found that managing people—knowing how to work with and direct the work of others; managing tasks—knowing how to manage and prioritize day-to-day tasks; managing self—knowing how to maximize one's performance and productivity; and managing career—knowing how to establish and enhance one's reputation were tacit knowledge areas particularly important for managerial success. While those studies did not involve educational administrators, the four domains are supported by Nestor-Baker and colleagues' (Nestor-Baker, 2002; Nestor-Baker & Hoy, 2001; Nestor-Baker & Tschannen-Moran, 2001) examinations of the tacit knowledge of superintendents.

Horvath and colleagues' (1994) study of military leadership found that, even though there is overlap, tacit knowledge changes based on hierarchical position, with individuals at higher levels evincing more complex forms of tacit knowledge. As military rank increased, officers' perceptions seemed to reflect the "big picture" of the organization, including a focus on the future rather than the individual level attended to at lower levels.

"The tacit-knowledge data on battalion commanders suggest that the officers ... at this level have developed a systems-level view of leadership. In general, they seem to see leadership in institutional rather than in strictly interpersonal terms" (p. 33).

While no published information exists at this point in time comparing tacit knowledge across different positions in school administration, the categories of tacit knowledge found by Horvath and colleagues (1994) provide interesting food for thought as we consider possible areas of similarity and difference across rank and level of responsibility within school systems. The military is certainly not the same as educational administration; however, both are concerned with the management, development, and supervision of groups of people functioning within the patterns and parameters of institutionalized organizations. Horvath and colleagues' categories are as follows, paired with possible conceptual linkages to positions in educational administration:

- **Battalion Commanders** (possible similarities to superintendents)
  Unique categories: Protecting the organization, managing organizational change and dealing with poor performers
  Shared categories: Developing subordinates, communicating, managing the self, motivating subordinates, establishing trust, and taking care of soldiers
- **Company Commanders** (possible similarities to principals or central office positions below the superintendency)
  Unique categories: Directing and supervising subordinates, cooperating with others, balancing mission and troops
  Shared categories: Influencing the boss, developing subordinates, communicating, managing the self, motivating subordinates, establishing trust, and taking care of soldiers
- **Platoon Leaders** (possible similarities to assistant principals)
  Unique category: Establishing credibility
  Shared categories: Influencing the boss, communicating, managing the self, motivating subordinates, establishing trust, and taking care of soldiers

Because most educational administrators move into administration from classroom teaching, the tacit knowledge they bring with them tends to be heavily oriented toward that particular professional and hierarchical level. Through education, experience, and reflection, those who are successful will develop additional reservoirs of tacit knowledge that utilize the effective aspects of the tacit knowledge used in their prior position and facilitate new knowledge more appropriate to managerial levels.

That hierarchical rise, with the concomitant development of related knowledge, has been de rigueur in education until recently. However, of late, we have experienced a push to provide alternative pathways into administrative practice. There has been and continues to be vociferous debate regarding the appropriateness of such pathways and the likelihood of success for nontraditional administrators. On the one hand are those who believe that successful administrative and educational leadership is most likely to occur when the administrator has an educational background and has been socialized and educated at different hierarchical levels in the world of education. This view suggests that the rivers and reservoirs of knowledge acquired while moving through the educational ranks are a necessity for effective supervision and leadership of educators. On the other hand are those who believe that the skills and knowledge needed for successful management and administration are remarkably similar in education and in other fields of leadership, such as the military or in business. In this view, necessary knowledge related to leadership is achievable through noneducation routes pursued prior to entering educational administration, while necessary knowledge related to education can be garnered through on-the-job training as needed.

Most of the debate focuses on explicit knowledge. However, it would appear that the stubborn irresolvability of the debate may actually be rooted in the implicit knowledge held by the debaters, the expectations they hold of administrators based on that knowledge, and the tacit knowledge they expect administrators to access. Value systems, assumptions, and organizational and personal goals are inextricably entwined with discussions of necessary administrative skill sets and organizational structures and competencies. Thus far, however, the implicit aspects of the debate have been largely ignored.

TACIT KNOWLEDGE IN ORGANIZATIONS

Eventually, all things merge into one, and a river runs through it. The river was cut by the world's great flood and runs over rocks from the basement of time. On some of the rocks are timeless raindrops. Under the rocks are the words, and some of the words are theirs.

—Norman Maclean (1976)

Knowledge management is of growing interest in the world of management, including interest in tacit knowledge as well as in the more traditional area of explicit, formalized knowledge. Effective use of tacit knowledge within business organizations is perceived to provide a competitive edge (Augier & Vendelo, 1999; Haldin-Herrgard, 2001). To paraphrase Nonaka and Takauchi (1995), if Hewlett-Packard knew what Hewlett-Packard knows, Hewlett-Packard would be unbeatable. Interestingly, that desire to capitalize on individual and organizational tacit knowledge is noticeably absent in the educational administration literature.

In order to effectively utilize tacit knowledge, the organization—whatever its field—needs to encourage the creation and enhancement of knowledge, both implicit and explicit. Von Krogh, Ichigo, and Nonaka (2000) suggest that an enabling context is necessary for knowledge creation and that such a context must foster a sense of trust and a reliance on relationships, thus providing tangential support for tacit knowledge development but wisely refraining from attempts to codify that knowledge. According to Von Krogh and colleagues, leadership that is effective in the development and transfer of tacit knowledge employs the following knowledge enablers:

- Instilling a knowledge vision;
- Managing conversations;
- Mobilizing knowledge activities;
- Globalizing local knowledge.

These enablers work to shape group norms, moving between concrete activities such as efforts to disseminate knowledge across the organization and symbolic representations of organizational beliefs such as vision creation. As in the individually focused studies by Horvath and colleagues (1994), Nestor-Baker and Hoy (2001), and Nestor-Baker and Tschannen-Moran (2001), there is a clear focus on interpersonal relationships. There is also an extensive utilization of small teams, or "microcommunities of knowledge." Ideally (though not always realistically), turnover in these microcommunities is slow, allowing for stable infusions of new relationships and new ideas and skills. Instability due to high turnover or rapidly changing organizational contexts leads to dissolution of microcommunities and the loss of much of the tacit knowledge developed within them. While some may argue that the dissolution of groups provides for dissemination of the group's tacit knowledge through those who were once group members, Van Krogh and colleagues (2000) argue that tacit knowledge is socially distributed within the group and can be retained only through its interactions.

Microcommunities are similar to the term "communities of practice" (Brown & Duguid, 1991; Leonard & Sensiper, 1998), which is more familiar in the field of education. Communities of practice share tacit understanding—group norms, assumptions, and knowledge—that "guide much of the interactions among group members" (Leonard & Sensiper, 1998, p. 126). Thus, the tacit knowledge of the group's members, as applied to the functioning of the organization, serves to embed the organization's culture and climate, whether positive or negative. Change in orientation, then, may require the development and institutionalization of new forms of tacit knowledge through the infusion of new people from different types of communities of practice or the rewarding of attempts to reframe tacit knowledge among existing group members.

Mascitelli (2000) adds further thoughts regarding the importance of groups to organizational tacit knowledge, saying "the first step toward harnessing the creative power of tacit knowledge is to foster the emotional commitment and deep personal involvement" (p. 179) of team members. Following Mascitelli's lead, educational administrators who seek to tap tacit knowledge for the good of the organization can open the gates by developing inspiring stories about administrative and educational innovation, encouraging reasonable risk taking, and displaying sure confidence in the abilities of group members. These efforts assist in developing a unique identity for the groups involved and assist in developing emotional commitment on the part of group members. However, Mascitelli cautions that tacit knowledge utilization requires physical interaction and group member stability.

This does not mean that movement across districts or schools is necessarily counterproductive, although rapid, continuing turnover could have negative ramifications as regards the development, transfer, and sustenance of tacit knowledge. Rather it is a cautionary note; boards and administrators making hiring decisions need to be aware of the need to create balance between the infusion of new knowledge and commonalities derived from overlapping experience within the organization. Furthermore, they need to consciously provide for cultural socialization to enhance the likelihood of acceptance of new blood from differing backgrounds.

Bringing in new blood is often seen as a way to stimulate innovation. The insertion of unknown entities or the fostering of creative abrasion is used to reduce the groupthink that can arise due to overabundant commonalities and that can result in an isolationism from the rest of the organization or from the field. However, the simple act of adding new people is not sufficient to stimulate innovation.

Leonard and Sensiper (1998) point to three ways that tacit knowledge is used in innovation, suggesting that the three are arranged in a hierarchy of increasing departure from what is obvious or expected and therefore are of increasing value to innovative effects. Most commonly, or at the lowest level of the hierarchy, tacit knowledge is used in problem solving, the understanding of appropriate actions to resolve issues. The second application of tacit knowledge in innovation is in framing or finding problems. A subhierarchy can be implied here in that there are differing levels of tacit knowledge application in defining a problem, possibly resulting in successively more creative, nonobvious reframing. Finally, the third level of the hierarchy, and that which is most remote from expectedness, relates to a deep understanding of how something works, an understanding that may be built on the extensive, partially conscious incubation of thoughts and experiences. Cattell (1971) provides a satisfying discourse on the mental rhythm that seems to run through the creative problem-solving process.

One detects a rhythm, in which there are phases, lasting days or months, such as a) clarifying the elements in the problem, b) deciding what the central question really is, c) experiencing a heightened tension as effort at solution mounts, d) marking time (apparently) in what is often a fairly long incubation period. Therein much work is done unconsciously, while consciously the individual feels in the doldrums, aware of no progress, e) a sudden, thrusting up from the subconscious of a solution, often rough, and sometimes as symbolic and poorly communicable as a dream, but generally true, and f) a working out of detail and explicitness and a tidying of the means of communication. (pp. 430–431)

While Cattell's words were oriented toward individuals, they are apropos to groups as well. "The process of innovation is a search and selection, exploration and synthesis, cycles of divergent thinking followed by convergence" (Leonard & Sensiper, 1998, p. 116).

Stability, trust, employee retention, support for reasonable risks, time to reflect and incubate ideas—these are all needed for the sustainable development and transfer of tacit knowledge within individuals and within organization. They may also be in short supply in the everyday world of a number of educational administrators.

The term "hindering bureaucracy," as used by Hoy and Sweetland (2001), suggests the type of organization that hinders collaborative development and sharing of tacit knowledge. Such a bureaucracy consists of a rigid, suspicious, highly controlling operational structure where mistakes are punished, problems are seen as constraints, and mistrust flourishes. This type of organization inhibits the sharing of tacit knowledge (Leonard & Sensiper, 1998).

The rigidity of a hindering bureaucracy brings to mind that time-worn cliché, "Throw the baby out with the bath water"; overzealous efforts to systematize, to be accountable and efficient and coldly rational, all too often result in a refusal to nurture the innovative aspects of individual and group tacit knowledge. That does not mean that tacit knowledge does not exist in a hindering bureaucracy—of course it does. However, the tacit knowledge rewarded in the organization will be that which furthers the organization's goals, which includes protection of its particular bureaucratic orientation.

This embedding is further cemented by the individuals hired into the organization. "Organizations hire individuals and groups not for their explicitly expressed knowledge alone, but for their anticipated overall impact on the performance of the organization...much of which derives from the tacit dimensions of knowledge" (Leonard & Sensiper, 1998, p.

126–127). The knowledge resources of the organization, then, are held and structured by the individuals who make up the organization, whose selection was influenced by assumptions about the implicit knowledge they possess. Thus, the hindering aspects of bureaucracy may be enhanced by individual and group tacit knowledge that blocks adaptation to change, hinders innovation, and leads to the continuation of practices that hinder effective organizational practices and individual behaviors (Ambrosini & Bowman, 2001).

In no way should it be suggested that all schools and school systems are under the iron rule imposed by hindering bureaucracies. "Enabling bureaucracies" (Hoy & Sweetland, 2001) provide a climate much more conducive to the spread of effective tacit knowledge. Marked by flexibility and cooperation, evincing helpful rules and procedures rather than rigid conformity, and promoting trust and risk taking, the enabling bureaucracy supports an organizational structure that is an incubator for innovative tacit knowledge. The existence of a structure and climate that encourages professionalization and collaboration provides psychological underpinnings supportive of the reflection and interaction helpful in creative problem solving's tacit knowledge resources.

Organizations' knowledge resources have been described as an iceberg, with the structured, explicit part of the knowledge as the visible top and the tacit knowledge beneath the surface (Haldin-Herrgard, 2000). This makes intuitive sense. It also raises a pertinent policy issue. There are various initiatives afoot to focus educator development on explicit content knowledge rather than on instructional methodology or the cognitive underpinnings of learning and instruction. Just as in the debate over alternative administrator pathways, the implicit arguments shape the explicit arguments for and against such practice. The arguments for increased content knowledge and decreased methodology have assumed significant prominence in government circles and in the press. Interestingly, in the lesser levels of refutation evidenced by the education community, we may be seeing an example of the difficulties inherent in explicating highly developed expertise. Noneducator policymakers and Sunday morning television hosts find it much easier to understand and argue the explicit content-based argument than to grapple with the implicit value of the "art" of educating. However, it is possible that a lopsided success of content-over-method initiatives could lead to increased difficulty in acquiring and transferring the tacit knowledge that is important to the development of effective instruction and improved student achievement.

In education we are fond of saying things like, "we have the knowledge to solve our problems." That may be so, but that message is not accepted by many of education's constituencies. We have not been remarkably successful in surfacing the tacit knowledge that could bolster our arguments or in building support by hooking onto tacit knowledge held by others. In fact, our current national context of legislated accountability, political dissension, upper level personnel upheaval (particularly in urban districts), and fiscal constraints suggests that the tacit knowledge being brought to bear on education's concerns increasingly belong to noneducators. This should not be construed as saying that knowledge of noneducators has no place in our educational systems. It is, however, a suggestion that we should seek to transfer, elucidate, and support tacit knowledge that is important to the field before the field is subsumed by tacit knowledge from other arenas.

TACIT KNOWLEDGE AND SOCIALIZATION

We sat on the bank and the river went by. As always, it was making sounds to itself, and now it made sounds to us. It would be hard to find three men sitting side by side who knew better what a river was saying.

—Norman Maclean (1976)

Socialization occurs through repeated exposure to artifacts, behaviors, and collective and individual memories. The process of socialization builds upon prior experiences and combines concrete, explicit manifestations of culture and expectations with implicit, abstract manifestations of the same. Socialization occurs over time as an individual implicitly absorbs the norms of the organization through observation, induction, and participation in its life (Knight, 2002). With the passage of time and repeated exposure to the organization, the meaning that the individual attributes to routine and explicit activities becomes deeply embedded and resistant to change.

As do those in other professions, administrators go through a process of professional socialization wherein they learn the skills and knowledge base of the profession (Bullough, 1990; Hart, 1991). In the typical career progression of a school administrator, this understanding of teaching and administration is developed as the individual progresses through various avenues of training (i.e., teaching experience, graduate school, field internships, principal assignments, central office). As the administrator absorbs this professional knowledge, he or she also is engaging in organizational socialization, learning behavioral expectations, values, and organizationally oriented knowledge. Hart (1991) states that organizational and professional socialization occur virtually simultaneously during the early part of an individual's induction into a profession but that organizational socialization takes precedence over professional socialization as time goes by, or as Hart explains, "the salience, immediacy, and power of the work context hold sway over education and training for many reasons" (p. 452). Looking at socialization from a tacit knowledge viewpoint, the goal specificity and contextual orientation of tacit knowledge generation and application may be related to the values and expectations internalized during organizational socialization.

We are all familiar with those large group orientations where new organizational members are exposed to the policies, procedures, rituals, and languages of the organization. While members of large groups can share these things and while individual socialization into the large group occurs through interaction and exposure to it, if tacit knowledge is to occur beyond the individual level, socialization within small groups is needed (Van Krogh et al., 2000). In other words, if the tacit knowledge held by the individual is to be transferred to others in the organization—and theirs to him or her—socialization within small groups is vitally important.

Efforts to assist socialization may benefit from intentional expression of concepts through nonverbal means. The use of object-based metaphors is effective in the socialization process, allowing the individual to make connections from the mental images existing in his or her tacit knowledge to the new organization. Thus, symbols and artifacts combine to create metaphors and analogies that are important in socialization.

Is the use of metaphor really that important to the socialization and tacit knowledge development processes? Metaphoric inference is a higher level of analogical reasoning (Sternberg, 1985) that is effective in addressing nonentrenched tasks. According to Sternberg (1985), metaphorical inferences require comprehension of explicit terms and the relations between those terms, and generation of implicit terms within the metaphor. "In comprehending and appreciating a metaphor, we conceive of something new in terms of something old" (p. 164). Therefore, the novelty of a situation is acted upon by relating the new information to existing knowledge schemas. Morgan (1986) states that individuals use metaphor whenever they attempt to understand one element or experience in terms of another, and that an individual's use of metaphor frames understanding in distinctive ways, as he or she determines how "A" is like "B." These understandings, then, are used to interpret novel situations. Morgan suggests that well-developed skill in the use of metaphoric inference is learned through experience coupled with natural ability, and becomes an almost subconscious application of knowledge. This deep application then presents across-domain information as images, symbols, impressions, or sensations (Cooper & Sawaf, 1996). Cooper and Sawaf (1996) call these "as...if loops." Though the semantics are different, the similarity to Horvath and colleagues' (1994) discussion of the procedural knowledge aspects of tacit knowledge is clear. They point out that proceduralized knowledge is often difficult to articulate, and may become so highly automatized that individuals lose articulative access to it completely. Thus, access to such knowledge may occur through images and sensations rather than through articulation. This access is a nonverbal use of metaphor. The lack of articulation, however, does not diminish the importance of deep procedural knowledge to the practical application of tacit knowledge. It merely reinforces the implicitness inherent in the observation and/or transfer of tacit knowledge.

The "hierarchy of intricate relations" that metaphorical inference allows leads to "a veritable conflagration of cognitive processes...which illuminates a whole landscape of ideas" (Cattell, 1971, p. 430). Through Cattell's, Cooper and Sawaf's (1996), Morgan's (1986), and Sternberg's (1985) discussion of metaphor and metaphorically driven insights, it can be argued that the development and embedding of tacit knowledge and related aspects of socialization involve repeated utilization of metaphoric inference for insight generation, and successful application of those insights to novelty.

THE DEVELOPMENT AND TRANSFER OF TACIT KNOWLEDGE

A fisherman even has a phrase to describe what he does when he studies the patterns of a river. He says he is "reading the water," and perhaps to tell his stories he has to do much the same thing.

Either we don't know what part to give or maybe we don't like to give any part of ourselves. Then, more often than not, the part that is needed is not wanted. And even more often, we do not have the part that is needed. It is like the auto supply shop over town where they always say, "Sorry, we are just out of that part."

—Norman Maclean (1976)

As we interact with others in our organizations, the tacit knowledge swirls and eddies through the comments made, the presentations given, the nonverbal responses expressed. It is seen in the work we choose to do, and in the work we choose to ignore. It is seen in the images we present and in the stories that we tell. Implicitly, we develop an understanding of what matters to the organization and what does not. Informally, we absorb and transfer tacit knowledge that we feel is relevant to our role and our goals within the organization.

The expansion of knowledge is more likely if the information is relevant and has aspects that are familiar to the learner (Herschel, Nemati, & Steiger, 2001). In other words, the development of useable tacit knowledge may hinge on whether the individual has a point of connection with the information he or she is to learn, and feels the relevance of that information. Tacit may build on tacit, tacit may build on explicit, but tacit needs something from which to build. Because knowledge is personalized, the interpretation and application of the knowledge will hinge on the prior experience base used as the foundation for the new knowledge.

That experience base in turn is built upon other experiences and understandings. And all are filtered through the individual's value system and goal objectives.

The implicit exchange of tacit knowledge and the transformation of tacit to explicit knowledge does not need to rely only on informal bases; deliberate utilization of tacit knowledge within the organization suggests that relying on informal transfer is haphazard at best. In our quest to develop tacit knowledge or to assist others in its development, three particular processes need to be applied to our efforts. Sternberg (1984, 1985, 1998) refers to these as selective encoding, selective combination, and selective comparison.

Selective encoding involves the use of existing knowledge to distinguish relevant information from irrelevant information, an important ability in our information-deluged world. Sternberg relates his informal finding that a major determiner of better from lesser scientists is the ability of better scientists to recognize what is important in their data, what findings to emphasize, and what findings to ignore. Lesser scientists appear unable to make those distinguishments. Because of the importance of using prior knowledge to encode new knowledge, "the (knowledge) rich get richer, the (knowledge) poor get poorer" (Sternberg, 1998, p. 710).

Selective combination combines crystallized pieces of information into a larger stream of information, thus combining pieces of information into a unified whole, and synthesizing what may appear to be unrelated parts. Once again referring to his informal study of scientists, Sternberg relates that better scientists are better able to see ways that their data fit together. Lesser scientists are more apt to present their findings as isolated facts rather than as part of an interwoven story.

Selective comparison refers to the ability to relate new information to previously acquired information, as in analogical and metaphorical reasoning. It draws on past information to understand and contextualize present information. The three processes work in harmony with each other and are linked to the acquisition and application of tacit knowledge (Horvath et al., 1994).

Herschel and colleagues (2001) agree with earlier research (Reber, 1989; Seger, 1994) that supports the effectiveness of using rich narratives to facilitate implicit knowledge transfer. While sharing narratives is accomplishable both informally and formally, Herschel and colleagues found that the use of narratives was most successful when paired with a structured recall process that increases individuals' abilities to articulate their thoughts. The articulation provides scaffolding for the narrative's recipient to build his or her tacit knowledge upon.

Eliciting tacit knowledge from domain experts is not an easy task. Chervinskaya and Wasserman (2000) suggest that it is impossible to elicit tacit knowledge by means of direct questioning of experts; they are not always able to articulate the how and why behind their decisions, and when they do attempt this explicitness, there are poor correlations between the experts' verbal reports and their behaviors (Ossipov, 1993). This is due not only to difficulties in expressing the rules and knowledge governing their behavior but is also due to their inability to recognize its importance in their work.

Transfer of knowledge from expert to novice or socialized to unsocialized is also hampered by the speed at which the expert passes from describing a problem to solving it, leaping over the intermediate steps necessary for the novice. There is, of course, no guarantee that such leaps always result in correct diagnoses/decisions. The knowledge accessed by the expert may be incorrectly applied or the expert may have leapt to decisional status by seeing a typically occurring problem when in fact it is unique.

Transfer of tacit knowledge is not a one-way proposition. Metaphors, analogies, maxims, and stories arising from tacit knowledge are not in themselves sufficient. The absorption and utilization of the information encoded in the tacit knowledge—that is, the completion of the transfer process—require recognition of the contexts and conditions where use of the knowledge is appropriate (Eraut, 2000). Tacit knowledge transfer can be conceived of as a partnership that relies on the ability to submit and receive coded information that is proceduralized through experience and reflection.

It is not uncommon to assign mentors to new administrators, particularly at the principal level. The mentor is to help the mentee by providing ideas, assistance, and a shoulder to cry or lean on. Embedded in much of the mentor's tasks is the assumption that organizational and professional "know how" will be passed along to the new person. However, the difficulties inherent in transfer of tacit knowledge as discussed above create issues in the mentor–mentee relationship. Development of mentor programs, assignments of mentors, and mentor–mentee activities should be examined in light of the implicit assumptions held for the relationship and should be structured with facilitation of tacit knowledge in mind.

In our efforts to assist in the development and transfer of tacit knowledge, we should not allow ourselves to be sucked into a belief that what is tacit must become explicit. Explicating all tacit knowledge should not be the goal. Setting aside the fact that it very likely is not possible, explication can lead to codification, which can result in the removal of the contextual interpretations that underlie adaptation of tacit knowledge. "The resourcefulness of such knowledge that is in fact made explicit may possibly be lower after the transformation than before" (Kreiner, 2002, p. 113). Or, as Polanyi (1966) said:

[In] general, an explicit integration cannot replace its tacit counterpart. The skill of a driver cannot be replaced by a thorough schooling in the theory of the motor car; the knowledge I have of my own body differs altogether from the knowledge of its physiology; and the rules of rhyming and prosody do not tell me what a poem told me without any knowledge of its rules. (p. 143)

While receiving inspiration from Polanyi, Nonaka (1994) believes that successful transformation from tacit to explicit knowledge is necessary for organizational success and suggests that there are four different patterns of interaction between tacit and explicit knowledge working together to create knowledge conversion processes. First, he suggests that tacit knowledge is transferred through socialization interactions between individuals. Second, explicit knowledge is transferred as individuals interact together to reconfigure existing explicit knowledge. The third and fourth modes of conversion are predicated on the idea that tacit and explicit knowledge are complementary (rather than existing on Polanyi's continuum) and can expand through repeated mutual interaction. Tacit becomes explicit by being externalized; explicit becomes tacit by becoming automatized and thus, internalized. In Nonaka's view, these four processes work together combining and recombining tacit and explicit categories of knowledge in a continuing spiral.

Our implicit understandings are at once individual and social, comprised of changing degrees of translucence and fluid levels of importance regarding goal specificity. The contexts in which we find ourselves and which we construct rely upon and, in turn, are relied upon by our tacit knowledge. Our success, individually and organizationally, depends on the appropriate internalization and application of the tacit knowledge we build through experience, observation, and socialization. Because of its importance, those who are and who would become educational administrators have the potential to benefit from the creation of pathways to assist in their development of tacit knowledge. Tacit knowledge will grow. The question becomes, how will it grow, and to what ends?

SUGGESTIONS FOR THE PREPARATION
OF EDUCATIONAL ADMINISTRATORS

Eventually, the watcher joined the river and there was only one.
I believe it was the river.

—Norman Maclean (1976)

Tacit knowledge is not just what we know; it is also a foundation for what we *will* know and for the likelihood of success we will achieve in reaching our goals and in enhancing our knowledge, whether it be implicit or explicit. Tacit knowledge is also practical. As such, it is fitting to consider the utility of this concept as it relates to the preparation of educational administrators.

Tacit knowledge areas of importance can be infused into aspects of most formal training. Attention to real-life scenarios that direct attention to areas important in day-to-day administrative operations would seem to be a helpful means for creating attention to the underlying structures of everyday professional problems. Whether through cases, simulations, observation of superintendents in action, or through the distillation of tacit knowledge from narratives, the learner should focus on ferreting out the interpersonal, intrapersonal, and organizational aspects associated with goal achievement. There is a need for reflective discussion, for weighing pros and cons, and for connecting to other situations and to formal knowledge bases. Using tacit knowledge categories and items in such ways may well provide an avenue for transmission and development of tacit knowledge.

Suggesting that the infusion of tacit knowledge transmission and development into the curricula for training administrators should not be construed as saying that formal, explicit training in areas related to school administration should be removed. Patel and colleagues state that "strong, formal, explicit knowledge instruction...may be necessary for tacit knowledge to develop" (1999, p. 93). They advocate that this formal background is needed in order to develop an understanding of the structure of a problem, rather than simply looking at a means–end analysis. Tacit knowledge development is not a substitute for formal, explicit knowledge, it is a full partner to that knowledge. It is, as Scribner said, "the mind in action" (1986, p.15).

Educational administration students clamor for practice-based knowledge, for tacit made explicit and explicit made comprehensible. They ask for "how-to" information, concrete facts, and tested ideas. Practicing administrators commonly say that their educational administration training did not prepare them for the realities of administrative life. In response, schools of educational administration have beefed up the practitioner aspects of their courses. In their efforts to meet student needs and desires, some have gone so far as to turn their programs into what amounts to a series of professional development workshops. While good arguments can be made for a number of those moves, we should not allow our focus on explicit practitioner-based education to cause us to ignore applicable aspects of the development of tacit knowledge. A student may feel secure as he or she clutches a how-to checklist in one hand and a list of procedures in the other. And those checklists and procedures will probably be helpful in addressing some common situations. However, we do our stu-

dents a serious disservice if our focus on practice does not include strategies for enhancing and transferring tacit knowledge. It is not enough to
place a student in an internship or to match a novice administrator with an
experienced mentor. While informal transfer of tacit knowledge may
occur, hopefully will occur, it is like the old "throw 'em in the river and
they'll learn to swim" method. They may learn, or they may drown. Supports such as small group involvement, verbalized reflection, structured
recall techniques used to elicit mentor knowledge, analysis of the meaning
of cultural artifacts, and problem based scenario creation and analysis can
all be used to provide students with access to the tacit knowledge they will
need. In so doing, we acknowledge the limitations of our preparation and
the correctness of Sternberg's (1998) comments.

> How many pieces of tacit knowledge do we have about the ways in which ...
> schools work?... No one can count, but certainly there are thousands—thou-
> sands of things we consider obvious that may be extremely non-obvious....
> These bits and pieces of tacit knowledge are so much a part of our cultural
> upbringing that we are unaware of them...but they are a product of many
> years accumulated experience, usually informal experience. We learn how to
> get around by being in an environment (Perkins, 1996), not by formal train-
> ing." (p. 705)

And in our acknowledgment, we nod to the rivers of tacit knowledge that
shape each of us, whether in the fast water by the rapids or the quiet waters
of the shallows, and recall the words of Norman Maclean in *A River Runs
Through It,*

> *As the heat mirages on the river in front of me danced with and through each other, I
> could feel patterns from my own life joining with them...at the time I did not know that
> stories of life are often more like rivers than books.*

REFERENCES

Allison, D., & Allison, P. (1993). Both ends of a telescope: Experience and expertise
    in principal problem-solving. *Educational Administration Quarterly, 29*(3),
    302–322.
Ambrosini, V., & Bowman, C. (2001). Tacit knowledge: Some suggestions for opera-
    tionalization. *Journal of Management Studies, 38*(6), 811–829.
Argyris, C. (1999). Tacit knowledge in management. In R. J. Sternberg & J. Horvath
    (Eds.), *Tacit knowledge in professional practice: Researcher and practitioner perspec-
    tives.* (pp.123–140). Mahwah, NJ: Erlbaum.
Augier, M., Shariq, S. Z., & Vendelo, M. T. (2001). Understanding context: Its
    emergence, transformation and role in sharing tacit knowledge. *Journal of
    Knowledge Management, 5*(2), 125–136.

Augier, M., & Vendelo, M. T. (1999). Networks, cognition, and management of tacit knowledge. *Journal of Knowledge Management, 3*(4), 252–261.

Bereiter, C., & Scardamalia, M. (1993). *Surpassing ourselves: An inquiry into the nature and implications of expertise.* Chicago: Open Court.

Berliner, P. F. (1994). *Thinking in jazz: The infinite art of improvisation.* Chicago: University of Chicago Press.

Berry, J. W., & Irvine, S. H. (1986). Bricolage: Savages do it daily. In R. J. Sternberg & R. K. Wagner (Eds.), *Practical intelligence* (pp. 271–306). Cambridge, UK: Cambridge University Press.

Brown, J. S., & Duguid, P. (1991). Organizational learning and communities of practice: Toward a unified view of working, learning and organization. *Organization Science, 2*(1), 40–57.

Bullough, R. V., Jr. (1990). Supervision, mentoring, and self-discovery: A case study of a first year teacher. *Journal of Curriculum and Supervision, 5,* 338–360.

Castillo, J. (2002). A note on the concept of tacit knowledge. *Journal of Management Inquiry, 11*(1), 46–57.

Cattell, R. B. (1971). *Abilities: Their structure, growth, and action.* Boston: Houghton Mifflin.

Chervinskaya, K. R., & Wasserman, E. L. (2000). Some methodological aspects of tacit knowledge elicitation. *Journal of Experimental and Theoretical Artificial Intelligence, 12,* 43–55.

Chi, M., Glaser, R., & Farr, M. (Eds.). (1988). *The nature of expertise.* Hillsdale, NJ: Erlbaum.

Cooke, N. M., & MacDonald, J. E. (1987). The application of psychological scaling techniques to knowledge elicitation for knowledge-based systems. *International Journal of Man–Machine Studies, 26,* 533–550.

Cooper, R. K., & Sawaf, A. (1996). *Executive EQ: Emotional intelligence in leadership and organizations.* New York: Grossett/Putnam.

Dervin, B. (1983). *An overview of sense-making research: Concepts, methods, and results* [Online]. Paper presented at the annual meeting of the International Communication Association, Dallas, TX. Available: http://communication.sbs.ohio-state.edu/sense-making/art/artdervin83.html

Eraut, M. (2000). Non-formal learning and tacit knowledge in professional work. *British Journal of Educational Psychology, 70,* 113–136.

Flanagan, J. C. (1954). The critical incident technique. *Psychological Bulletin, 51,* 327–358.

Ford, M. E. (1986). For all practical purposes: Criteria for defining and evaluating practical intelligence. In R. J. Sternberg & R. K. Wagner (Eds.), *Practical intelligence* (pp. 183–202). Cambridge, UK: Cambridge University Press.

Gardner, H. (1993). *Frames of mind* (2nd ed.). New York: Basic Books.

Glass, T. (1992). *The 1992 study of the American school superintendency.* Arlington, VA: American Association of School Administrators.

Glass, T., Bjork L., & Brunner, C. (2000). *The 2000 study of the American school superintendency.* Arlington, VA: American Association of School Administrators.

Gore, C., & Gore, E. (1999). Knowledge management: The way forward. *Total Quality Management, 10*(4-5), 554–560.

Grant, R. M. (1991). The resource-based theory of competitive advantage: Implications for strategy formulation. *California Management Review, 33*(3), 114–135.

Haldin-Herrgard, T. (2000). Difficulties in diffusion of tacit knowledge in organizations. *Journal of Intellectual Capital, 1*(4), 357–365.

Hart, A. W. (1991). Leader succession and socialization: A synthesis. *Review of Educational Research, 61*(4), 451–474.

Hennart, J. F. (1992). The transaction costs theory of joint ventures: An empirical study of Japanese subsidiaries in the United States. *Management Science, 37*(4), 483–497.

Herschel, R. T., Nemati, H., & Steiger, D. (2001). Tacit to explicit knowledge conversion: Knowledge exchange protocols. *Journal of Knowledge Management, 5*(1), 107–116.

Horvath, J. A., Williams, W. M., Forsythe, G. B., Sweeney, P. J., Sternberg, R. J., McNally, J. A., & Wattendorf, J. (1994). *Tacit knowledge in military leadership: Evidence from officer interviews* (Technical report no. 1018). Alexandria, VA: United States Army Research Institute for the Behavioral and Social Sciences.

Horvath, J. A., Forsythe, G. B., Bullis, R. C., Sweeney, P. J., Williams, W. M., McNally, J. A., Wattendorf, J., & Sternberg, R. J. (1999) Experience, knowledge, and military leadership. In R. J. Sternberg & J. Horvath (Eds.), *Tacit knowledge in professional practice: Researcher and practitioner perspectives* (pp.39–48). Mahwah, NJ: Erlbaum.

Hoy, W. K., & Sweetland, S. R. (2001). Designing better schools: The meaning and nature of enabling school structure. *Educational Administration Quarterly, 37,* 296–321.

Johnson, S. M. (1996). *Leading to change: The challenge of the new superintendency.* San Francisco: Jossey-Bass.

Kennedy, M. M. (1987). Inexact sciences: Professional education and the development of expertise. In E. Z. Rothkopf (Ed.), *Review of research in education.* Washington, DC: American Educational Research Association.

Klemp, G. O., & McClelland, D. C. (1986). What characterizes intelligent functioning among senior managers? In R. J. Sternberg & R. K. Wagner (Eds.), *Practical intelligence* (pp. 31–50). Cambridge, UK: Cambridge University Press.

Knight, P. (2002). A systematic approach to professional development: Learning as practice. *Teaching and Teacher Education, 18,* 229–241.

Kreiner, K. (2002). Tacit knowledge management: The role of artifacts. *Journal of Knowledge Management, 6*(2), 112–123.

Leithwood, K., & Steinbach, R. (1995). *Expert problem solving: Evidence from school and district leaders.* Albany: State University of New York Press.

Leonard, D., & Sensiper, S. (1998). The role of tacit knowledge in group innovation. *California Management Review, 40*(3), 112–132.

Levine, H. G., McGuire, C. H., & Nattress, L. W. (1970). The validity of multiple-choice achievement test as measures of competence in medicine. *American Educational Research Journal, 7,* 69–82.

Maclean, N. (1976). *A river runs through it and other stories.* Chicago: University of Chicago Press.

Marchant, G., & Robinson, J. (1999). Is knowing the tax code all it takes to be an expert? On the development of legal expertise. In R.J. Sternberg & J.A. Horvath (Eds.), *Tacit knowledge in professional practice* (pp. 155–182). Mahwah, NJ: Lawrence Erlbaum.

Mascitelli, R. (2000). From experience: Harnessing tacit knowledge to achieve breakthrough innovation. *Journal of Product Innovation Management, 17*(3), 179–194.

Miele, F. (1995). Skeptic Magazine interview with Robert Sternberg on The Bell Curve. *Skeptic, 3*(3) [Online], 72–80. Available: www.elib.com

Minsky, M. 1980. K-lines: A theory of memory. *Cognitive Science, 4,* 117–133.

Morgan, G., (1986). *Images of organizations.* Newbury Park, CA: Sage.

Nestor-Baker, N. S. (2002). Knowing when to hold 'em and fold 'em: Tacit knowledge of place and career bound superintendents. *Journal of Educational Administration, 40*(3), 230–256.

Nestor-Baker, N. S., & Hoy, W. K. (2001). Tacit knowledge of school superintendents: Its nature, meaning, and content. *Educational Administration Quarterly, 37*(1), 59–86.

Nestor-Baker, N. S., & Tschannen-Moran, M. (2001, November). *Tacit knowledge and trust development: First year efforts of two newly-hired superintendents.* Paper presented at the meeting of the University Council of Educational Administration, Cincinnati, OH.

Nonaka, I. (1994). A dynamic theory of organizational knowledge creation. *Organization Science, 5*(1), 14–37.

Nonaka, I., & Takauchi, H. (1995). *The knowledge creating company.* New York: Oxford University Press.

Ossipov, G. S. (1993). Knowledge-based information technologies. *Novosti Iscusstvennogo Intellecta, 1,* 7–14.

Patel, V., Arocha, J., & Kaufman, D. (1999) Expertise and tacit knowledge in medicine. In R. J. Sternberg & J. Horvath (Eds.), *Tacit knowledge in professional practice: researcher and practitioner perspectives* (pp. 75–100). Mahwah, NJ: Erlbaum.

Perkins, D. (1996). *Outsmarting IQ: The emerging science of learnable intelligence.* New York: Free Press.

Polanyi, M. (1966). *The tacit dimension.* Garden City, NY: Doubleday Anchor.

Rapport, N. (1999). Context as an act of personal externalisation. In R. Dilley (Ed.), *The problem of context* (pp. 187–211). New York: Berghahn.

Reber, A. (1989). Implicit learning and tacit knowledge. *Journal of Experimental Psychology: General, 118,* 219–235.

Salovey, P., & Mayer, J. (1990). Emotional intelligence. *Imagination, Cognition, and Personality, 9*(3), 185–211.

Schmidt, F. L., & Hunter, J. E. (1981). Employment testing: Old theories and new research findings. *American Psychologist, 36,* 1128–1137.

Schön, D. A. (1983). *The reflective practitioner.* New York: Basic Books.

Scribner, S. (1984). Studying working intelligence. In B. Rogoff & J. Lave (Eds.), *Everyday cognition: Its development in social context* (pp. 9–40). Cambridge, MA: Harvard University Press.

Scribner, S. (1986). Thinking in action: Some characteristics of practical thought. In R. J. Sternberg & R. K. Wagner (Eds.), *Practical Intelligence: Nature and origins of competence in the everyday world* (pp. 13–30). Cambridge, UK: Cambridge University Press.

Seger, C. (1994). Implicit learning. *Psychological Bulletin, 115*, 163–196.

Shaw, R. E., & Hazelett, W. M. (1986). Schemas in cognition. In V. McCabe & G. Balzano (Eds.), *Event cognition: An ecological perspective* (pp. 45–58). Hillsdale, NJ: Erlbaum.

Spender, J. C. (1993). *Competitive advantage from tacit knowledge? Unpacking the concept and its strategic implications.* Paper presented at the annual meeting of the Academy of Management, Atlanta, GA.

Sternberg, R. J. (1981). Intelligence and nonentrenchment. *Journal of Educational Psychology, 73*(1), 1–16.

Sternberg, R. J. (1984). Toward a triarchic theory of human intelligence. *Behavioral and Brain Sciences, 7*(2), 269–315.

Sternberg, R. J. (1985). *Beyond IQ: A triarchic theory of human intelligence.* Cambridge, UK: Cambridge University Press.

Sternberg, R. J. (1995). The triarchic model applied to identifying, teaching, and assessing gifted children. *Roeper Review* [Online]. Available: www.elib.com

Sternberg, R. J. (1996). *Successful intelligence: How practical and creative intelligence determine success in life.* New York: Simon & Schuster.

Sternberg, R. (1998). Enhancing education for immigrants: The role of tacit knowledge. *Educational Policy, 12*(6), 705–719.

Sternberg, R. J., & Horvath, J.A. (1999). *Tacit knowledge in professional practice: Researcher and practitioner perspectives.* Mahwah, NJ: Erlbaum.

Sternberg, R. J., Wagner, R. K., Williams, W. M., & Horvath, J. A. (1995). Testing common sense. *American Psychologist, 50*(11), 912–927.

Van Krogh, G., Ichigo, K., & Nonaka, I. (2000). *Enabling knowledge creation: How to unlock the mystery of tacit knowledge and release the power of innovation.* New York: Oxford University Press.

Wagner, R. K. (1987). Tacit knowledge in everyday intelligent behavior. *Journal of Personality and Social Psychology, 52*(6), 1236–1247.

Wagner, R. K., Sujan, H., Sujan, M., Rashotte, C., & Sternberg, R. J. (1999). Tacit knowledge in sales. In R. J. Sternberg & J. A. Horvath (Eds.), *Tacit knowledge in professional practice* (pp. 155–182). Mahwah, NJ: Erlbaum.

Wagner, R. K., & Sternberg, R. J. (1985). Practical intelligence in real-world pursuits: The role of tacit knowledge. *Journal of Personality and Social Psychology, 49*(2), 436–458.

Wagner, R. K., & Sternberg, R. J. (1986). Tacit knowledge and intelligence in the everyday world. In R. J. Sternberg & R. K. Wagner (Eds.) *Practical intelligence* (pp. 51–83). Cambridge, UK: Cambridge University Press.

Wagner R. K., & Sternberg, R. J. (1991). *Tacit Knowledge Inventory for Managers.* San Antonio, TX: Psychological Corporation.

Wagner, R. K., & Sternberg, R. J. (1993). The g-ocentric view of intelligence and job performance is wrong. *Current Directions in Psychological Science 2*(1), 1–5.

Ward, W. C., Frederiksen, N., & Carlson, S. (1980). Construct validity of free-response and multiple-choice versions of a test. *Journal of Educational Psychology, 17*, 11–29.

Weick, K. E. (1993). The collapse of sensemaking in organizations: The Mann Gulch disaster. *Administrative Science Quarterly, 41*, 301–313.

Weick, K. E. (1998). Improvisation as a mindset for organizational analysis. *Organization Science, 9*(5), 543–555.

Weick, K. E. (1999). That's moving: Theories that matter. *Journal of Management Inquiry, 8*(2), 134–142.

Wigdor, A. K., & Garner, W. R. (Eds.). (1982). *Ability testing: Uses, consequences, and controversies.* Washington, DC: National Academy Press.

CHAPTER 6

FOSTERING ORGANIZATIONAL CITIZENSHIP IN SCHOOLS

Transformational Leadership and Trust

Megan Tschannen-Moran

ABSTRACT

To meet the challenging new standards that have been set for schools, school personnel must go well beyond minimum performance of their duties. Educational theorists assume that transformational leadership behavior on the part of principals will motivate teachers and other school personnel to work beyond their formally prescribed job responsibilities and to give their very best to the task. This study challenges that assumption. In this study, trust emerged as an important correlate to the organizational citizenship behaviors of school personnel, while the transformational leadership behavior of the principal was unrelated. Implications for research as well as the preparation of school leaders are discussed.

Studies in Leading and Organizing Schools, pages 157–179
Copyright © 2003 by Information Age Publishing
All rights of reproduction in any form reserved.

CHALLENGING AN ASSUMPTION

To meet the demanding new standards that have been set for schools, school personnel must go well beyond minimum performance of their duties. They must be inspired to give their very best. Schools look to transformational leadership on the part of principals to set the tone and motivate teachers and other school personnel to work beyond formally prescribed job responsibilities. These extra-role behaviors have been called *organizational citizenship behaviors* (OCBs). Because of the important role that leaders play in the cultivation of organizational citizenship, much research interest has focused on the skills and behaviors that make for transformational leadership. This study challenges the assumption that transformational leadership behaviors lead to greater OCBs, and instead posits that the cultivation of trust is an important factor in fostering such citizenship.

TRANSFORMATIONAL LEADERSHIP

In the current era of educational reform, school leaders are increasingly looked upon to bring about the transformation of schools. Without strong leadership, it seems unlikely that schools will make the kinds of changes that are being demanded of them. But not all leaders are created equal. Some seem to evoke extraordinary effort from their followers, while others simply maintain the status quo. Scholars have been interested in the former, who they have labeled "transformational leaders." A rich body of literature is developing on leaders with transformational qualities and the differential impact that these leaders can have on the organizations they lead and its participants. Scholars report that transformational leaders:

- Cause followers to "do more than they are expected to do" (Yukl, 1989, p. 272).
- Motivate followers to perform at a level "over and above mechanical compliance with the routine directives of the organization" (Katz & Kahn, 1978, p. 528).
- Are able to "shape and elevate the motives and goals of followers" (Bennis & Nanus, 1985, p. 217).
- "Transform or change the basic values, beliefs, and attitudes of followers so that they are willing to perform beyond the minimum levels specified by the organization" (Podsakoff, MacKenzie, Moorman, & Fetter, 1990, p. 108).
- "Lift ordinary people to extraordinary heights" (Boal & Bryson, 1988, p. 11).

Going beyond minimum expected performance has been called "organizational citizenship." In order to foster such citizenship, transformational leaders "stimulate others to view their work from new perspectives, generate an awareness of the mission and vision of the organization, develop colleagues and followers to higher levels of ability and potential, and motivate them to look beyond their own interests toward those that will benefit the group" (Hoy & Miskel, 2001, p. 415). Transformational leadership builds commitment to the organization's objectives and empowers followers to achieve these objectives (Yukl, 1998). Increased capacities and commitment are assumed to result in greater subordinate effort, productivity, and satisfaction (Bass, 1985, 1998; Burns, 1978).

To accomplish these productive outcomes, transformational leadership has been defined in terms of the four I's: individualized influence, inspirational motivation, intellectual stimulation, and individualized consideration (Bass, 1985, 1998). Transformational leaders exercise individualized influence when they serve as role models for followers such that followers identify with and want to emulate them. These leaders demonstrate high standards of ethical and moral conduct, using power to move individuals and groups toward accomplishing their common mission and not for personal gain. Through inspirational motivation, leaders provide meaning and challenge to followers so as to promote enthusiasm, optimism, a shared vision, goal commitment, and team spirit. Transformational leaders clearly communicate expectations that followers want to meet (Bass & Avolio, 1994). In cultivating intellectual stimulation, transformational leaders stimulate creative and innovative thinking in followers by questioning assumptions, reframing problems, and approaching old situations in new ways. Individualized consideration is fostered as leaders, serving as mentors, take stock of individuals' needs for achievement and growth (Avolio, 1994). These leaders recognize and accept individual differences in needs and values, and create learning opportunities in a supportive climate.

Although work on transformational leadership has been largely theoretical, several studies support the claim that transformational leadership is related to positive organizational outcomes. Employees in a large engineering firm reported that they exerted extra effort on behalf of managers who were transformational leaders (Bass, 1990). Between 75% and 82% of the employees of managers who scored in the top quartile on various aspects of transformational leadership reported that they frequently exerted extra effort on their jobs, while for managers in the bottom quartile only 22–24% of workers indicated they regularly put forth extra effort. In schools, transformational leadership behavior was related to a number of important school conditions including goals and purposes, structure and organization, planning, organizational culture, and information collection and decision making, as well as classroom conditions such as instructional services, policies, and procedures (Leithwood & Jantzi, 2000). When middle school teachers rated their principals on five leadership behaviors including "models behavior," "inspires group purpose," "provides contingent rewards," "holds high performance expectations," and "provides support" (Leithwood & Steinbach, 1993), these behaviors were only modestly related to teachers' sense of efficacy, with correlations ranging from .12 to .23 (Hipp & Bredeson, 1995).

The construct of transformational leadership has generated excitement as a model for school leadership in this time of reform and change (Leithwood, Jantzi, & Steinbach, 1999). However, further empirical research is needed about how transformational leadership functions in the context of schools. Does the transformational leadership of principals really lead to greater organizational citizenship among teachers? To begin to answer this question, we need to know more about organizational citizenship.

ORGANIZATIONAL CITIZENSHIP

Within effective organizations, employees often go beyond formal job responsibilities, performing nonmandatory tasks with no expectation of recognition or compensation. These altruistic acts are neither prescribed nor required, yet they contribute to the smooth functioning of the organization. Organ coined the phrase "organizational citizenship behavior" (OCB) to denote such organizationally beneficial gestures (Bateman & Organ, 1983). Organ's interest in organizational citizenship was sparked as he reflected on his experience as a young factory worker. He was struggling with the use of a piece of equipment until an older worker noticed his difficulty and left his own work to instruct the floundering young man in the proper use of the tool. It was not in the job description of the older worker to offer such assistance, but his efforts aided both young Organ and the organization as a whole.

Organizational citizenship behavior is defined as "performance that supports the social and psychological environment in which task performance takes place" (Organ, 1997, p. 95). OCBs can be said to "lubricate the social machinery of the organization" (Bateman & Organ, 1983, p. 588). The willingness of participants to go beyond the formal requirements of their positions has long been recognized as an essential component of effective organizations. More than six decades ago, Barnard (1938) stated that the willingness of individuals to contribute cooperative efforts to the organization was indispensable. OCBs are generally considered extra-role behaviors; those neither required nor prescribed, yet critical to the smooth functioning and efficiency of the organization. Katz and Kahn (1978) pointed to extra-role behaviors that do not directly conform to the usual notion of job performance and how those behaviors improve the effectiveness of organizations. They argued that any organization in which cooperation is limited so that individuals only perform prescribed duties is doomed to failure. More recently, Borman and Motowidlo (1993) proposed that individuals contribute to organizational effectiveness by doing things that are not main task functions but are important because they shape the organizational and social context that supports task activities. Although OCBs are not accounted for, or monitored, by the organization's reward system, they provide the organization with the adaptation and innovation necessary for long-term survival and growth (Graham, 1986; Katz, 1964).

By delineating and defining these helpful behaviors, we can hope to structure an organization so as to evoke them. Citizenship behaviors contribute to organizational performance because these behaviors provide an effective means of managing the interdependencies between members of a work unit and, as a result, increase the collective outcomes (Organ, 1988, 1990, 1997; Smith, Organ, & Near, 1983). Workers perceived to be the most effective by managers were those who were not only productive themselves but who also made those around them more productive "by helping, by being good sports, and/or exhibiting civic virtue" (Podsakoff & MacKenzie, 1994, p. 359). Both greater efficiency and increased satisfaction were the result.

Organizational charts, employment agreements, and job descriptions fail to address all the contingencies that arise in schools (Stewart, 1985). They generally can do no more than specify minimum performance requirements. Teachers in well-functioning schools consistently go well beyond the minimum expectations of formal job descriptions and contracts. School organizations count on teachers doing so and could not achieve their goals if teachers limited their contributions to those specified in their job descriptions. In fact, "working to rule" is a tactic employed by teacher unions to punish school districts when contracts have expired or when contract negotiations are at an impasse. This is viewed as an extreme measure and generally brings a quick response because it demonstrates how crucial goodwill and working beyond minimum specifications are to the smooth functioning and efficiency of school organizations.

In attempting to define organizational citizenship behaviors, Organ (1988) identified five specific categories of discretionary behavior and explained how each helps to maximize efficiency in the organization. Altruism (e.g., helping new colleagues, giving of time to others) is generally directed toward other individuals, but contributes to efficiency by enhancing individuals' performance. Conscientiousness (e.g., efficient use of time, high attendance rates) contributes to the efficiency of both an individual and the group. Sportsmanship (e.g., avoids complaining and petty grievances) maximizes the total amount of time spent on constructive endeavors in the organization. Courtesy (e.g., advance notices, reminders, passing along appropriate information) helps prevent problems and maximizes use of time. Civic virtue (e.g., serving on committees, attending functions not required that help the image of the organization) serves the interests of the organization. Although Organ (1990) proposed five categories of OCBs, factor analyses of data in organizations have most often revealed just two underlying dimensions: citizenship behaviors directed toward helping individuals and citizenship behaviors performed in service of the organization.

Because the work in schools is such that it cannot be comprehensively prescribed in teachers' job descriptions or contracts, it is important that scholars and practitioners alike learn more about organizational citizenship behaviors and their antecedents in school settings. Greater understanding of the role of leaders in cultivating citizenship behaviors will make an important contribution toward nurturing school effectiveness. In a pair of studies in secondary schools, DiPaola and Tschannen-Moran (2001) demonstrated a strong link between the collegial leadership style of principals and organizational citizenship. In other settings, Organ and Ryan (1995) also found that leader supportiveness was related to OCBs. Although transformational leadership behaviors are presumed to result in greater organizational citizenship, this assumption has not been tested in schools.

TRUST

Trust is increasingly recognized as a critical element of leadership. Trust is "the mortar that binds leader to follower" and forms the basis for a leader's legitimacy (Nanus, 1989, p. 101). Kouzes and Posner (1987, 1993) reported that the leader characteristics most valued by followers were honesty, integrity, and truthfulness—behaviors that contributed to leaders' credibility. Faculty trust in the principal is based on what teachers feel they ought to be able to expect from a person who occupies that role.

Trust is a complex concept with a variety of facets. In a general sense, trust is the assurance that another will not exploit one's vulnerability or take excessive advantage of one even when the opportunity is available (Cummings & Bromily, 1996). A comprehensive definition of trust, drawn from recurring themes that emerge across various contexts in which it has been studied (e.g., philosophical, economic, organizational, or individual) is that "trust is one party's willingness to be vulnerable to another party based on the confidence that the latter party is benevolent, reliable, competent, honest, and open" (Tschannen-Moran, 1998, 2001). Greater comprehension of trust requires a deep understanding of each facet of trust. Each of the facets—benevolence, reliability, competence, honesty, and openness—are played out in the behavior of principals and in teachers' willingness to trust principals. There is empirical evidence that all of these facets are important aspects of trust relations in schools. A factor-analytic study demonstrated that the facets covary and form a coherent construct of trust (Hoy & Tschannen-Moran, 1999; Hoy & Tschannen-Moran, Chapter 7, this volume). These facets are discussed in more depth below.

Willingness to Risk Vulnerability

A necessary condition of trust is interdependence, a relationship in which the interests of one party cannot be achieved without reliance upon another (Rousseau, Sitkin, Burt, & Camerer, 1998). Where there is no interdependence, there is no need for trust. Interdependence brings with it vulnerability. The trustor is cognizant of the potential for betrayal and harm from the other (Granovetter, 1985; Kee & Knox, 1970; Lewis & Weigert, 1985), and uncertainty concerning whether the other intends to and will act appropriately is a source of risk (Rousseau et al., 1998). Trust, then, is a willingness to be vulnerable under conditions of risk and interdependence.

Benevolence

One of the most pervasive facets of trust is a sense of benevolence, the confidence that one can count on the goodwill of another to act in one's best interest. In an ongoing relationship, the actions or deeds required of the other may not be specified but only that there will be a mutual attitude of goodwill. In situations in which a person is vulnerable to another, he or she must count on this faith in the altruism of the other to feel at ease.

Principals who earn the trust of their faculties demonstrate goodwill and genuine concern for teachers' well-being both on and off the job. Principals promote trust by demonstrating benevolence by showing consideration and sensitivity for teachers' needs and interests, acting in a way that protects employees' rights, and refraining from exploiting others for the benefit of personal interests. In a qualitative study of faculty trust, the facet of trust in the principal most frequently mentioned by teachers concerned issues of benevolence or supportiveness (Tschannen-Moran, 1998). In situations of high trust, teachers do not hesitate to seek help because they do not fear that others will think they are inadequate. They will not feel threatened by being seen as dependent upon another person, nor be as concerned about incurring indebtedness to another person (Jones & George, 1998).

Reliability

It is not enough to show support from time to time or to demonstrate benevolence sporadically. The sense that one can consistently depend on another is an important element of trust. One must be confident that one can count on the other to come through, without investing energy worrying about the possibility that he or she will not, for trust to characterize a relationship. Teachers may acknowledge that their principal is a nice person and means well, and even that he or she is very capable and helpful if you can get his or her attention; however, if poor self-management behaviors are observed, such as difficulty handling the time demands of the job, overcommitment, or being easily distracted, teachers may doubt whether the principal will come through for them when needed and trust will not characterize the relationship.

Teachers will have greater confidence when they feel they can predict the behavior of their principal. For principals to garner the trust of their faculty, they need to demonstrate predictability and to behave consistently enough to inspire confidence that teachers can count on them in their time of need. In a study of leadership in schools, Evans (1996) found that trust derived from consistency in personal beliefs, organizational goals, and work performance. Similarly, Bryk and his colleagues (Bryk & Driscoll, 1988; Bryk, Lee, & Holland, 1993; Bryk & Schneider, 1996) found that consistency, competence, and even-handedness in principals' behavior promoted strong and healthy school communities.

Competence

When a certain level of skill is involved for a person to fulfill the expectation of another, as is the case in any of the professions, then a person who means well may nonetheless not be trusted (Baier, 1986; Butler & Cantrell, 1984; Mishra, 1996). If the lack of skill, however, is evidenced in an apprentice, such as a student teacher, the lack of competence is expected and not a breach of trust because the person is expected to make some mistakes (Solomon & Flores, 2001). In such cases, failure should not be confused with betrayal, because the person did not purport to have the requisite skill. The system is presumed to have safeguards in place to protect clients or subordinates from the harm of the mistakes of an apprentice.

In interviews, teachers often mentioned incidents in which the competence of their principal mattered (Tschannen-Moran, 1998). Principals who were trusted were regarded with respect and even admiration on the basis of their competence. High-trust principals not only set high standards, they also held teachers accountable in ways that seemed fair and reasonable to their staff. One way that principals demonstrated their competence was in the willingness to handle difficult situations and to buffer teachers, such as in dealing with difficult or distressed parents or in dealing discretely with problems among the faculty and staff.

Honesty

Honesty is a pivotal facet of trust (Baier, 1986; Butler & Cantrell, 1984; Cummings & Bromily, 1996; Hoy & Tschannen-Moran, 1999). Without the confidence that a person's words can be relied upon and that they accurately predict future actions, trust is unlikely to develop. Attributions of integrity result from telling the truth and keeping promises (Dasgupta, 1988). A correspondence between a person's statements and deeds, that is, the perceived degree of congruence between the values expressed in words and those expressed through action, characterizes integrity (Simons, 1999). Inconsistencies between words and deeds destroy trust (McGregor, 1967). Another dimension of honesty is authenticity, or accepting responsibility for one's actions and avoiding distorting the truth in order to shift blame to another. Authenticity has been linked to faculty trust in principals (Hoy & Kupersmith, 1985; Tschannen-Moran & Hoy, 1998).

Integrity and authenticity were the hallmarks of the kind of honesty teachers sought from their principals. Among teachers, the integrity of their principals was assumed until there was evidence to the contrary. Once a principal had been caught in even a single lie, however, trust was damaged and difficult to reestablish, as the communication necessary to restore trust was now suspect. Simon (1999) observed that, "words are one of a manager's most potent tools for guiding subordinates....When credibility is sacrificed, the manager damages that tool, and is forced into additional actions to show when he or she 'really means' what he or she says" (p. 95). Trust might survive a broken promise if an explanation was given, however, a pattern of broken promises provoked a serious threat to trust.

Openness

Openness is a process by which leaders make themselves vulnerable to others by sharing information, influence, and control (Butler & Cantrell, 1984; Mishra, 1996; Zand, 1997). Such openness signals the extending of trust, a confidence that neither the information nor the individual will be exploited. The strategy is one of building trust by taking the initiative to make oneself vulnerable with the hope that it will build more trust in the collective. The belief or expectation is that, by engaging in acts of trust oneself, one may be able to induce others to do the same (Horsburgh, 1960; Kramer, Brewer, & Hanna, 1996). A spiral of trust is thus initiated.

Patterns of communication have an impact on employees' trust. People who are guarded or closed about the information they share provoke suspicion because people wonder what is being hidden and why. Employees view managers as trustworthy when their communication is both accurate and forthcoming. Open communication, in which managers disclose facts, alternatives, judgments, intentions, and feelings freely with employees, enhances perceptions of trust (Butler, 1991; Gabarro, 1978). Adequate explanations and timely feedback on decisions lead to higher levels of trust (Sapienza & Korsgaard, 1996). Principals who are open and honest promote supportive and trusting climates for teachers (Bryk et al., 1993; Rosenholtz, 1989). Openness is important for the development of subordinates' trust in their superiors because the withholding of important information might be one way that superiors use to maintain power or manipulate employees (Gabarro, 1978; Kramer, 1996; Mishra, 1996).

Openness concerning control also connotes a willingness to be vulnerable through accepting dependence and a reliance on others through delegation. Openness in influence allows others to initiate and accept change to goals, concepts, plans, criteria, and resources. Research has shown that subordinates perceive greater trustworthiness on the part of superiors who share control. Employees' trust is higher when they are satisfied with their level of participation in decisions (Driscoll, 1978). Similarly, teachers' trust is positively related to empowerment and shared decision making (Short, Greer, & Melvin, 1994; Tschannen-Moran, 2001). This control provides greater protection of employees' interests and reduces the risk of opportunism on the part of superiors. Principals who had earned the trust of the faculty had done so in part by extending trust and making themselves vulnerable through sharing of both information and decision-making power (Tschannen-Moran, 1998).

Among teachers and their principals, all aspects of trust have been shown to carry significant importance (Hoy & Tschannen-Moran, 1999). Above all, teachers seemed to expect a sense of benevolence or goodwill from their principal. Furthermore, because they felt vulnerable to the problems that emerged from an incompetent or disengaged principal, they also relied heavily on competence as a basis for trust. Principals who are disposed to help teachers solve problems, encourage open communication, and consistently help teachers do their jobs are principals who are likely to earn the trust of their teachers.

LEADERSHIP, CITIZENSHIP, AND TRUST

Transformational leaders must have the trust of their followers in order to be effective. Yukl (1989) proposed that "one of the key reasons why followers are motivated by transformational leaders to perform beyond expectations is that followers trust and respect them" (p. 272). Boal and Bryson (1988) also highlight the critical role of trust and loyalty to the leader in their model of transformational leadership. As leaders keep their word and promises with followers over time, the followers will come to trust those leaders, making transformative processes more likely. "It is this higher level of trust and identification," Hoy and Miskel (2001) noted, "that transformational leaders use as a foundation for achieving exemplary performance" (p. 414). The relationship between other forms of leadership, specifically collegial and supportive leadership, and trust has been demonstrated through empirical studies. Principals who demonstrated collegial (Hoy, Sabo, & Barnes, 1996) and supportive leadership (Hoy, Tarter, & Witkoskie, 1992; Tarter, Bliss, & Hoy, 1989; Tarter, Sabo, & Hoy, 1995; Tschannen-Moran & Hoy, 1998) enjoyed high levels of faculty trust. The link between transformational leadership and trust has not been as extensively studied.

One intriguing study that examined transformational leadership and organizational citizenship proposed that the link would be mediated by trust and worker satisfaction. Transformational leadership behaviors are purported to increase organizational citizenship behaviors. Podsakoff and colleagues (1990) found, however, that transformational leadership behaviors had a primarily indirect effect on followers' organizational citizenship and that the relationship was mediated by worker trust in the leader. The direct relationship, as well as the effect of worker satisfaction, was negligible. When workers trusted their superiors, transformation leadership behaviors were likely to be related to greater organizational citizenship. When trust was absent, however, those same behaviors were unlikely to kindle greater citizenship among workers. Thus, these researchers concluded that trust plays an important mediating role in the transformational leadership process.

The purpose of this study was to discover whether a similar link would be found in educational settings. On the one hand, research has shown that in a professional organization with a service mission, organizational citizenship behaviors may be somewhat different than in other work settings. On the other hand, it seems plausible that teachers' trust in their principal would mediate the relationship of leadership and citizenship behaviors evident in schools as in other settings. With the current emphasis being placed on the importance of good leadership in schools, it would be useful to know if the relationship between leadership and citizenship is found in schools, and if so, whether it is mediated by trust or a direct link is found.

METHODOLOGY

This study explored whether the mediating role of trust between transformational leadership behaviors and organizational citizenship found by Podsakoff and colleagues (1990) would also be found in schools. Modifications were made in the measures and methodology that may affect the outcome. Nonetheless, greater understanding of the relationship between transformational leadership, organizational citizenship, and trust will be useful to understanding what makes for productive schools.

Sample

In this study, the school was the unit of analysis. The collective level of organizational citizenship and of trust in the principal was considered to be more meaningful in the context of this study than the levels of trust and citizenship of particular individuals within the school. The sample for this study was 55 middle schools in a mid-Atlantic state. Approximately a quarter of the schools were in urban settings, with another 25% in rural contexts and the remaining 50% in suburban districts. The mean of students receiving free and reduced-price lunch in the middle schools sampled was .37 with a range of .01–.94. The mean of students receiving free and reduced-price lunch for the middle schools in the state not participating in the study was .33 with a range of .01–.86. Data were collected from a total of 3,066 middle school teachers within those schools, with approximately one third responding to each of three surveys.

Data Collection

Data were collected at regularly scheduled faculty meetings. Participants were informed of the purpose of the study and told that their participation was voluntary. They were also told that their responses were anonymous and that they could skip any items they chose not to answer. Three different surveys were distributed randomly, so that different respondents completed separate surveys for each of the constructs under study. This procedure was used to reduce common method bias.

Measures

Three measures were used to gather data for this study. Each was distributed on a separate survey to approximately one third of the faculty at each school. Two of the measures have been used in previous research, while the third is a new measure.

Transformational leadership. Much of the research in transformational leadership has made use of Bass' 1985 Multifactor Leadership Questionnaire (MLQ). However, because the principalship differs from leadership in a business context, a measure specific to schools was desirable. Consequently, a new measure developed by Nicholson (2002) at Ohio State University was selected for this study. The measure has nine items that capture each of the four aspects of transformational leadership: idealized influence, inspirational motivation, intellectual stimulation, and individualized consideration. Responses were on a 5-point scale from 0 to 4, anchored at 0—"Not at all," 1—"Once in a while," 2—"Sometimes," 3—"Fairly often," and 4—"Frequently, if not always." Each item completed a sentence stem beginning "The principal in this school."

Sample items for the principal of this school are:

- Instills pride in me for being associated with him/her (*idealized influence*)
- Gives me a sense of being important (*inspirational motivation*)
- Seeks differing perspectives when solving problems (*intellectual stimulation*)
- Provides moral support by making me feel appreciated (*individualized consideration*)

Organizational citizenship behaviors. Organizational citizenship behaviors were measured with an instrument developed specifically to capture OCBs in schools (DiPaola & Tschannen-Moran, 2001). The measure was adapted from a measure used by Smith, Organ, and Near (1983) for OCBs in private sector organizations. The measure consists of nine items assessed on a 5-point scale with the following anchors: 1—"Never," 2—"Rarely," 3—"Sometimes," 4—"Often," and 5—"Continuously."

Sample items are:

- Teachers voluntarily help new teachers.
- Teachers schedule personal appointments at times other than during the school day.
- Teachers make innovative suggestions to improve the overall quality of our school.

Because the items asked teachers about their perceptions of the organization as a whole, data were aggregated to the school level for analysis. Reliabilities for the longer 15-item measure used in two previous studies were .87 and .96 (DiPaola & Tschannen-Moran, 2001).

Trust in the principal. Trust was defined as "one party's willingness to be vulnerable to another based on the confidence that the other is benevolent, reliable, competent, honest, and open." Trust in the principal was measured with an eight-item measure with a 6-point Likert scale from Strongly Disagree (1) to Strongly Agree (6).

Sample items include:

- The teachers in this school have faith in the integrity of the principal.
- The principal of this school typically acts with the best interest of the teachers in mind.
- Teachers in this school can rely on the principal.

The mean score for teachers who responded to this measure was used for the analysis. Reliability from a previous study was .95 (Hoy & Tschannen-Moran, 1999).

Data Analysis

Data from each measure were subjected to factor analysis using Principal Axis Factor Analysis to ensure that each measure tapped a unitary construct. Reliability of the measures was checked using Cronbach's Alpha for Internal Consistency. Finally, Structural Equation Modeling using AMOS 4.0 was used to test the direct and indirect effects of transformational leadership and trust on organizational citizenship.

RESULTS

Factor analysis of the transformational leadership measure demonstrated good construct validity (Kerlinger, 1986). All nine items loaded onto one strong factor with an eigenvalue of 7.23 that explained 80% of the variance. The factor loadings ranged from .97 to .78 (see Table 6.1). The reliability of the instrument, tested using Cronbach's alpha of internal consistency, was .97 (reported on the diagonals in Table 6.4). Although Avolio (1999) proposed that idealized influence and inspirational motivation were the most effective and satisfying elements of transformational leadership, while intellectual stimulation and individualized consideration have somewhat less effect, in this sample of middle schools, all four elements of transformational leadership varied together and formed one unitary construct with high internal consistency.

**Table 6.1.   Factor Loadings of Teachers' Rating
of Transformational Leadership**

The principal in this school:	*Factor Loadings*
Acts in ways that build my self-respect	.97
Provides moral support by making me feel appreciated	.95
Gives me a sense of being important	.94
Instills pride in me for being associated with him/her	.91
Practices what he or she preaches	.86
Leads by example	.86
Helps staff to learn from each other	.86
Seeks differing perspectives when solving problems	.81
Treats me as an individual rather than just a member of a group	.78
Eigenvalue	7.23
Percent of variance explained	80.36

Likewise, factor analysis of the organizational citizenship measure revealed acceptable validity. Again, all nine items loaded onto one factor, although the proportion of variance explained and the factor loadings were not as strong as the transformational leadership items. The eigenvalue for the organizational citizenship items was 5.78 and 48% of the variance was explained. These results are reported in Table 6.2. The factor loadings ranged from .85 to a minimally acceptable level of .43 for one item. Reliability was not improved with the removal of that item and so it was retained. The Cronbach's alpha of reliability, reported in Table 6.4, was .91.

Finally, factor analysis of the faculty trust in the principal items demonstrated good validity. The eight items loaded onto one strong factor with an eigenvalue of 6.78 that explained 85% of the variance. The factor loadings ranged from .98 to .82 (see Table 6.3). Reliability, reported in Table 6.4, was .98 using Cronbach's alpha.

In sum, each of these measures demonstrated good reliability and construct validity using both exploratory and confirmatory factor analyses. Although the measure of organizational citizenship had the lowest factor loadings overall, it was within an acceptable range.

The intercorrelations between these three variables revealed some surprising results. Transformational leadership was not significantly related to organizational citizenship (see Table 6.4). Trust in the principal, on the other hand, was significantly and moderately related to the citizenship behavior of teachers ($r = .38$, $p < .01$). The strongest correlation occurred

**Table 6.2.   Factor Loadings of Teachers' Rating
of Organizational Citizenship**

	Factor Loadings
Teachers arrive to work and meetings on time	.85
Teachers are rarely absent	.72
Teachers give advance notice of changes in schedule or routine	.71
Teachers begin class promptly and use class time effectively	.69
Teachers schedule personal appointments at times other than during the school day	.67
Teachers take the initiative to introduce themselves to substitutes and assist them	.64
Teachers voluntarily help new teachers	.64
Teachers make innovative suggestions to improve the quality of our school	.56
Teachers volunteer to serve on committees	.43
Eigenvalue	5.78
Percent of variance explained	48.14

Table 6.3.   Factor Loadings of Teachers' Rating of Trust in the Principal

	Factor Loadings
Teachers in this school trust the principal	.98
The principal in this school typically acts with the best interest of the teachers in mind	.96
Teachers in this school can rely on the principal	.95
The teachers in this school have faith in the integrity of the principal	.95
The principal in this school is competent in doing his or her job	.91
*The principal of this school does not show concern for teachers	.88
*The principal doesn't tell teachers what is going on	.83
*Teachers in this school are suspicious of most of the principal's actions	.82
Eigenvalue	6.78
Percent of variance explained	84.77

* Items were reverse-coded prior to factor analysis.

between perceived transformational leadership behaviors and faculty trust in the principal ($r = .75$, $p < .01$).

These intriguing findings led to further analyses. Structural equation modeling using AMOS was applied. Several models were tried, including

Table 6.4. Correlation Matrix of Transformational Leadership, Citizenship, and Trust

	Transformational Leadership	Organizational Citizenship	Trust in the Principal
Transformational leadership	.97	.16	.75**
Organizational citizenship		.91	.38**
Trust in the principal			.98

* p < .05; ** p < .01; Cronbach's alpha for internal consistency shown on the diagonals.

testing the direct contribution of transformational leadership behaviors to organizational citizenship, as well as utilizing trust as a mediating variable. None of these models, however, reached adequate fit, as might have been expected given the low correlations between the constructs. The model that came closest to an adequate fit was a simple model including trust and organizational citizenship. This model had a chi square of 238.6 (134), a Comparative Fit Index (CFI) of .89, an Adjusted Goodmess of Fit Index (AGFI) of .64, and a Root Mean Square Error of Approximation (RMSEA) of .12.

DISCUSSION

These findings differ from what was expected based on the theory of transformational leadership as well as from those found by Podsakoff and his colleagues (1990). Based on the theoretical foundations of transformational leadership, one would expect transformational leadership behaviors to be strongly related to organizational citizenship behaviors among the followers. However, this was not the case. The relationship between transformational leadership behaviors of the principal and organizational citizenship among teachers was nonsignificant. Furthermore, even a model of transformational leadership that was mediated by trust, as indicated by Podsakoff and colleagues, did not reach acceptable fit in relation to organizational citizenship. Trust in the principal was significantly correlated to organizational citizenship, although the correlation was of moderate strength.

The only relationship that fell within the range that might have been predicted was the strong relationship between perceptions of the transformational leadership behaviors of principals and teachers' trust in principals. Indeed, some scholars discuss trust as a byproduct or even an element of transformational leadership, drawing connections to the idealized influence aspect of transformational leadership behaviors (Boal & Bryson 1988; Hoy & Miskel, 2001; Yukl, 1989). Rather than thinking of trust as an element of transformational leadership, in light of the findings it may be more instructive to think of the competencies of transformational leadership as but one element of trustworthy leadership. Recall that competence is one of the five elements of trust. But competence alone does not appear to create the conditions that promote organizational citizenship. Indeed, benevolence, reliability, honesty, and openness seem to be required as well before workers are likely to go beyond their formally prescribed job descriptions and give of their best for the organization.

It is clear that school leaders need to be cognizant of the power of trust. Trust was related to citizenship where transformational leadership was not. Teachers are apparently unlikely or unwilling to extend themselves beyond formal expectations where trust in the principal is absent. Even so, only about 15% of the variance in organizational citizenship was explained by trust. Other factors were apparently at work. These might be factors beyond the control of the principal, such as negative media coverage of teachers, resentment over top-down changes brought about as a result of the standards movement, or low salaries. Teachers in the state under study did not receive cost-of-living raises during the year the study was conducted due to a budget crisis in the state. Other factors within the school, such as the accepted norms, the culture of various factions, or the power and influence of informal leaders, might also affect the organizational citizenship of teachers.

The findings invite further study. Studies using other samples and perhaps other measures to tap the constructs under study would no doubt add to the findings of this study. Although each of the instruments held up under rigorous statistical tests, there were perhaps elements or dimensions of the constructs that were not adequately captured by our study. For example, the measure of organizational citizenship we used included citizenship behaviors directed at individuals as well as the organization. Previous studies outside of K–12 school settings have frequently found these two dimensions of citizenship to have loaded on separate factors. In this study, they loaded together. This may be because schools are professional organizations where service to clients is the hallmark of professional behavior (DiPaola & Tschannen-Moran, 2001). On the other hand, if organizational citizenship directed toward the organization alone were tested, the results might align more closely with the behavior of the principal.

CONCLUSION AND DIRECTIONS FOR FUTURE RESEARCH

For schools to meet the high standards now expected of them, teachers must be inspired to perform at high levels. When teachers spontaneously go beyond formally prescribed job responsibilities and perform nonmandatory tasks, the impact on the school organization is significant. Tension such as that produced by the vague and generalized job descriptions of professionals in school organizations is reduced. OCBs also contribute to the overall effectiveness of the school and reduce the time the administrator must devote to management activities. We need to know more about how to evoke organizational citizenship behaviors in schools. The study of organizational citizenship behavior has produced many important insights in various organizational settings (Organ, 1988; Organ & Ryan, 1995), however, it has rarely been studied in school organizations.

The results of this study are both perplexing and challenging. Transformational leadership behaviors are presumed to inspire followers to greater citizenship. Yet there was no significant correlation between those behaviors and the perceived organizational citizenship of teachers in the middle schools studied. At the same time, trust emerged as an important factor in relation to citizenship. This goes beyond the findings of Podsakoff and colleagues (1990) that trust mediated the relationship between leadership and citizenship. Instead, we found that it was primarily trust alone that led to greater citizenship among teachers.

In light of these findings, we need a greater focus on the study of trust to understand the dynamics that foster trust and how to repair trust that has been damaged. Principal preparation programs need to focus on the development of trust as a crucial component of leadership. The behavior of principals plays a critical role in setting the tone within a school. Because of the hierarchical nature of the relationships within schools, it is the responsibility of the person with greater power to take the greater initiative to build and sustain trusting relationships (Whitener, Brodt, Korsgaard, & Werner, 1998). If schools are to garner the benefits of greater citizenship behaviors among the faculty, fostering a trusting work environment through trustworthy leadership on the part of principals is a good place to start.

REFERENCES

Avolio, B. J. (1994). The alliance of total quality and the full range of leadership. In B. M. Bass & B. J. Avolio (Eds.), *Improving organizational effectiveness through transformational leadership* (pp. 121–145). Thousand Oaks, CA: Sage.

Avolio, B. J. (1999). *Full leadership development.* Thousand Oaks, CA: Sage.

Baier, A. C. (1986). Trust and antitrust. *Ethics, 96,* 231–260.

Barnard, C.I. (1938). *The functions of the executive.* Cambridge, MA: Harvard University Press.

Bass, B. M. (1985). *Leadership and performance beyond expectations.* New York: Free Press.

Bass, B. M. (1990). From transactional to transformational leadership: Learning to share the vision. In B. M. Bass & R. M. Stogdill (Eds.), *Bass & Stogdill's handbook of leadership* (3rd ed., pp. 628–640). New York: Free Press.

Bass, B. M. (1998). *Transformational leadership: Industrial, military, and educational impact.* Mahwah, NJ: Erlbaum.

Bass, B. M., & Avolio, B. J. (Eds.). (1994). *Improving organizational effectiveness through transformational leadership.* Thousand Oaks, CA: Sage.

Bateman, T. S., & Organ, D. W. (1983). Job satisfaction and the good soldier: The relationship between affect and employee citizenship. *Academy of Management Journal, 26,* 587–595.

Bennis, W., & Nanus, B. (1985). *Leaders: The strategies for taking charge.* New York: Harper & Row.

Boal, K. B., & Bryson, J. M. (1988). Charismatic leadership: A phenomenological and structural approach. In J. G. Hunt, B. R. Baliga, H. P. Dachler, & C. A. Schriesheim (Eds.), *Emerging leadership vistas* (pp. 5–28). Lexington, MA: Lexington.

Borman, W. C., & Motowidlo, S. J. (1993). Expanding the criterion domain to include elements of contextual performance. In N. Schmitt & W. C. Borman (Eds.), *Personality selection* (pp. 71–98). San Francisco: Jossey-Bass.

Bryk, A. S., & Driscoll, M. E. (1988). *The high school as community: Contextual influences and consequences for students and teachers.* Madison: University of Wisconsin, National Center on Effective Secondary Schools.

Bryk, A. S., Lee, V. E., & Holland, P. B. (1993). *Catholic schools and the common good.* Cambridge, MA: Harvard University Press.

Bryk, A. S., & Schneider, B. (1996). *Social trust: A moral resource for school improvement.* Chicago: University of Chicago, Center for School Improvement.

Burns, J. M. (1978). *Leadership.* New York: Harper & Row.

Butler, J. K. (1991). Towards understanding and measuring conditions of trust: Evolution of a conditions of trust inventory. *Journal of Management, 17,* 643–663.

Butler, J. K., & Cantrell, R. S. (1984). A behavioral decision theory approach to modeling dyadic trust in superiors and subordinates. *Psychological Reports, 55,* 81–105.

Cummings, L. L., & Bromily, P. (1996). The Organizational Trust Inventory (OTI): Development and validation. In R. Kramer & T. Tyler (Eds.), *Trust in organizations: Frontiers of theory and research* (pp. 302–330). Thousand Oaks, CA: Sage.

Dasgupta, P. (1988). Trust as a commodity. In D. Gambetta (Ed.), *Trust: Making and breaking cooperative relations* (pp. 213–238). Cambridge, MA: Basil Blackwell.

DiPaola, M., & Tschannen-Moran, M. (2001). Organizational citizenship behavior in schools and its relationship to school climate. *Journal of School Leadership, 11,* 424–447.

Driscoll, J. W. (1978). Trust and participation in organizational decision making as predictors of satisfaction. *Academy of Management Journal, 21,* 44–56.

Evans, R. (1996). *The human side of change: Reform, resistance, and real-life problems of innovation.* San Francisco: Jossey-Bass.

Gabarro, J. J. (1978). The development of trust, influence and expectations. In A. G. Athos & J. J. Gabarro (Eds.), *Interpersonal behavior: Communication and understanding in relationships* (pp. 290–303). Englewood Cliffs, NJ: Prentice-Hall.

Graham, J.W. (1986). *Organizational citizenship informed by political theory.* Paper presented at Academy of Management meeting, Chicago.

Granovetter, M. (1985). Economic action and social structure: The problems of embeddedness. *American Journal of Sociology, 91,* 481–510.

Hipp, K. A., & Bredeson, P. V. (1995). Exploring connections between teacher efficacy and principals' leadership behavior. *Journal of School Leadership. 5,* 136–150.

Horsburgh, H. J. N. (1960). The ethics of trust. *Philosophical Quarterly, 10,* 343–354.

Hoy, W. K., & Kupersmith, W. J. (1985). The meaning and measure of faculty trust. *Educational and Psychological Research, 5,* 1–10.

Hoy, W. K., & Miskel, C. G. (2001). *Educational administration: Theory, research and practice* (6th ed.). Boston: McGraw-Hill.

Hoy, W. K., Sabo, D., & Barnes, K. (1996, Spring). Organizational health and faculty trust: A view from the middle level. *Research in Middle Level Education Quarterly,* 21–39.

Hoy, W. K., Tarter, C. J., & Witkoskie, L. (1992). Faculty trust in colleagues: Linking the principal with school effectiveness. *Journal of Research and Development in Education, 26,* 38–45.

Hoy, W. K., & Tschannen-Moran, M. (1999). Five faces of trust: An empirical confirmation in urban elementary schools. *Journal of School Leadership, 9,* 184–208.

Jones, G. R., & George, J. M. (1998). The experience and evolution of trust: Implications for cooperation and teamwork. *Academy of Management Review, 23,* 531–546.

Katz, D. (1964). The motivational bases of organizational behavior. *Behavioral Science, 9,* 131–133.

Katz, D., & Kahn, R. L. (1978). *The social psychology of organizations* (2nd ed.). New York: Wiley.

Kee, H. W., & Knox, R. E. (1970). Conceptual and methodological considerations in the study of trust and suspicion, *Journal of Conflict Resolution, 14,* 357–365.

Kerlinger, F. N. (1986). *Foundations of behavioral research* (3rd ed.). New York: Holt, Rinehart & Winston.

Kouzes, J. M., & Posner, B. Z. (1987). *The leadership challenge: How to get extraordinary things done in organizations.* San Francisco: Jossey-Bass.

Kouzes, J. M., & Posner, B. Z. (1993). *Credibility: How leaders gain and lose it, why people demand it.* San Francisco: Jossey-Bass.

Kramer, R. M. (1996). Divergent realities and convergent disappointments in the hierarchic relation: Trust and the intuitive auditor at work. In R. Kramer & T. Tyler (Eds.), *Trust in organizations* (pp. 216–245). Thousand Oaks, CA: Sage.

Kramer, R. M., Brewer, M. B., & Hanna, B. A. (1996). Collective trust and collective action: The decision to trust as a social decision. In R. Kramer & T. Tyler (Eds.), *Trust in organizations* (pp. 357–389). Thousand Oaks, CA: Sage.

Leithwood, K., & Jantzi, D. (2000). The effects of transformational leadership on organizational conditions and student engagement with school. *Journal of Educational Administration, 38,* 112–129.

Leithwood, K., Jantzi, D., & Steinbach, R. (1999). *Changing leadership for changing times.* Philadelphia: Open University Press.

Leithwood, K., & Steinbach, R. (1993). Total quality leadership: Expert thinking plus transformational practice. *Journal of Personnel Evaluation in Education, 7,* 311–337.

Lewis, J. D., & Weigert, A. (1985). Trust as a social reality. *Social Forces, 63,* 967–985.

McGregor, D. (1967). *The professional manager.* New York: McGraw-Hill.

Mishra, A. K. (1996). Organizational responses to crisis: The centrality of trust. In R. Kramer & T. Tyler (Eds.), *Trust in organizations: Frontiers of theory and research* (pp. 261–287). Thousand Oaks, CA: Sage.

Nanus, B. (1989). *The leader's edge: The seven keys to leadership in a turbulent world.* Chicago: Contemporary Books.

Nicholson, M. (2002). *Transformational leadership, collective efficacy, and student achievement.* Unpublished dissertation, Ohio State University.

Organ, D.W. (1988). *Organizational citizenship behavior.* Lexington, MA: D. C. Heath.

Organ, D.W. (1990). The motivational basis of organizational citizenship behavior. *Research in Organizational Behavior, 12,* 43–72.

Organ, D.W. (1997). Organizational citizenship behavior: It's construct clean-up time. *Human Performance, 10*(2), 85–97.

Organ, D. W., & Ryan, K (1995). A meta-analytic review of attitudinal and dispositional predictors of organizational citizenship behavior. *Personnel Psychology, 48,* 775–802.

Podsakoff, P. M., & MacKenzie, S. B. (1994). Organizational citizenship behaviors and sales unit effectiveness. *Journal of Marketing Research, 31,* 351–363.

Podsakoff, P. M., MacKenzie, S. B., Moorman, R. H., & Fetter, R. (1990). Transformational leader behaviors and their effects on followers' trust in leader, satisfaction, and organizational citizenship behaviors. *Leadership Quarterly 1,* 107–142.

Rosenholtz, S. (1989). *Teachers workplace.* New York: Longman.

Rousseau, D., Sitkin, S. B., Burt, R., & Camerer, C. (1998). Not so different after all: A cross-discipline view of trust. *Academy of Management Review, 23,* 393–404.

Sapienza, H. J., & Korsgaard, M. A. (1996). Managing investor relations: The impact of procedural justice in establishing and sustaining investor support. *Academy of Management Journal 39,* 544–574.

Short, P. M., Greer, J. T., & Melvin, W. M. (1994). Creating empowered schools: Lessons in change. *Journal of Educational Administration, 32,* 38–52.

Simons, T. L. (1999). Behavioral integrity as a critical ingredient for transformational leadership. *Journal of Organizational Change, 12,* 89–104.

Smith, C. A., Organ, D. W., & Near, J. P. (1983). Organizational citizenship behavior: Its nature and antecedents. *Journal of Applied Psychology, 68,* 653–663.

Solomon, R. C., & Flores, F. (2001). *Building trust in business, politics, relationships, and life.* New York: Oxford University Press.

Stewart, R. (1985). *The reality of management.* London: Heinemann.

Tarter, C. J., Bliss, J. R., & Hoy, W. K. (1989). School characteristics and faculty trust in secondary schools. *Educational Administration Quarterly 25,* 294–308.

Tarter, C. J., Sabo, D. J. & Hoy, W. K. (1995). Middle school climate, faculty trust, and effectiveness: A path analysis. *Journal of Research and Development in Education 29*(1), 41–49.

Tschannen-Moran, M. (1998). *Trust and collaboration in urban elementary schools.* Unpublished doctoral dissertation, Ohio State University.

Tschannen-Moran, M. (2001). Collaboration and the need for trust. *Journal of Educational Administration 39,* 308–331.

Tschannen-Moran, M., & Hoy, W. K. (1998). A conceptual and empirical analysis of trust in schools. *Journal of Educational Administration, 36,* 334–352.

Whitener, E. M., Brodt, S. E., Korsgaard, M. A., & Werner, J. M. (1998). Managers as initiators of trust: An exchange relationship framework for understanding managerial trustworthy behavior. *Academy of Management Review, 23*(3), 513–530.

Yukl, G. A. (1989). Managerial leadership: A review of theory and research. *Yearly Review of Management, 15,* 251–289.

Yukl, G. A. (1998). *Leadership in organizations* (4th ed.). Upper Saddle River, NJ: Prentice Hall.

Zand, D. E. (1971). Trust and managerial problem solving. *Administrative Science Quarterly, 17,* 229–239.

Zand, D. E. (1997). *The leadership triad: Knowledge, trust, and power.* New York: Oxford University Press.

CHAPTER 7

THE CONCEPTUALIZATION AND MEASUREMENT OF FACULTY TRUST IN SCHOOLS

The Omnibus T-Scale[1]

Wayne K. Hoy
Megan Tschannen-Moran

ABSTRACT

Trust has long been a subject of philosophers and politicians, but the systematic study of the construct is of more recent vintage. Trust means many things; in fact, most people intuitively know what it is, but it is quite a different matter to articulate a definition of trust because it is a complex, multifaceted concept. The purpose of this inquiry is threefold: first, to conceptualize the many facets of trust and develop a working definition; second, to explore empirically four referents of trust in schools—faculty trust in students, in teachers, in the principal, and in parents; and finally, to develop a short, valid, and reliable measure of faculty trust for use in both elementary and secondary schools—the Omnibus T-Scale.

Studies in Leading and Organizing Schools, pages 181–208

Most of us notice a given form of trust most easily after its sudden demise or severe injury. We inhabit a climate of trust as we inhabit an atmosphere and notice it as we notice air, only when it becomes scarce or polluted.

—Baier (1994, p. 98)

Trust is a critical ingredient of all human learning (Rotter, 1967), one that is especially important in schools where learning is the central mission. Moreover, trust is crucial in facilitating cooperation (Deutsch, 1958; Tschannen-Moran, 2001), in developing open school cultures (Hoffman, Sabo, Bliss, & Hoy, 1994), in promoting group cohesiveness (Zand, 1971, 1997), in school leadership (Sergiovanni, 1992), in student achievement (Goddard, Tschannen-Moran, & Hoy, 2001; Hoy, 2002), and in increasing the quality of schooling (Hoy & Sabo, 1998).

Although trust has long been the subject of philosophers and politicians, the systematic investigation of trust by social scientists is of more recent vintage. In the late 1950s, the impetus for the empirical study of trust came from the escalating suspicion of the Cold War and optimism that science could provide answers to the dangerous and costly arms race (Deutsch, 1958). In the late 1960s, in response to a generation of young people who had become disillusioned with established institutions and authority, the study of trust shifted to individual personality traits (Rotter, 1967). In the 1980s, with soaring divorce rates and radical changes in the American family, research on trust next turned to interpersonal relationships (Johnson-George & Swap, 1982; Larzelere & Huston, 1980; Rempel, Holmes, & Zanna, 1985). In the 1990s, with shifts in technology and society, trust continues as a subject of study in sociology (Coleman, 1990), in economics (Fukuyama, 1995), and in organizational science (Gambetta, 1988; Kramer & Tyler, 1996; Shaw, 1997). Thus, it should not be surprising that the nature and meaning of trust in schools has recently taken on added importance.

Trust is good. Everyone wants to trust and be trusted. But trust means many things. Everyone knows intuitively what it is to trust, yet articulating a precise definition is no simple matter. Trust is difficult to define because it is so complex; in fact, Hosmer (1995) has observed, "There appears to be widespread agreement on the importance of trust in human conduct, but unfortunately there also appears to be an equally widespread lack of agreement on a suitable definition of the construct" (p. 380).

Trust is a multifaceted construct, which may have different bases and phases depending on the context. It is also a dynamic construct that can change over the course of a relationship. The purpose of this inquiry, which builds on earlier work (Hoy & Tschannen-Moran, 1999; Tschannen-Moran & Hoy, 1998), is to examine the meaning and measure of faculty trust in schools. The current analysis has three goals: First, to conceptualize the many facets of faculty trust in schools and then to provide a working definition of faculty trust; second, to explore empirically four referents of faculty trust—in students, in teachers, in the principal, and in parents; and third, to develop reliable and valid measures of faculty trust for use in both elementary and secondary schools.

TRUST

A review of the extant literature on trust (Tschannen-Moran & Hoy, 1998) led to the identification of a host of different definitions. With one exception (Frost, Stimpson, & Maughan, 1978), all were multifaceted definitions. Most were based on common beliefs that individuals or groups would act in ways that were in the best interest of the concerned party. The literature on trust is diverse and yet it has some common threads running through it regardless of whether the focus is on the individual, organization, or society itself.

Trust relationships are based upon interdependence; that is, the interests of one party cannot be achieved without reliance upon another (Rousseau, Sitkin, Burt, & Camerer, 1998). If there is no interdependence, there is no need for trust. Interdependence in a relationship typically creates vulnerability, and vulnerability is a common feature of most definitions of trust (Baier, 1986; Bigley & Pearce, 1998; Coleman, 1990; Mayer, Davis, & Schoorman, 1995; Mishra, 1996). Trust involves taking risk and making oneself vulnerable to another with confidence that the other will act in ways that are not detrimental to the trusting party.

Facets of Trust

There are at least five facets of trust that can be gleaned from the literature on trust (Hoy & Tschannen-Moran, 1999; Tschannen-Moran & Hoy, 1998). Benevolence, reliability, competence, honesty, and openness are all elements of trust.

Benevolence

Perhaps the most common facet of trust is a sense of benevolence—confidence that one's well-being or something one cares about will be protected and not harmed by the trusted party (Baier, 1986; Butler & Cantrell, 1984; Cummings & Bromily, 1996; Deutsch, 1958; Frost et al., 1978; Gambetta, 1988; Hosmer, 1995; Hoy & Kupersmith, 1985; Mishra, 1996). Trust is the assurance that others will not exploit one's vulnerability or take advantage even when the opportunity is available (Cummings & Bromily,

1996). Benevolence is the "accepted vulnerability to another's possible but not expected ill will" (Baier, 1986, p. 236).

In situations of interdependence, faith in the altruism of the other is especially important. Parents who trust educators to care for their children are confident that teachers will act with the best interests of their child in mind and that their child will be treated not only with fairness but with compassion. When trust in the benevolence of the other is missing, there are costs in productivity because energy is invested in anticipating and in making alternative plans. Teachers who don't trust their students spend much of their time planning for expected or imagined student misbehavior. Benevolence is an important element of trust relationships because a mutual attitude of goodwill is so important in interpersonal relationships.

Reliability

At its most basic level trust has to do with predictability, that is, consistency of behavior and knowing what to expect from others (Butler & Cantrell, 1984; Hosmer, 1995). In and of itself, however, predictability is insufficient for trust. We can expect a person to be invariably late, consistently malicious, inauthentic, or dishonest. When our well-being is diminished or damaged in a predictable way, expectations may be met, but the sense in which we trust the other person or group is weak.

Reliability combines a sense of predictability with benevolence. In a situation of interdependence, when something is required from another person or group, the individual can be relied upon to supply it (Butler & Cantrell; Mishra, 1996; Rotter, 1967). Reliability implies that there is a sense of confidence that one's needs will be met in positive ways. Hence, one need neither invest energy worrying about whether the person will come through nor make alternative mental provisions.

Competence

Good intentions are not always enough. When a person is dependent on another but some level of skill is involved in fulfilling an expectation, an individual who means well may nonetheless not be trusted (Baier, 1986; Butler & Cantrell, 1984; Mishra, 1996). Competence is the ability to perform as expected and according to standards appropriate to the task at hand. Many organizational tasks rely on competence. In situations of interdependence, when a team's project depends on the participation of others, trust will depend on an "assured confidence" that deadlines will be met and that the work will be of sufficient quality to meet project goals. In schools, principals and teachers depend upon one another to accomplish the teaching and learning goals of the school. Students are dependent on the competence of their teachers. A student may believe that her teacher is benevolent and wants to help her learn, but if the teacher lacks knowledge of the subject matter or cannot adequately communicate that knowledge, then the student's trust in her teacher may be limited.

Honesty

Honesty is the person's character, integrity, and authenticity. Rotter (1967) defined trust as "the expectancy that the word, promise, verbal or written statement of another individual or group can be relied upon" (p. 651). Statements are truthful when they conform to "what really happened" from that person's perspective and when commitments made about future actions are kept. A correspondence between a person's statements and deeds demonstrates integrity. Moreover, acceptance of responsibility for one's actions and not distorting the truth in order to shift blame to another exemplifies authenticity (Tschannen-Moran & Hoy, 1998). Many scholars and researchers see honesty as a pivotal feature of trust (Baier, 1986; Butler & Cantrell, 1984; Cummings & Bromily, 1996). Indeed, honesty is assumed when we think of what is entailed in trust.

Openness

Openness is the extent to which relevant information is shared; it is a process by which individuals make themselves vulnerable to others. The information shared may be strictly about organizational matters or it may be personal information, but it is a giving of oneself (Butler & Cantrell, 1984; Mishra, 1996). Such openness signals reciprocal trust, a confidence that neither the information nor the individual will be exploited, and recipients can feel the same confidence in return.

Just as trust breeds trust, so too does distrust breed distrust. People who are guarded in the information they share provoke suspicion; people wonder what is being hidden and why. Individuals who are unwilling to extend trust through openness end up isolated (Kramer, Brewer, & Hanna, 1996). For example, principals in closed school climates engender distrust by withholding information and spinning the truth in order to make their view of reality the accepted standard (Sweetland & Hoy, 2001); most teachers are not fooled by such behavior and the principal's future actions become even more suspect.

Definition

The review of the extant literature on trust identified a myriad of definitions of trust. Most were multifaceted definitions and were based upon expectations or common beliefs that individuals or groups would act in ways that were in the best interest of the concerned party. The analysis led to the following definition of trust: *Trust is an individual's or group's willing-*

ness to be vulnerable to another party based on the confidence that the latter party is benevolent, reliable, competent, honest, and open.

Faculty trust is a collective property—the extent to which the faculty as a group is willing to risk vulnerability. Notice that this definition includes multiple facets:

- *Benevolence*—confidence that one's well-being will be protected by the trusted party.
- *Reliability*—the extent to which one can count on another person or group.
- *Competency*—the extent to which the trusted party has knowledge and skill.
- *Honesty*—the character, integrity, and authenticity of the trusted party.
- *Openness*—the extent to which there is no withholding of information from others.

Trust is embedded in relationships, and the referent of trust influences the meaning. In the current analysis four referents of faculty trust are of interest:

- Faculty trust in students
- Faculty trust in colleagues
- Faculty trust in the principal
- Faculty trust in parents

DEVELOPING MEASURES OF FACULTY TRUST— THE TRUST SCALE

Using the conceptual formulation of trust developed above, items were written by a team of researchers. For each trust referent (student, colleagues, principal, parent), items were written to include all five facets of trust. Although there were no extant measures for trust that fitted the proposed conceptual framework, Hoy and Kupersmith (1985) had developed scales to measure faculty trust in colleagues and in principals. Their work was a starting point for this research. An analysis of their items, however, revealed that none of them tapped competency or openness; hence, new items were added to the existing ones to measure the missing facets of trust. In addition, sets of items were written for faculty trust in students and in parents, making sure that each facet of trust was represented for each referent group.

The format of the Trust Scales was a 6-point Likert response set from strongly agree to strongly disagree. Teachers were asked to indicate the extent to which they agreed with the items. Sample items from each of the four levels of trust being measured include:

- Teachers in this school are suspicious of students.
- The principal is unresponsive to teachers' concerns.
- Teachers in this school are reliable.
- Teachers can count on parents in this school to support them.

Items were developed that tapped each proposed facet of trust. The development of the instrument went through a number of phases:

1. The researchers created a pool of items.
2. A panel of experts reacted to the items.
3. A preliminary version was field tested with teachers.
4. A pilot study was done with a small group of schools to test the factor structure, reliability, and validity of the instrument.
5. Two large-scale studies were conducted to assess psychometric properties of the measures.

Developing Items

Using the conceptual framework developed above, the researchers created a pool of items to measure the facets and referents of faculty trust. Specifically, willingness to risk vulnerability and five facets of trust were considered—benevolence, reliability, competency, honesty, and openness—as the items were written, and four referents of faculty trust—student, teacher, principal, and parent—guided the creation of the four separate sets of trust items.

Panel of Experts

To check the content validity of the items, the Trust Scale was submitted to a panel of experts, all professors at Ohio State University from the College of Education and the Fisher Business School. The panel was asked to judge which facet of trust each item measured. There was strong agreement among the judges, and in those few cases where the panelists disagreed, the items were retained and the question of the appropriate category was left to an empirical test using factor analysis. There was consensus that the items measured all the facets of trust for each referent group.

Field Test

A field test was conducted to test the clarity of instructions, appropriateness of the response set, and face validity of the items. Six experienced teachers were asked to examine, respond to the items, and give some feedback. Again there was general agreement that the items were clear, reasonable, and had face validity. In a few instances, specific comments led to minor modification of an item.

Pilot Study

After the panel review and field test, 48 items remained and were used in a pilot study to explore the factor structure, reliability, and validity of the measure.

Sample

A sample of 50 teachers from 50 different schools in five states was selected to test the psychometric properties of the Trust Scales. Half of the schools selected were schools with reputations of relatively high conflict and the other half had relatively low conflict among the faculty.

Instruments

In addition to the 48-item Trust Scales survey, teachers were asked to respond a self-estrangement scale (Forsyth & Hoy, 1978), a sense of powerlessness scale (Zielinski & Hoy, 1983), a teacher sense of efficacy scale (Bandura, n.d.), and one item measuring the perception of conflict in the school. These additional measures were used to check the validity of the trust measure. It was predicted that each aspect of trust would be positively related to sense of teacher efficacy and negatively related to self-estrangement, sense of powerlessness, and degree of conflict.

Data collection

Data were collected from 50 different schools through two procedures. University professors identified about one third of the schools as coming from either low-trust or high-trust schools, and the other two thirds were sent the questionnaire by mail. Ninety-one percent of those contacted agreed to participate and returned usable questionnaires.

Results

The items were submitted to a factor analysis to test whether they loaded strongly and as expected. Although we anticipated four factors, only three strong factors emerged. The three-factor solution was supported by a scree test and made conceptual sense. Surprisingly, trust in students and trust in parents items loaded together on a single factor. Teachers did not distinguish between trusting students and trusting parents. Thus, the two sets of items combined into a single factor, which was called "Trust in Clients." The clients in this case are students and parents; both are recipients of the services offered by schools. The other two factors, as predicted, were Trust in the Principal and Trust in Colleagues. On the whole, factor loadings were strong and loaded together with other items from the same subtest. Results are reported in Table 7.1.

Table 7.1. Factor Analysis of Trust Items (Pilot Study, n = 50)

	F1	F2	F3
1. The principal is unresponsive to teachers' concerns.	−.93	−.12	.06
2. Teachers in this school can rely on the principal.	.92	.10	.14
3. Teachers in this school trust the principal.	.88	.10	.28
The principal in this school typically acts with the best interests of teachers in mind.	.84	.21	.15
5. The principal of this school does not show concern for teachers.	−.79	−.10	−.12
6. The principal doesn't really tell teachers what is going on.	−.78	−.27	−.12
7. The principal in this school keeps his or her word.	.77	.20	.23
8. The principal takes unfair advantage of teachers in this school.	−.74	−.21	−.06
9. Teachers in this school have faith in the integrity of the principal.	.73	.11	.46
10. Teachers in this school are suspicious of most of the principal's action.	−.71	−.03	−.23
11. Teachers in this school often question the motives of the principal.	−.70	.09	−.42
12. The principal openly shares personal information with teachers.	.63	−.01	.26
13. When the principal commits to something teachers can be sure it will get done.	.61	.26	.19
14. The principal in this school is competent in doing his or her job.	.60	.33	−.02
15. Teachers feel comfortable admitting to the principal they have made a mistake.	.51	.02	.35
16. Teachers in this school believe in each other.	.27	.20	.86
17. Even in difficult situations, teachers in this school can depend on each other.	.19	.15	.86
18. Teachers in this school are open with each other.	.28	.10	.82

Table 7.1.   Factor Analysis of Trust Items (Pilot Study, n = 50) (Cont.)

	F1	F2	F3
19. When teachers in this school tell you something, you can believe it.	.19	.06	.82
20. Teachers in this school typically look out for each other.	.29	.19	.80
21. Teachers in this school trust each other.	.29	.25	.79
22. Teachers in this school have faith in the integrity of their colleagues.	.16	.37	.76
23. Teachers here only trust teachers in their clique.	−.31	−.30	−.64
24. If I had a school-age child, I would feel comfortable putting my own child in most anyone's classroom in this school.	.11	.54	.61
25. Teachers take unfair advantage of each other in this school.	−.11	−.41	−.59
26. Teachers in this school are suspicious of each other.	−.31	−.39	−.58
27. Teachers in this school are reliable.	.30	.55	.50
28. Teachers in this school do their jobs well.	.31	.59	.40
29. Teachers in this school don't share much about their lives outside of school.	−.36	−.23	−.20
30. Students in this school are reliable.	.10	.81	.18
31. Students in this school can be counted on.	.05	.80	.12
32. Teachers think that most of the parents do a good job.	.07	.79	.24
33. The students in this school have to be closely supervised.	−.16	−.78	.02
34. Parents in this school are reliable in their commitments.	.06	.75	.44
35. Teachers in this school trust their students.	.06	.75	.43
36. Students in this school care about each other.	−.08	.72	.29
37. Teachers can count on the parental support.	.06	.71	.19
38. Students here are secretive.	−.17	−.70	−.10
39. Students in this school cheat if they have a chance.	−.09	−.65	−.06
40. Students in this school can be counted on to do their work.	.16	.66	.21
41. Teachers in this school are suspicious of students.	−.32	−.61	−.20
42. Teachers avoid making contact with parents.	−.24	−.60	−.22
43. Teachers in this school show concern for their students.	.29	.45	.35
44. Teachers are suspicious of parents' motives.	−.21	−.49	−.31
45. Teachers in this school believe what students say.	.11	.47	.65
46. Teachers in this school trust parents.	.04	.45	.56
47. The students in this school talk freely about their lives outside of school.	.07	.04	.40
48. Teachers are guarded in what they say to parents.	−.36	−.27	−.22

Table 7.1. Factor Analysis of Trust Items (Pilot Study, n = 50) (Cont.)

	F1	F2	F3
Eigenvalue	19.00	6.20	3.79
Cumulative variance explained	39.60	52.50	60.40

New items:

49. **Teachers here believe that students are competent learners.**

50. **Teachers can believe what parents tell them.**

Bold items composed the next version of the instrument.

Decisions of whether to retain, eliminate, or modify each of the items were based on theoretical (conceptual fit) and empirical (factor loadings) grounds. When an item loaded at .40 or above on more than one factor, it typically was removed. In a few cases, however, such items were retained because either the conceptual fit was strong or the item could be modified to enhance the conceptual fit. For example, the item, "Teachers in this school trust their students," loaded strongly on Trust in Clients at .75 but also loaded on Trust in Colleagues at .43. This item was retained because of its strong conceptual fit with trust in clients. Any item that failed the empirical test of loading .40 or higher on at least one factor was eliminated. Likewise, regardless of the factor loading, any item that loaded on the wrong factor conceptually was eliminated. Finally, a few redundant items were also eliminated when another item measured the same property of trust and had an even stronger loading.

As a result of the factor analysis, four items from Trust in the Principal, five from Trust in Colleagues, and four in the Trust in Clients factor were eliminated. Some of the eliminated items revealed interesting patterns. Whether teachers shared information about their lives outside of school with their colleagues was not strongly related to trust factors. And when teachers were asked whether they would feel comfortable putting their own child in their school, judgments of their colleagues' competence were confounded with trust for clients. Teachers were apparently as concerned about their level of trust in students as in their trust in colleagues in determining how comfortable they would be in enrolling their own child in the school. In brief, the pilot study produced a 35-item survey that reliably measured three kinds of trust: Trust in the Principal (alpha = .95), Trust in Colleagues (alpha = .94), and Trust in Clients (alpha = .92).

Next, a content analysis was performed. That is, each level of trust was examined to make sure that all the facets of trust (benevolence, reliability, competence, honesty, and openness) were represented in each scale, and indeed that was the case. The factor structure also supported the construct validity of the trust measures; items generally loaded correctly for each referent of trust. Moreover, all the facets of trust covaried together for a coherent pattern of trust for each referent group—principal, colleagues, and clients. Nevertheless, two items were added for the next iterations of the trust scale, one to tap the competence of students ("Teachers here believe that students are competent learners") and one to measure the honesty of parents ("Teachers can believe what parents tell them"), which yielded a 37-item instrument for further analysis.

We examined the validity of the measures and their ability to distinguish trust from other related constructs. Discriminant validity of the measures of trust was strong. As predicted, self-estrangement, powerlessness, and conflict were all negatively related to dimensions of trust, and teacher sense of efficacy was positively related to the subscales of trust. The results of the correlational analyses are summarized in Table 7.2.

**Table 7.2. Some Validity Evidence:
Correlations between Trust and Criterion Variables**

Subscale	1	2	3	4	5	6	7
1. Trust in Principal	(.95)	.54**	.40**	−.47**	−.22	−.28**	.46**
2. Trust in Colleagues		(.94)	.62**	−.32**	−.31**	−.76**	.30*
3. Trust in Clients			(.92)	−.51**	−.31*	−.56**	.47**
4. Powerlessness				(.83)	.42**	.38**	−.55**
5. Self-estrangement					(.88)	.36**	−.61**
6. School Conflict						—	−.28*
7. Teacher Efficacy							(.87)

*p < .05, **p < .01
Alpha coefficients of reliability are on the diagonal.

A TEST OF THE REVISED TRUST SCALE

Having developed a measure of trust in field and pilot studies, the next step was to evaluate the Trust Scale in a more comprehensive sample. In particular, the goal was to refine the scales and check their reliability and validity. To that end, we tested the 37-item Trust Scale (which included two new items along with 35 original items) along with a measure of parent collaboration in a sample of elementary schools (Hoy & Tschannen-Moran, 1999).

The Elementary Sample

The population for this phase of the study was the elementary schools within one large urban Midwestern school district. Permission to conduct research was requested following school district procedures. Schools were selected at random. Ninety percent of the schools contacted agreed to participate, resulting in a sample of 50 elementary schools.

Halpin (1956) has provided strong evidence that average scores on descriptive questionnaire items such as the LBDQ computed on the basis of 5–7 respondents per school yield reasonably stable scores; thus, schools with fewer than five teachers responding to the instruments were not used. Of the 50 schools surveyed, 45 returned a sufficient number of each of the two surveys to be included in the sample. A total of 898 teachers completed surveys and over 99% of forms returned were useable.

Data Collection

Data were collected from the urban elementary schools at a regularly scheduled faculty meeting. A member of the research team explained the purpose of the study, assured the confidentiality of all participants, and requested that the teachers complete the surveys. The instruments, which had been printed on scannable forms, were distributed along with pencils. Half the teachers present responded to the trust questionnaire and half completed the questionnaire on collaboration. The separation was to ensure methodological independence of the responses. No attempt was made to gather data from faculty who were not present at the meetings.

Factor Analysis and Reliability of the Trust Scale

A factor analysis was conducted to check the stability of the factor structure of trust, to refine the measure, to ensure that all items loaded on the appropriate scale, and to assess the construct validity. Varimax orthogonal rotation was guided by simple structure; items were expected to load high on one factor and low or near zero on the other factors. Moreover, it was anticipated that all faces of trust—benevolence, reliability, competence, honesty, and openness—would be represented in each scale and form a coherent pattern of trust for each of the three referent groups—principal, colleagues, and clients.

A factor analysis of the 37-item trust measure resulted in the elimination of three items due to poor factor loadings. On the Trust in Colleagues sub-scale, one item, "Teachers in this school do their jobs well," was eliminated because it loaded on more than one factor—it loaded on Trust in Colleagues (.72) but also on Trust in Clients (.46). "Teachers avoid making contact with parents" loaded almost equally with Trust in Clients and Trust in Colleagues (.49 and .50, respectively), and "Teachers in this school show concern for their students" loaded as expected on Trust in Colleagues (.58) but was confounded by the level of trust in the principal (.66); hence, both items were eliminated, reducing the number of items on the Trust Scale to 34.[2]

Factor loadings of the items for the Trust in the Principal subscale ranged from .44 to .94 with a subscale reliability of .98 using Cronbach's alpha. Loadings for the Trust in Colleagues ranged from .84 to .93 and the reliability for the subscale was also .98. Loadings for Trust in Clients ranged from .62 to .91 and the alpha for subscale was .97. The results of the factor analysis are found in Table 7.3.

Table 7.3.   Factor Analysis of Trust Items (n = 45 elementary schools)

	F1	*F2*	*F3*
1. The principal is unresponsive to teachers' concerns.	−.22	−.93	.01
2. Teachers in this school can rely on the principal.	.19	.94	.17
3. Teachers in this school trust the principal.	.21	.88	.16
4. The principal in this school typically acts in the best interests of teachers.	.14	.94	.19
5. The principal of this school does not show concern for teachers.	−.21	−.91	−.07
6. The principal doesn't really tell teachers what is going on.	−.16	−.89	−.19
7. The principal in this school keeps his or her word.	.19	.85	.10
8. Teachers in this school have faith in the integrity of the principal.	.17	.92	.28
9. Teachers in this school are suspicious of most of the principal's actions.	−.20	−.86	−.29
10. The principal in this school is competent in doing his or her job.	.20	.92	.12
11. The principal openly shares personal information with teachers.	.09	.44	.15
1. Teachers in this school believe in each other.	.16	.18	.92
2. Even in difficult situations, teachers in this school can depend on each other.	.10	.20	.93
3. Teachers in this school are open with each other.	.14	.11	.91
4. When teachers in this school tell you something, you can believe it.	.27	.19	.84

Table 7.3.   Factor Analysis of Trust Items (n = 45 elementary schools)

	F1	F2	F3
5. Teachers in this school typically look out for each other.	.09	.19	.91
6. Teachers in this school trust each other.	.05	.19	.91
7. Teachers in this school have faith in the integrity of their colleagues.	.28	.09	.92
8. Teachers in this school are suspicious of each other.	−.02	−.14	−.89
9. * Teachers in this school do their jobs well.	.45	.21	.71
1. Students in this school are reliable.	.91	.20	.12
2. Students in this school can be counted on to do their work.	.90	.18	.22
3. Teachers think that most of the parents do a good job.	.90	.11	.18
4. The students in this school have to be closely supervised.	−.89	.03	−.15
5. Parents in this school are reliable in their commitments.	.91	.11	.07
6. Teachers in this school trust their students.	.79	.24	.32
7. Students in this school care about each other.	.89	.23	.23
8. Teachers can count on parental support.	.91	.12	.14
9. Students here are secretive.	−.75	−.26	−.04
10. Students in this school cheat if they have a chance.	−.72	−.25	−.31
11. Teachers can believe what parents tell them.	.84	.23	.09
12. Teachers in this school believe what students say.	.80	.32	.14
13. Teachers in this school trust parents (to support them).	.89	.16	.15
14. The students in this school talk freely about their lives outside of school.	.62	.05	.11
15. Teachers here believe that students are competent learners.	.75	.19	.38
16. * Teachers avoid making contact with parents.	−.49	−.26	−.50
17. * Teachers in this school show concern for their students	.57	.18	.65
Eigenvalues	18.32	6.08	5.44
Cumulative variance explained	49.50	65.90	80.60

* Items deleted.

The factor structure for the Trust Scale was very similar to that found in the pilot study and demonstrated a stable factor structure. In addition, reliabilities for the three subscales were even higher than those found in the pilot study. Kerlinger (1973) argues that factor analysis is perhaps the most powerful method of construct validation, and the findings of this study support the construct validity of faculty trust. The proposed faces or facets of trust—benevolence, reliability, competence, honesty, and openness—vary together and belong to an overall conception of trust that is coherent. Moreover, the facets of trust are present for each referent of trust. In brief, the Trust Scale provides reasonably valid and reliable measures of faculty trust in principals, colleagues, and clients.

Not surprisingly, the three measures of faculty trust were moderately related to each other. Faculty trust in the principal was related to faculty trust in colleagues ($r = .37$, $p <. 01$) and in clients ($r = .42$, $p <. 01$), and faculty trust in colleagues was correlated with faculty trust in clients ($r = .35$, $p <. 01$).

Another Validity Check

The extent to which parents are included and have influence in school decision making varies from school to school. Teachers sometimes resist the intrusion of parents into school affairs; life is simpler for teachers without interference from outsiders, especially parents (Hoy, Tarter, Kottkamp, 1991; Hoy & Sabo, 1998). Yet there has been increasing demand to get parents involved in school decision making. In this study, we measured parent collaboration with a collaboration index (Tschannen-Moran, 2001), which was constructed by asking teachers how much influence parents had over the outcomes of the following important school activities: "planning school activities," "determining school rules," "resolving problems with community groups," "fostering community relations," "determining curriculum priorities," "determining areas in need of improvement," "determining how to comply with mandates and legislation," "approving extracurricular activities," and "determining how to allocate school resources (the school budget)." These items formed a parent collaboration index that had reliability in this sample of .94.

It was theorized that parent collaboration would be more likely in schools in which the faculty was trusting. For example, it seems unlikely that teachers will want to engage in any authentic collaboration with parents if they do not trust them. Thus, we expected that faculty trust in clients would be strongly related to collaboration with parents. The general hypothesis was supported—the greater the degree of faculty trust, the stronger the degree of parental collaboration in decision making as perceived by teachers. The correlations for all three dimensions of trust were statistically significant with parental collaboration, for faculty trust in the principal ($r = .45$, $p < .01$), for faculty trust in colleagues ($r = .37$, $p <. 01$), and for faculty trust in clients ($r = .79$, $p < .01$)

The multiple relationships between the dimensions of faculty trust and parental collaboration was also examined. Parental collaboration was regressed on the three dimensions of faculty trust. Although the simple correlations indicated that all three aspects of trust were related to parental collaboration, the multiple regression analysis demonstrated that trust in clients overwhelmingly explains the degree of parental collaboration in school decision making: in fact, only faculty trust in clients had a significant independent relationship with parental collaboration in decision making (b =. 72, p < . 01). Not surprisingly, when the faculty trusts the parents and students, parental collaboration is greatest. The multiple R^2 of .64 (p < . 01) indicates that almost two thirds of the variance in parental collaboration in decision making is explained by faculty trust. The results of this analysis also support the predictive validity of the items that measure trust.

FACULTY TRUST IN SECONDARY SCHOOLS

To this point, the analysis of trust focused on elementary schools. Would the same structure of trust emerge in secondary schools? Would faculty trust in students and parents combine into a unitary measure of trust or would it separate into two aspects of trust? Would the trust scales used at the elementary level work as well at the secondary level? Next, attention turned to these questions.

Secondary Sample

The secondary sample consisted of 97 high schools in Ohio. Although procedures were not used to ensure a random sample from the population of high schools, care was taken to select urban, suburban, and rural schools from diverse geographic areas of the state, and the sample proved to be fairly representative of secondary schools in Ohio. Only schools with 15 or more faculty members were considered candidates for the study. One hundred fifty high schools were contacted and invited to participate, but for a variety of reasons only 97 agreed to participate (65%). High schools were defined by grade span levels that included grades 9–12 and grades 10–12. Schools in the sample represented the entire range of socioeconomic status (SES); in fact, data from the Ohio Department of Education support the representativness of the sample in terms of size, SES, and urban–rural balance.

Data Collection

Data were collected from the high schools at a regularly scheduled faculty meeting. After the purpose of the study was explained and the confidentiality of all participants was guaranteed, teachers were asked to complete the surveys. In this study, we were interested in a number of other variables; hence, the Trust Scale was given to one group of teachers selected at random while those in another random group responded to an organizational climate index. The separation was to assure methodological independence of the responses. No attempt was made to gather data from faculty who were not present at the meetings.

Factor Analysis and Reliability of the Trust Scale

The trust scale that was developed at the elementary level had 34 items. To use this scale for the secondary schools, we added the item, "Teachers in this school do their jobs well" (which had been eliminated from the elementary scale), because we needed a competency item for the Trust in Colleagues subscale. The following four items: "The principal is unresponsive to teachers' concerns," "Teachers in this school believe in each other," "The students in this school have to be closely supervised," and "The students in this school talk freely about their lives outside of school" were eliminated because another item tapped the same facet of trust for each group. Hence, a 31-item scale was used in the analysis of secondary schools.

Would trust in students and trust in parents merge into one aspect of client trust as they did in elementary schools or remain separate aspects of trust? In fact, the results were the same in both kinds of schools. Regardless of level, elementary or secondary, trust in students and trust in parents combined to form one unitary construct of trust—faculty trust in clients. Once again, the three-factor solution was best and explained about 70% of the variance. Indeed the factor-analytic results of the two samples were remarkably similar. The factor structure remained stable; all items loaded as predicted and defined three dimensions of trust—faculty trust in the principal, in colleagues, and in clients (students and teachers). The results of the factor analysis for secondary schools are summarized in Table 7.4. Alpha coefficients of reliabilities for the three scales were also high for this sample—faculty trust in principal (.98), faculty trust in colleagues (.93), and faculty trust in clients (.93).

Table 7.4. Factor Analysis of Trust Items (n = 97 secondary schools)

		F1	F2	F3
1.	Teachers in this school trust the principal.	.97	.05	.12
2.	The teachers in this school are suspicious of most of the principal's actions.	−.90	−.07	−.07
3.	The principal in this school typically acts in the best interests of teachers.	.94	.08	.16
4.	The principal of this school does not show concern for teachers.	−.83	−.06	−.14
5.	Teachers in this school can rely on the principal.	.97	.04	.06
6.	The principal in this school is competent in doing his or her job.	.91	.03	.15
7.	The principal in this school keeps his or her word.	.85	.02	.13
8.	The teachers in this school have faith in the integrity of the principal.	.92	.02	.17
9.	The principal doesn't really tell teachers what is going on.	−.83	−.10	−.09
10.	The principal openly shares personal information with teachers.	.88	.08	.17
1.	Teachers in this school trust each other.	.19	.24	.85
2.	Teachers in this school are suspicious of each other.	−.06	−.31	−.65
3.	Teachers in this school typically look out for each other.	.13	.21	.83
4.	Even in difficult situations, teachers in this school can depend on each other.	.25	.31	.78
5.	Teachers in this school do their jobs well.	.04	.65	.42
6.	When teachers in this school tell you something, you can believe it.	.24	.41	.64
7.	Teachers in this school have faith in the integrity of their colleagues.	.10	.40	.74
8.	Teachers in this school are open with each other.	.32	.08	.75
1.	Teachers in this school trust their students.	.07	.73	.32
2.	Teachers in this school trust parents (to support them).	.06	.89	.23
3.	Students in this school care about each other.	.03	.79	.24
4.	Teachers can count on parental support.	.14	.82	.16
5.	Students in this school are reliable.	.05	.89	.18
6.	Students in this school can be counted on to do their work.	.01	.83	.10
7.	Parents in this school are reliable in their commitments.	.18	.80	.22
8.	Teachers here believe that students are competent learners.	.13	.82	.16
9.	Teachers think that most of the parents do a good job.	−.02	.90	.11

Table 7.4.   Factor Analysis of Trust Items (n = 97 secondary schools)

		F1	F2	F3
10.	Students in this school cheat if they have a chance.	−.02	−.28	−.09
11.	Teachers can believe what parents tell them.	.13	.72	.30
12	Teachers in this school believe what students say.	.12	.61	.17
13.	Students here are secretive.	−.07	−.27	−.05
	Eigenvalue	12.19	7.12	2.35
	Cumulative variance Explained	39.30	62.30	69.87

OMNIBUS TRUST SCALE

At this point in the instrument development, there were two slightly different versions of the trust scale—one for elementary schools and one for secondary schools. To simplify things, it was decided to develop a single scale that could be used for either elementary or secondary schools. The goal was to create a scale, such that:

1. each of the three referents of faculty trust was measured by a subscale,
2. each trust subscale contained all facets of trust,
3. each subscale had high reliability,
4. each subscale was relatively parsimonious, and
5. each subscale correlated strongly with the original elementary and secondary subscales.

The analysis started with the 31-item secondary version of the trust scale. All the facets of trust were represented on each subscale (see Table 7.5).

Table 7.5.   Common Items for Trust Scale (Elementary and Secondary)

	Facet of Trust
Faculty Trust in Principal	
1. Teachers in this school can rely on the principal.	Reliability
2. Teachers in this school trust the principal.	Vulnerability
3. The principal in this school typically acts in the best interests of teachers.	Reliability
4. The principal of this school does not show concern for teachers.	Benevolence
5. The principal doesn't really tell teachers what is going on.	Openness
6. The principal in this school keeps his or her word.	Honesty
7. The teachers in this school have faith in the integrity of the principal.	Honesty

Table 7.5. Common Items for Trust Scale (Elementary and Secondary)

	Facet of Trust
8. The teachers in this school are suspicious of most of the principal's actions.	Vulnerability
9. The principal in this school is competent in doing his or her job.	Competence
10. The principal openly shares personal information with teachers.	Openness
Faculty Trust in Colleagues	
1. Teachers in this school do their jobs well.	Competence
2. Even in difficult situations, teachers in this school can depend on each other.	Reliability
3. Teachers in this school are open with each other.	Openness
4. When teachers in this school tell you something, you can believe it.	Honesty
5. Teachers in this school typically look out for each other.	Benevolence
6. Teachers in this school trust each other.	Vulnerability
7. Teachers in this school have faith in the integrity of their colleagues.	Honesty
8. Teachers in this school are suspicious of each other.	Vulnerability
Faculty Trust in Clients (students and parents)	
1. Students in this school are reliable.	Reliability
2. Students in this school can be counted on to do their work.	Reliability
3. Teachers think that most of the parents do a good job.	Competence
4. Parents in this school are reliable in their commitments.	Reliability
5. Teachers in this school trust their students.	Vulnerability
6. Students in this school care about each other.	Benevolence
7. Teachers can count on parental support.	Reliability
8. Students here are secretive.	Openness
9. Students in this school cheat if they have a chance.	Honesty
10. Teachers can believe what parents tell them.	Honesty
11. Teachers in this school believe what students say.	Honesty
12. Teachers in this school trust parents.	Vulnerability
13. Teachers here believe that students are competent learners.	Competence

Next, a comparison was made on the factor loadings on the items for elementary and secondary samples. The factor loadings were quite high for all the items. Even the competency item that we added had reasonably high loadings (see Table 7.6). In fact, only two items had low loadings. The item, "The students in this school cheat if they get a chance," loaded high on the elementary sample but low on the secondary sample. Because we

Table 7.6.   Items and Factor Loadings for the Omnibus Trust Scale (T-Scale)

		Factor Loadings	
Subscales and Items		*Elementary*	*Secondary*
Trust in Principal			
1H	The teachers in this school have faith in the integrity of the principal.	.92	.92
2R	The principal in this school typically acts in the best interests of the teachers.	.94	.94
3O	The principal doesn't tell teachers what is really going on.*	−.89	−.84
4V	Teachers in this school trust the principal.	.88	.97
5B	The principal of this school does not show concern for teachers.*	−.91	−.84
6V	The teachers in this school are suspicious of most of the principal's actions.*	−.86	−.91
7R	Teachers in this school can rely on the principal.	.94	.97
8C	The principal in this school is competent in doing his or her job.	.92	.91
Trust in Colleagues			
1B	Teachers in this school typically look out for each other.	.91	.83
2V	Teachers in this school trust each other.	.91	.74
3R	Even in difficult situations, teachers in this school can depend on each other.	.93	.79
4H	Teachers in this school have faith in the integrity of their colleagues.	.92	.73
5V	Teachers in this school are suspicious of each other.*	.89	−.66
6C	Teachers in this school do their jobs well.	.71	.43
7H	When teachers in this school tell you something, you can believe it.	.84	.63
8O	Teachers in this school are open with each other.	.91	.74
Trust in Clients (students and parents)			
1V	Teachers in this school trust their students.	.79	.72
2R	Students in this school can be counted on to do their work.	.90	.83
3B	Students in this school care about each other.	.89	.80
4O	Students here are secretive.*	−.75	−.30
5C	Teachers here believe that students are competent learners.	.75	.81
6R	Teachers can count on parental support.	.91	.82
7H	Teachers in this school believe what parents tell them.	.84	.72

Table 7.6.   Items and Factor Loadings for the Omnibus Trust Scale (T-Scale) (Cont.)

	Factor Loadings	
Subscales and Items	*Elementary*	*Secondary*
8C Teachers think that most of the parents do a good job.	.90	.90
9R Parents in this school are reliable in their commitments.	.91	.81
10V Teachers in this school trust the parents.	.89	.89

H=Honesty; B=Benevolence; C=Competence; O=Openness; V=Risk of Vulnerability; R=Reliability. * Reverse the scoring

had another honesty item with high loading for both samples, we deleted this item from the omnibus measure. The other item with a low loading in the secondary sample was an openness item, "Students here are secretive," which loaded only at –.30; however, because it was the only openness item on the trust in clients subscale, we retained it for conceptual reasons. Next, we eliminated some of the redundant items on the other subscales, making sure that all facets of trust were measured for each subscale. The result was an omnibus trust scale of 26 items that measured three aspects of faculty trust—faculty trust in colleagues, in the principal, and in clients. The alpha coefficients of reliability were high in both samples—trust in principal (.98), trust in colleagues (.93), and trust in clients (.94). Moreover, the omnibus subscales correlated very highly with the longer subscale versions for both samples—none were lower than .96.

SUMMARY

Trust was conceptualized as a concept with multiple facets; the willingness to risk or be vulnerable is inherent in all trust relations as are the facets of benevolence, reliability, competence, honesty, and openness. Thus our constitutive definition of trust was *an individual's or group's willingness to be vulnerable to another party based on the confidence that the latter party is benevolent, reliable, competent, honest, and open.*

This conceptual perspective of trust proved useful and was supported. All the conditions of trust were found empirically; in fact, factor-analytic techniques demonstrated all facets of trust for each of the three referents—principals, colleagues, and clients. Moreover, the trust subscales yielded reliable and valid measures for faculty trust in principals, in colleagues, and in clients. As predicted, faculty trust in each of these three groups were moderately related to each other. Faculty trust in schools tends to be pervasive. When teachers trust their principal, for example, they are also more likely to trust each other and their clients. Conversely, distrust also tends to breed distrust. Broken trust is likely to ripple through the system.

The analyses of referents of faculty trust indicated that they were related to other school variables in predictable ways. On the one hand, teachers' sense of powerlessness and estrangement were negatively related to trust. On the other hand, trust was positively related to teacher sense of efficacy; the greater the degree of perceived trust in a school, the stronger the belief in teachers' ability to organize and execute courses of action that lead to success. Also, not unexpectedly, the greater the degree of faculty trust in a school, the less the degree of conflict. All of the aspects of trust measured by the trust scales were related to other school variables as predicted.

The research also tested the hypothesis that faculty trust was related to the degree of schools' collaboration with parents on important aspects of school decision making. The assumption that trust was a key element in collaboration with parents on school decision making was supported by the results. Although all aspects of faculty trust were correlated with parental collaboration and explained about two thirds of the variance in collaboration, it was faculty trust in clients that proved the strongest predictor of collaboration; in fact, it was the only dimension of trust that was independently related to parental collaboration in decision making. The greater the faculty trust in clients, the more influence teachers say parents have in making important decisions.

Another intriguing finding of the study was that for both elementary and secondary samples, faculty trust in students and parents converged. The relationship was so strong that the trust for the two groups was indistinguishable. Faculty trust for the two referents merged to form a single factor, which we called faculty trust in clients. When teachers trust the students, they also trust their parents, and vice versa.

In sum, a multifaceted definition of trust was developed based on an extensive review of the literature. That definition was operationalized and confirmed with Trust Scales for elementary and secondary schools. Each scale had three reliable and valid subscales of faculty trust. Finally, a measure of faculty trust, the Omnibus T-Scale, was constructed and tested for use in both elementary and secondary schools. The omnibus measure is short and has the added general advantage of being useful regardless of the school level—elementary or secondary. A chronology of the development of the Omnibus Trust Scale and the resulting items in the various iterations are found in the grid in Table 7.7.

The final Omnibus T-Scale can be found online at www.coe.ohio-state.edu/whoy under research instruments. Students and professors are invited to use the scale for research purposes and administrators for professional and organizational development. Just download the scale, copy it, and use it.

Table 7.7. Chronology of Omnibus T-Scale Development

Number of Items	48	37	34	31	26
Iterations	1	2	3	4	5
1. The principal is unresponsive to teachers' concerns.	x	x	x		
2. Teachers in this school can rely on the principal.	x	x	x	x	x
3. Teachers in this school trust the principal.	x	x	x	x	x
4. The principal in this school typically acts in the best interests of teachers.	x	x	x	x	x
5. The principal of this school does not show concern for teachers	x	x	x	x	x
6. The principal doesn't really tell teachers what is going on.	x	x	x	x	x
7. The principal in this school keeps his or her word.	x	x	x	x	
8. The principal takes unfair advantage of the teachers in this school.	x				
9. The teachers in this school have faith in the integrity of the principal.	x	x	x	x	x
10. The teachers in this school are suspicious of most of the principal's actions.	x	x	x	x	x
11. Teachers in this school often question the motives of the principal.	x				
12. The principal openly shares personal information with teachers.	x	x	x	x	
13. When the principal commits to something teachers can be sure it will get done.	x				
14. The principal in this school is competent in doing his or her job.	x	x	x	x	x
15. Teachers feel comfortable admitting to the principal they have made a mistake.	x				
16. Teachers in this school believe in each other.	x	x	x		
17. Even in difficult situations, teachers in this school depend on each other.	x	x	x	x	x
18. Teachers in this school are open with each other.	x	x	x	x	x
19. When teachers in this school tell you something, you can believe it.	x	x	x	x	x
20. Teachers in this school typically look out for each other.	x	x	x	x	x
21. Teachers in this school trust each other.	x	x	x	x	x
22. Teachers in this school have faith in the integrity of their colleagues.	x	x	x	x	x
23. Teachers here only trust teachers in their clique.	x				
24. If I had a school-age child, I would feel comfortable putting my own child in most anyone's classroom in this school.	x				
25. Teachers take unfair advantage of each other in this school.	x				

Table 7.7.   Chronology of Omnibus T-Scale Development (Cont.)

Number of Items	48	37	34	31	26
Iterations	1	2	3	4	5
26. Teachers in this school are suspicious of each other.	x	x	x	x	x
27. Teachers in this school are reliable.	x				
28. Teachers in this school do their jobs well.	x	x		x	x
29. Teachers in this school don't share much about their lives outside of school.	x				
30. Students in this school are reliable.	x	x	x	x	
31. Students in this school can be counted on.	x				
32. The students in this school have to be closely supervised.	x	x	x		
33. Teachers think that most of the parents do a good job.	x	x	x	x	x
34. Parents in this school are reliable in their commitments	x	x	x	x	x
35. Teachers in this school trust their students.	x	x	x	x	x
36. Students in this school care about each other.	x	x	x	x	x
37. Teachers can count on the parental support.	x	x	x	x	x
38. Students here are secretive.	x	x	x	x	x
39. Students in this school cheat if they have a chance.	x	x	x	x	
40. Students in this school can be counted on to do their work.	x	x	x	x	x
41. Teachers in this school are suspicious of students.	x				
42. Teachers avoid making contact with parents	x	x			
43. Teachers in this school show concern for their students.	x	x			
44. Teachers are suspicious of parents' motives.	x				
45. Teachers in this school believe what students say.	x	x	x	x	
46. Teachers in this school trust parents.	x	x	x	x	x
47. The students in this school talk freely about their lives outside of school.	x	x	x		
48. Teachers are guarded in what they say to parents.	x				
New items:					
— Teachers here believe that students are competent learners.		x	x	x	x
— Teachers can believe what parents tell them.		x	x	x	x

Iterations 1–5:
1 = All pilot items (see Table 7.1);
2 = Surviving pilot items plus new items (see Table 7.1);
3 = Final elementary items (see Table 7.3);
4 = Final secondary items (see Table 7.4);
5 = Final omnibus items (see Table 7.6).

NOTES

1. Page A. Smith of the University of Texas at San Antonio was part of the research team at various points in the research, and we are grateful for his help. This research builds on our previous work (Hoy & Tschannen-Moran, 1999).
2. We (Hoy & Tschannen-Moran, 1999) suggested adding another item, but subsequent analysis proved that unnecessary.

REFERENCES

Baier, A. C. (1986). Trust and antitrust. *Ethics, 96,* 231–260.

Baier, A. C. (1994). *Moral prejudices: Essays on ethics.* Cambridge, MA: Harvard University Press.

Bandura, A. (n.d.). *Teacher self-efficacy scale.* Unpublished manuscript.

Bigley, G. A., & Pearce, J. L. (1998). Straining for shared meaning in organization science: Problems of trust and distrust. *The Academy of Management Review, 23,* 405–421.

Butler, J. K., & Cantrell, R.S. (1984). A behavioral decision theory approach to modeling dyadic trust in superiors and subordinates. *Psychological Reports, 55,* 81–105.

Deutsch, M. (1958). Trust and suspicion. *Journal of Conflict Resolution, 2,* 265–279.

Coleman, J. S. (1990). *Foundations of social theory.* Cambridge, MA: Belknap Press of Harvard University Press.

Cummings, L. L., & Bromily, P. (1996). The organizational trust inventory (OTI): Development and validation. In R. Kramer & T. Tyler (Eds.), *Trust in organizations.* Thousand Oaks, CA: Sage.

Forsyth, P. B., & Hoy, W. K. (1978). Isolation and alienation in educational organizations. *Educational Administration Quarterly, 14,* 80–96.

Frost, T., Stimpson, D. V., & Maughan, M. R. (1978). Some correlates of trust. *Journal of Psychology, 99,* 103–108.

Fukuyama, F. (1995). *Trust: The social virtues and the creation of prosperity.* New York: Simon & Schuster.

Gambetta, D. (1988). Can we trust? In D. Gambetta (Ed.), *Trust: Making and breaking cooperative relations* (pp. 213–238).Cambridge, MA: Basil Blackwell.

Goddard, R. D., Tschannen-Moran, M., & Hoy, W. K. (2001). A multilevel examination of the distribution and effects of trust in students and parents in urban elementary schools. *Elementary School Journal, 102,* 3–17.

Halpin, A. W. (1956). *The leader behavior of school superintendents.* Columbus, OH: College of Education, Ohio State University.

Hoffman, J., Sabo, D., Bliss, J., & Hoy, W. K. (1994). Building a culture of trust. *Journal of School Leadership, 4,* 484–501.

Hosmer, L. T. (1995). Trust: The connecting link between organizational theory and philosophical ethics. *Academy of Management Review, 20* (2), 379–403.

Hoy, W. K. (2002). Faculty trust: A key to student achievement. *Journal of School Public Relations, 23,* 88–103.

Hoy, W. K., & Kupersmith, W. J. (1985). The meaning and measure of faulty trust. *Educational and Psychological Research, 5,* 1–10.

Hoy, W. K., & Sabo, D. J. (1998). *Quality middle schools: Open and healthy.* Thousand Oaks, CA: Corwin.

Hoy, W. K., Tarter, C. J., & Kottkamp, R. B. (1991). *Open schools, healthy schools: Measuring organizational climate.* Newbury Park, CA: Sage.

Hoy, W. K., & Tschannen-Moran, M. (1999). Five faces of trust: An empirical confirmation in urban elementary schools. *Journal of School Leadership, 9,* 184–208.

Johnson-George, C. E., & Swap, W. C. (1982). Measurement of specific interpersonal trust: Construction and validation of a scale to assess trust in a specific other. *Journal of Personality and Social Psychology, 43,* 1306–1317.

Kerlinger, F. N. (1973). *Foundations of behavioral research* (2nd ed.). New York: Holt, Rinehart, and Winston.

Kramer, R. M., & Tyler, T. (Eds.). (1996). *Trust in organizations.* Thousand Oaks, CA: Sage.

Kramer, R. M., Brewer, M. B., & Hanna, B.A. (1996). Collective trust and collective action: The decision to trust as a social decision. In R. Kramer & T. Tyler (Eds.), *Trust in organizations.* Thousand Oaks, CA: Sage.

Larzelere, R. E., & Huston, T. L. (1980). The dyadic trust scale: Toward understanding interpersonal trust in close relationships. *Journal of Marriage and the Family, 42,* 595–604.

Mayer, R. C., Davis, J. H., & Schoorman, F. D. (1995). An integrative model of organizational trust. *Academy of Management Review, 20,* 709–734.

Mishra, A. K. (1996). Organizational responses to crisis: The centrality of trust. In R. Kramer & T. Tyler (Eds.), *Trust in organizations.* Thousand Oaks, CA: Sage.

Rempel, J. K., Holmes, J. G., & Zanna, M. D. (1985). Trust in close relationships. *Journal of Personality and Social Psychology, 49,* 95–112.

Rotter, J. B. (1967). A new scale for the measurement of interpersonal trust. *Journal of Personality, 35,* 651–665.

Rousseau, D., Sitkin, S. B., Burt, R., & Camerer, C. (1998). Not so different after all: A cross-discipline view of trust. *Academy of Management Review, 23*(3), 393–404.

Sergiovanni, T. J. (1992). *Moral leadership: Getting to the heart of school improvement.* San Francisco: Jossey-Bass.

Shaw, R. B. (1997). *Trust in the balance: Building successful organizations on results, integrity and concern.* San Francisco: Jossey-Bass.

Solomon, R. C., & Flores, F. (2001). *Building trust in business, politics, relationships, and life.* New York: Oxford University Press.

Sweetland, S. R., & Hoy, W. K. (2001). Varnishing the truth: Principals and teachers spinning reality. *Journal of Educational Administration, 39,* 282–293.

Tschannen-Moran, M. (2001). Collaboration and the need for trust. *Journal of Educational Administration, 39,* 308–331.

Tschannen-Moran, M., & Hoy, W. K. (1998). A conceptual and empirical analysis of trust in schools. *Journal of Educational Administration, 36,* 334–352.

Zand, D. E. (1971). Trust and managerial problem solving. *Administrative Science Quarterly, 17,* 229–239.

Zand, D. E. (1997). *The leadership triad: Knowledge, trust, and power.* New York: Oxford University Press.

Zielinski, A. E., & Hoy, W. K. (1983). Isolation and alienation in elementary schools. *Educational Administration Quarterly, 19,* 27–45.

CHAPTER 8

INVESTING IN TEACHER QUALITY

A Framework for Estimating the Cost of Teacher Professional Development[1]

Jennifer King Rice

ABSTRACT

The current policy emphasis on teacher quality has stimulated efforts to reform the preparation and ongoing professional development of teachers in America's schools. As with any type of reform, the ability of schools, school systems, universities, and other organizations to adopt and implement high-quality professional development programs depends in large part on the availability and allocation of appropriate resources to support the initiatives. A first step involves gaining a better understanding of what those resources are. Currently, there is no comprehensive framework for the cost elements that must be taken into consideration when planning and implementing professional development initiatives. If initiatives are to find necessary resources, especially for replicating or scaling up existing small-scale successes, a complete understanding of the costs that must be covered is necessary. This chap-

Studies in Leading and Organizing Schools, pages 209–233

ter considers the costs of professional development for teachers, with the ultimate goal of developing a cost framework to guide decision makers as they think about the resources required to support such initiatives.

COST OF TEACHER PROFESSIONAL DEVELOPMENT

A great deal of attention among researchers, policymakers, and others interested in improving the quality of public education in the United States has focused on high quality teachers as a key to realizing success for all students. Better teachers, most would agree, lead to better learning. So, it is not surprising that the growing emphasis on high standards for student performance evident across the United States has triggered a movement to improve the quality of the teaching workforce. In particular, attention has focused on upgrading preparation programs for new teachers as well as improving inservice professional development opportunities for practicing teachers to enhance the human capital available in schools. This emphasis on improving the quality of teacher training is evident in the recent efforts of several research groups and organizations to better understand and define the characteristics of effective teacher preparation and professional development (American Council on Education, 1999; Center for the Study of Teaching and Policy, 1998; Holmes Group, 1986; National Commission on Teaching and America's Future, 1996; National Foundation for the Improvement of Education, 1996). At the same time, efforts must also be made to reach a better understanding of what these sorts of activities cost. As with any type of intervention or reform, the ability of schools, school systems, universities, and other organizations to adopt and implement high-quality professional development programs depends in large part on the availability and allocation of appropriate resources to support the initiatives. A first step involves gaining a better understanding of what those resources are.

Currently, there is no comprehensive framework for the cost elements that must be taken into consideration when planning and implementing professional development initiatives. If initiatives are to find necessary resources, especially for replicating or scaling up existing small-scale successes, a complete understanding of the costs that must be covered is necessary. This chapter considers the costs of professional development for teachers, with the ultimate goal of developing a cost framework to guide decision makers as they think about the resources required to support such initiatives. The chapter takes an economic approach to cost analysis that recognizes the full opportunity cost of all resources devoted to the initiative.

A vexing difficulty associated with estimating the costs of education policies and programs is the hidden nature of many of the cost elements. The distinction between costs and expenditures is an important one. The total cost is the value of all resources that are required to accomplish the goals of an initiative, while expenditures are the monetary outlays associated with the initiative. Expenditures may overstate costs to the degree that more valuable resources are being used than necessary (e.g., overqualified staff). On the other hand, expenditures may understate costs to the extent that some resources necessary to meet the goals of the initiative are not associated with fiscal outlays. A key example related to teacher professional development is the uncompensated time that teachers and teacher candidates devote to their own professional development. Certainly, to the degree that these individuals are willing to donate their time, the overall price tag of the initiative will decrease. However, this time is still a cost, and must be recognized as such. Likewise, to the degree that the cost burden is distributed in such a way that external sources of support cover substantial portions of the cost, the burden on the school or school system will decrease. However, the overall cost of the initiative remains unchanged. The point here is that the many hidden and widely dispersed costs embedded in teacher professional development initiatives must be recognized so that decision makers have a complete picture of the resources required to support the effort. The framework developed in this chapter is intended to identify the full opportunity cost of teacher professional development in order to guide decision makers as they think about the array of resources needed to support such initiatives. Once the total cost is determined, decision makers can apply local conditions (e.g., the potential to reallocate time, the willingness of teachers to give of their time, the availability of external support) to assess the amount of fiscal resources needed to support the initiative.

The development of this framework proved to be a challenging task due in part to the contested nature of many issues related to teacher professional development. Unresolved issues range from the definition and scope of teacher professional development to the individual cost elements that should be included in a framework such as this. The general approach taken here is to be as comprehensive and inclusive as possible with the goal of casting a broad net to capture all costs associated with teacher professional development. While this runs the risk of inflating the estimated costs of professional development, next steps that test the framework will help to further refine this tool. The goal for this step is to lay out all possible resources required to support effective teacher professional development. In the process, I take care to recognize factors that are controversial to help policymakers, planners, and researchers think through some of the difficult issues associated with the cost of teacher professional development. The contested nature of these issues underscores the significance and importance of the task.

The next section of the chapter describes what constitutes professional development and what forms these activities take. The section that follows lays out the cost elements associated with teacher professional development, and discusses the distribution of the cost burden. The final section highlights directions for future work in this area.

WHAT DOES TEACHER PREPARATION AND PROFESSIONAL DEVELOPMENT LOOK LIKE?

The first major challenge in thinking about the costs of professional development involves identifying what counts as teacher professional development in the first place. More conventional interpretations have tended to limit professional development to the formal activities that practicing teachers engage in (usually outside of the classroom) to further develop their teaching skills, learn new skills or content, and/or familiarize themselves with new education policies that affect their teaching (e.g., changes to the curriculum, new standards and assessment programs). These activities generally require after-school time, inservice days, or release time during the school day for teachers to participate, and participation in some form of professional development is generally part of a teacher's contractual agreement.

More recent work acknowledges a new understanding of professional development that is far more inclusive and comprehensive. First, professional development includes both preservice preparation of teachers as well as the inservice activities that expand the skills and knowledge base of practicing teachers. In fact, many argue that considering both preservice and inservice professional development together as a seamless process is necessary to promote the most effective and efficient system for developing teachers' skills and knowledge base.[2] Second, professional development activities extend well beyond the conventional delivery structure through which, for example, the school system provides workshops on specific topics for teachers. Rather, professional development is increasingly being recognized as an ongoing series of experiences that are embedded in the collaborative work of teachers and are directly linked with outcomes and standards. This chapter considers the costs of this broader understanding of both preservice and inservice professional development.

Preservice Professional Development

Teacher preparation programs are the preservice component of professional development. These programs are many and varied with numerous promising innovations on the horizon. Almost all approaches include instruction in an academic discipline or content area, instruction in the areas of child development and pedagogy, and a practical element that involves applying the content and pedagogical knowledge in a teaching context through clinical experiences and supervised student teaching. Traditionally, most teacher preparation programs have been university-based bachelor's degrees that include all of these elements and meet the certification requirements of the state. Recently, these programs have been criticized on multiple grounds, most notably for the disconnect between the coursework and the practical world of teaching (National Association of School Boards of Education [NASBE], 1998). This criticism has invited a number of alternative approaches to the preparation of teachers to emerge. Some popular examples include the following:

- *Extended teacher preparation programs.* A number of states currently require that teachers earn a master's degree to be fully certified. Some extended teacher preparation programs link a content-specific bachelor's degree with a one-year master' s degree program focused on child development theories, pedagogy, and clinical teaching experiences. Others admit students from a variety of disciplines and offer a two-year teacher education master's degree.

- *Alternative approaches to teacher certification.*[3] Programs that offer aspiring teachers nontraditional alternatives for entering the profession often target geographic areas facing substantial teacher shortages. The programs, sponsored by a wide variety of organizations, vary in terms of requirements, length of time to complete, and availability of external support. One example is the Pathways to Teaching Careers program, which targets individuals who are currently teaching without certification, who work as paraprofessionals in the schools, and who have participated in the Peace Corps and would like to become teachers in high-need geographic areas. The program is a cooperative effort between local districts and university teacher preparation programs (see Rice & Brent, in press).

- *Professional development schools (PDSs).* PDSs are partnerships between local school systems and universities to provide teacher preparation and inservice professional development for teachers. As described in a recent NASBE (1998) report, "Teachers and administrators work alongside university faculty and teacher preparation students to influence the development of their profession, to increase the pro-

fessional relevance of their work, and to undertake mutual delibera-
tion on issues of student learning" (p. 31).
* *District-based teacher preparation programs.* In some cases, large urban
  districts recruit and train teachers locally with district staff and partnerships with local higher education institutions. In these programs,
  "teacher candidates spend most of their course of study working in
  local public schools, often receiving a stipend for their school-based
  work" (NASBE, 1998, p. 32).

State and district officials along with university-based personnel and,
increasingly, individuals associated with a variety of nongovernmental organizations offering alternative teacher preparation programs are active in the
administration and coordination of preservice professional development.

Inservice Professional Development[4]

Echoing the heterogeneity of preservice teacher preparation programs,
inservice professional development initiatives for practicing teachers have
long taken a variety of forms. A 1998 National Center for Education Statistics (NCES) analysis of data from the Schools and Staffing Survey (SASS)
identified five broadly recognized categories of professional development:
(1) district-sponsored workshops or inservice programs; (2) school-spon-
sored workshops or inservice programs; (3) university extension or adult
education programs; (4) college courses in the teacher's subject area; and
(5) growth activities sponsored by professional associations. While these
sorts of activities continue to characterize inservice teacher professional
development, new conceptualizations of professional development have
begun to emerge that involve changes along at least three dimensions:
point of origination (e.g., district mandated, school based), content (e.g.,
subject matter, pedagogy), and form (e.g., workshops, college courses)
(Rice, 2000). In general, the shift involves moving from an understanding
of professional development as a district-driven, transmissive process
using a menu of alternative activities to an approach that emerges from
local needs and interests; is relevant to the teachers, students, and school
communities; and is open to a wide variety of methods (Little, 1993;
National Foundation for the Improvement of Education, 1996; Sparks,
1995; Sykes, 1996).

The National Partnership for Excellence and Accountability in Teaching asserts eight research-based principles to promote high-quality professional development (Hawley & Valli, 1998). Professional development
should (1) be based on analyses of the differences between actual student
performance and student learning goals; (2) involve teachers in the identi-

fication of what they need to learn and in the development of the learning experiences in which they will be involved; (3) be primarily school-based and built into the day-to-day work of teaching; (4) be organized around collaborative problem solving; (5) be ongoing and involve follow-up and support for further learning—including support from sources external to the school that can provide necessary resources and new perspectives; (6) incorporate evaluation of multiple sources of information on student outcomes and instruction; (7) provide opportunities to gain an understanding of the theory underlying the knowledge and skills being learned; and (8) be connected to a comprehensive change process focused on improving student learning.

This change in understanding has allowed a wide array of activities to emerge as valid forms of professional development that give rise to meaningful teacher learning. These include, but are certainly not limited to, the following: providing opportunities for collaborative problem solving; requiring legitimate long-term professional development plans for individual teachers to guide learning experiences over time; providing time for teachers to collectively and systematically discuss problems using test data; structuring mentoring relationships for new as well as veteran teachers; scheduling common planning time for teachers of the same subject and/ or grade; and encouraging teacher networks. To correspond with the evolving nature of staff development, these types of activities must be generated by the teachers themselves, consistent with the long-term goals and mission of the school community, integrated into the school day, continuous with ongoing follow-up, and designed to improve the educational outcomes of the students.

In addition to the practices described above, more conventional approaches such as workshops and university courses may be aligned with the evolving conceptualization of professional development, so long as they reflect these same principles. Indeed, it would be artificial as well as inaccurate to try to categorize this diverse set of practices as conforming to either traditional or "enlightened" conceptions of what professional development is (or should be). Rather, these practices fall along a continuum where they more or less reflect the characteristics associated with newer conceptualizations of teacher professional development. This wide range of different approaches to professional development implies a wide range of possible costs associated with teacher professional development.

A variety of different offices and actors are typically responsible for the administration and oversight of inservice teacher professional development (Education Commission of the States, 1997). Some researchers have recognized the authority structure as "fragmented" (Miles, Bouchard, Winner, Cohen, & Guiney, 1999). Included in the oversight of professional development are district professional development offices; other district offices whose primary responsibility is not professional development, but who have some secondary responsibility for professional development; state professional development offices; regional service centers; for-profit and nonprofit developers and providers of models of school reform who may assume responsibility for teacher professional development; and schools themselves. Furthermore, a variety of professional organizations and private companies (including several electronic businesses) are active in the provision of inservice professional development for teachers. Because all of these institutional units and organizations involve personnel and other resources, this complex administrative structure has direct implications for the costs of professional development (and potentially the effectiveness as well).

UNDERSTANDING THE COSTS
OF PROFESSIONAL DEVELOPMENT

Research has been conducted to estimate the costs of teacher professional development in different places, focused on specific programs, under a variety of local circumstances, and using an array of assumptions. These studies provide some sense of the costs of particular cases of professional development, and they illustrate the difficulties that arise when estimating these costs. For example, research estimating the costs of inservice professional development for practicing teachers has shown that investments range from about 2% (Little et al., 1987; Miller, Lord, & Dorney, 1994) to over 5% (Moore & Hyde, 1981) of districts' annual operating budgets. However, many argue that these estimates fall short of representing the full cost of inservice professional development since they neglect important cost elements that are often associated with significant value. For instance, the uncompensated time that teachers devote to professional development activities and the contractual student-free periods that teachers have built into the school day are often not included in the cost estimates. These issues are discussed below. For now, the important point is that while we have some estimates of the costs of teacher professional development, we need an overarching framework that identifies the full range of cost elements associated with these initiatives.

Though preservice and inservice teacher professional development initiatives have traditionally been recognized as separate processes (and the descriptions above reflect that differentiation), the cost structure presented in this chapter encourages moving toward a more seamless approach to these two stages of professional development. Until recently, there has been little evidence of coordination, or even interaction, among these two phases of the teacher professional development pipeline—they typically are administered by different institutions, are supported by different actors, and involve different sorts of activities. Professional development schools, however, have introduced a new approach that encourages greater levels of coordination. Arguably, a more comprehensive, seamless approach to teacher professional development could lead to greater effectiveness and a higher level of efficiency in terms of the costs and benefits of the investment. Forging a cost framework that can be applied to both stages of teacher professional development could help to promote a higher level of coordination.

The framework presented here uses a single set of cost categories to help organize the cost elements associated with both stages of professional development. This shared set of categories is intended to enable a more comprehensive understanding of and planning strategy around teacher professional development initiatives. Eight broad categories,[5] most of which involve human resources, frame the cost elements of both preservice and inservice programs: teacher time; trainers and coaches; administration; materials, equipment, and facilities; travel and transportation; tuition and conference fees (not covered in other categories); future salary obligations;[6] and research, development, and dissemination.

Table 8.1 illustrates specific cost elements associated with each of these categories for inservice and preservice teacher professional development. In some cases, a particular cost element could reasonably be classified in more than one category. The descriptions below lay out the conceptual divisions; future application of the framework will test those decisions. Where appropriate, I describe how the cost categories apply specifically to preservice and inservice initiatives. A discussion of the distribution of the cost burden follows.

Table 8.1.   Representative Cost Elements for Each Cost Category: By Preservice and Inservice Stage of Professional Development

Cost Category	Preservice Cost Elements	Inservice Cost Elements
Teacher Time	Time teachers invest in preparation program	Contracted student-free time—free periods, inservice days, sabbaticals
		Reallocation of time and personnel
		Additional personnel—substitute and more regular teachers
		Additional teacher compensation
		Teacher-donated time

**Table 8.1.   Representative Cost Elements for Each Cost Category:
By Preservice and Inservice Stage of Professional Development (Cont.)**

Cost Category	Preservice Cost Elements	Inservice Cost Elements
Trainers and Coaches	*Instruction component*	State officials
	Instructors	District personnel
	University professors	University faculty
	District and school personnel	School administrators
		Mentor teachers
	Field component	Reform model trainers
	School teachers	Professional association personnel
	School administrators	PD instructors
	Field supervisor	Consultants
Administration	State officials	State officials
	District personnel	District personnel
	University certification officer	Professional association personnel
		School personnel
Facilities, Materials, and Equipment	Classrooms	Facility rent charges
	Curriculum	Materials
	Instructional materials	Equipment
	Technology and library resources	Technology
	Books and course materials	
Travel and Transportation	Resulting from excessive distance between university and school site	Conferences
		Professional meetings
		External trainers/speakers
Tuition and Fees	University tuition	Conference fees
		University tuition
Future Salary Obligations	N/A	From additional coursework and degrees
Research, Development, and Dissemination	Federal/state/district data bank	Federal/state/district data bank

Note: The cost elements included in this table are representative of the kinds of costs that fall
under each broad cost category. While this table presents examples of the most common cost
elements, it is not fully inclusive of all possible cost elements that might arise.

Teacher Time

The time that teachers devote to their own professional development is a serious consideration in calculating the costs of these activities and initiatives. The costs associated with teacher time can be quite sizeable, particularly as school systems place additional demands on new teachers entering the profession, and as schools move toward more progressive visions of inservice professional development that involve teachers in the planning and delivery of more collaborative and job-embedded professional development activities (Rice, 2000, 2001).

Preservice costs

With respect to preservice preparation, teacher time relates to the time that students invest in their own preparation to become teachers, an opportunity cost that warrants some attention. While this time is rarely included in analyses of teacher preparation programs, it should be recognized as a cost since it could be used in other productive ways (i.e., paid employment, other professional preparation programs). This cost element is particularly interesting when comparing the costs of competing alternatives to teacher preparation that vary in their duration. Many teacher preparation programs involve earning a four-year bachelor's degree. Others require students to continue on for an additional year to earn a master's degree, adding a year of tuition and subtracting a year of earning power.[7] To the degree that the additional program requirements are longer, the associated costs related to student time grow higher. While extended teacher education programs have been advocated by many, some research has suggested that the costs of extending teacher education programs outweigh the benefits (Hawley, 1987). Conversely, alternative teacher certification programs that involve only the course requirements necessary for teacher certification can be relatively low in cost.[8]

Inservice costs

The costs associated with the time of personnel are, by all estimates, the most significant component of inservice teacher professional development. Moore and Hyde's (1981) study of the costs of professional development in three districts found that in all cases the largest portion of accounted-for dollars spent on staff development was devoted to the salaries and benefits of teachers and district staff (ranging from 65–80% of total reported professional development expenditures in the three districts). Likewise, Miller and colleagues (1994) estimated costs associated with personnel to range between 56–89% of total costs, and Elmore (1997) reported the personnel share of total professional development costs to range from 80–85%. Furthermore, donated teacher time has emerged as a critical cost component of inservice professional development. Few studies have included donated time as an explicit cost category, but those that have estimate that donated teacher time accounts for almost 40% of the total investment (time and money) in professional development (Little et al., 1987; Stern, Gerritz, & Little, 1989). Furthermore, the trends in professional development suggest an even greater reliance on teacher time commitments in the future. Teacher time investments in professional development can take at least five forms that have implications for cost.[9] While several require no additional expenditures, they are still costs in the sense that they use resources that could be used in other productive ways.

First, most school systems include in their teacher contracts "student-free" or "release" time for teachers to participate in professional development activities (NCES, 1998). For example, teacher inservice days and student-free periods used for professional development purposes should be included in the cost of teacher professional development. This cost element could be estimated using an average teacher salary figure and the typical contract provisions.

Second, time and personnel could be reallocated to find more time for teacher professional development activities in the existing school day or school year. Proposals here range from reallocating uses of existing time (National Foundation for the Improvement of Education, 1996) to completely restructuring how time is used in schools (National Education Commission on Time and Learning, 1994) to find more time for teachers to plan and participate in professional development activities. Researchers have acknowledged student-free planning periods within the regular school day as potentially valuable time for teacher professional development (Miles et al., 1999). While these periods may not be recognized as professional development time, they could be a focal point for finding time within the school day to accommodate professional development. For example, traditional planning periods could be restructured in ways that allow teachers of the same subject or grade level to come together to plan collaboratively, as well as identify areas where further assistance and professional development might be needed to meet the educational goals of the school. This strategy might also involve reallocating personnel (e.g., aides, librarians) to free teachers from their responsibilities for professional development purposes. The cost of such approaches is the value of the teacher time devoted to the professional development activity plus any student opportunity costs in the form of lost learning opportunities.

Third, additional personnel could be employed to provide greater slack during the school day for teacher professional development activities while maintaining current class sizes. Schools often accomplish this by hiring substitute teachers to cover classes for those participating in professional development. Given that the costs of substitute teachers are sizeable (Stern et al., 1989), other options should also be considered. For instance, more full-time teachers could be hired. This "overstaffing" of schools would avoid the use of substitutes on a regular basis to provide time for teacher professional development while keeping class sizes stable. Other options include using aides, parent volunteers, and other members of the broader school community. These individuals could also provide the slack time needed to create professional development time opportunities for teachers. Again, it is important to be certain that under any of these arrangements, students do not pay through lost learning opportunities (an important opportunity cost that could be associated with these new forms of professional development if great care is not taken). The cost of these kinds of strategies includes the time of the teachers and additional personnel hired, plus any student opportunity costs.

Fourth, the out-of-contract time that teachers devote to their professional development could translate into additional expenditures in the form of compensation for participating teachers. One option exercised by many school systems is to provide stipends to teachers who dedicate evening or summer hours to professional development. Another alternative for creating more time to support teacher professional development made by the National Foundation for the Improvement of Education (1996) is to make new time available by lengthening the work year (or the work day). Clearly, this has financial implications. For instance, consider a state education system employing 75,000 teachers. A policy to lengthen the school year by even five days could translate into a statewide cost of almost $100 million statewide per year (assuming annual salary and benefits equal to $50,000/teacher and depending on district–teacher negotiations).

Finally, the out-of-contract time that teachers devote to professional development could go uncompensated. In other words, teachers routinely give their own time to their own professional development.[10] In this case the cost is incurred by the teacher and could be estimated using salary figures.

While this is not the only way to construct the allocation of teacher time to inservice professional development, the point is that the costs of teacher time may be incurred in a variety of ways: contractual student-free time, reallocated time and personnel, additional personnel, additional compensation for teachers, and teacher-donated time. These different mechanisms for supporting teacher participation in professional development have implications not only for the cost of the enterprise, but also for how that cost burden is distributed across different stakeholders. Failure of policymakers to consider the high demand on teacher time may result in the failure of the professional development initiative altogether. Professional development initiatives that assume a high level of donated teacher time when it is not readily forthcoming have little chance of succeeding. A corollary to these issues related to teacher time involves the time of school building administrators. Under newer conceptualizations of professional development, principals assume greater responsibilities for leadership, management, implementation, evaluation, and continuous follow-up of teacher professional development activities. All of these responsibilities require time and have implications for cost.

Trainers and Coaches

A second personnel-intensive cost category associated with professional development is the investment of trainers and coaches.[11] This cost category includes all of the time that individuals spend providing professional development experiences.

Preservice costs

In terms of program delivery, trainers and coaches are associated with the instruction and the field components of preservice teacher preparation programs. The instruction component of the teacher preparation program involves the costs of all of the individuals who develop and deliver the formal coursework required in the program, including university professors, adjunct course instructors, and other staff dedicated to the teacher preparation program. In cases where PDSs are active in preservice teacher preparation, the time of district- and school-level personnel who contribute to instructional activities should also be considered. Likewise, to the degree that the school district is heavily involved with recruiting and preparing its own teaching force, district employees are likely to have time-intensive responsibilities associated with the instructional program that translate into costs.

The field component of the preservice teacher preparation program includes the time of personnel who coordinate and monitor student teaching or other clinical experiences of the students in the field. At the university level, this includes the time of the field supervisor (or other similar position). At the school level, the time of teachers and administrators who are active in the oversight of student teachers should be included. While these individuals at the school level may receive some compensation for their responsibilities related to students' field experiences, in calculating the costs, the full value of all of their time devoted to these responsibilities should be considered.

Inservice costs

A variety of individuals including state officials, district personnel, university faculty, school administrators, mentor teachers, reform model trainers, professional association personnel, and so forth, provide inservice professional development to teachers. Some of these people are hired for the explicit purpose of providing professional development (e.g., consultants, professional development instructors, and mentors/coaches in the schools), while others may devote just a portion of their work to these activities (e.g., school administrators, mentor teachers). Furthermore, schools affiliated with comprehensive school reform models (e.g., Accelerated Schools, Success for All) may incur additional costs since many of these models require that central staff be brought to the school site for periodic staff training sessions to ensure consistency and coordination across sites. In all cases, the cost of trainers and coaches should reflect the value of all time devoted to professional development by these different individuals, and should include salary and benefits.

Administration

A number of individuals participate in the administration, planning, and coordination of teacher professional development. In the case of traditional university-based teacher preparation programs, these functions are generally the responsibility of university personnel in cooperation with state officials who oversee teacher preparation and certification. As teachers complete their initial preparation programs, they are typically required to be certified to teach in a particular state. Often, universities pay an individual (sometimes a professor, sometimes not) to monitor the certification process and students' progress toward meeting the requirements. This type of position has become more important with the increasingly common use of student portfolios to document what students in teacher education programs know and can do. In addition, a number of individuals at the state level are generally involved in overseeing the teacher certification process and granting certification to new teachers.

The administration of inservice professional development tends to be more diffuse including state and district officials as well as school personnel, professional organizations, for-profit and nonprofit developers, and private companies. This cost category includes the value of the time of all individuals who administer and monitor professional development.

Facilities, Materials, and Equipment

All professional development initiatives incur costs related to facilities, materials, and equipment. Preservice teacher preparation programs—whether provided by colleges and universities or by others (e.g., private providers, local government)—require facilities used for instructional purposes, instructional materials and supplies, library and technology resources available to support the program, and books and course materials generally purchased by the students enrolled in the program. Many of these resources may not translate into additional fiscal expenditures, but are costs nonetheless.

Likewise, inservice professional development programs require materials, equipment, and facilities, and, in some cases, the fiscal value of these resources can be quite sizeable. For example, a full-day retreat could involve rent charges for a facility, as well as extensive materials for the various activities. In other cases, these resources may not translate into additional expenditures. For instance, to the degree that the professional development experiences are integrated into the regular school day, one would not expect much in the way of additional expenditures related to facilities. However, materials and equipment may still factor in as additional costs.

The increasing role of technology in the provision of teacher professional development warrants particular attention. Internet-based professional development modules and telecommunications offer important opportunities as alternative delivery systems. While these strategies are largely untested in terms of their use and impact, they have potentially important implications for cost, particularly over the long term.

Travel and Transportation

Preservice teacher preparation programs involve limited travel and transportation costs. To the degree that students travel to the university setting for their training, costs can be incurred, but these are typically small unless the travel requirements related to the program are extensive (e.g., a long distance from the university to the school site where the student teaching will occur). Furthermore, professional development schools may involve travel and transportation costs that are more or less extensive than those associated with more traditional university-based teacher preparation programs. Finally, travel costs may be related to research, development, planning, and administration of teacher preparation programs.

In contrast to preservice teacher professional development, off-site inservice training can require noteworthy travel and transportation costs. For example, conferences and professional meetings often gather educators from across a broad region, or even across the nation. These sorts of learning opportunities to exchange ideas with others come with a travel cost that includes transportation, lodging, and meals. Clearly the cost grows proportionately with the number of people who attend these sorts of meetings. To the degree that these interactions are possible through telecommunications, travel and transportation costs may decrease. In addition, on-site professional development activities that involve presentations by outside individuals may involve costs for their travel and transportation. From a development perspective, travel costs may also be related to the research and design activities related to inservice teacher professional development programs in order to allow for participant input and site observation. Finally, administration, planning, and coordination activities may also involve some travel and transportation costs.

Tuition and Conference Fees

The cost of tuition is typically a substantial component of the overall cost of preservice teacher preparation programs. In most cases, individuals cover the cost of their own tuition. With respect to inservice professional development, NCES (1998) reports that 50.6 percent of practicing public school teachers reported participating in inservice professional development through course taking at local colleges and universities during the 1993–94 school year. Depending on contractual arrangements, the tuition for these courses is covered either by the school system or by individuals themselves. In addition, 51.4% of teachers report participating in conferences, meetings, and other growth activities sponsored by professional associations during the same academic year (NCES, 1998). The costs of these activities involve both travel-related expenses (covered above) as well as conference fees that can be quite substantial, particularly if numerous individuals attend. As discussed below in the section on the distribution of the cost burden, these tuition and fee payments typically offset other costs.[12]

Future Salary Obligations[13]

Additional credits earned by practicing teachers through graduate coursework are generally rewarded in the salary schedules of school systems. In their study of the costs of teacher professional development in California, Little and colleagues (1987) report that the additional salary commitments that teachers earn through university course credits amounted to almost $600 million annually, equaling 160% of the direct costs of professional development in that state. When included in the analysis, this category represents the taxpayers' largest investment in teacher professional development. Ross's (1995) analysis of teacher development and salary incentives in Los Angeles reports that salary credits (i.e., the transfer of professional development credits into higher salaries) are a powerful incentive to encourage teachers' participation in inservice professional development, and that such incentives could be used more effectively to promote higher levels of student performance. Others have argued that future salary obligations should not factor into estimates of the cost of professional development, but should be considered as a routine personnel cost (rather than a training cost).

Given the high cost associated with future salary obligations, careful attention should be paid to the appropriateness of including this as a cost element of teacher professional development. One way of resolving this issue lies in determining whether the additional salary increments are design elements of the school system's professional development policy or part of routine human capital development apparent in education and business sectors alike. Consider the first possibility—that the future salary obligations are a design element of professional development policies intended to promote certain desirable behaviors. In other words, professional development policies could be designed in such a way that additional salary increments serve as a mechanism used by school system administrators as incentives to encourage teachers to engage in certain types of professional development, to do this at particular stages of their careers, and to achieve certain levels of performance. The award of the salary increments is dependent on teachers meeting these kinds of criteria. Since this approach could be viewed as an alternative to "pay-up-front" approaches (e.g., providing teachers with stipends and/or paying for their tuition), not including future salary obligations as a cost of professional development could seriously distort the cost estimates, favoring districts that rely on these kinds of salary incentives in their professional development programs.

On the other hand, the future salary obligations associated with teachers' participation in professional development could be viewed as a routine investment in human capital. From this perspective, upgrading skills through professional development (as is routinely done in many professions) leads to higher levels of productivity. The employer rewards the increase in employee productivity through salary hikes. The increase in productivity realized by the firm (or school system in this case) presumably outweighs the additional salary payments made to the employees. In sum, participation in professional development leads to greater productivity, which is subsequently reflected in salary increases. Since the salary increases are a reflection of greater productivity, it wouldn't make sense to include them as a cost of professional development. Although viewing professional development this way is a plausible approach, it is complicated in education by the questionable causal relationship between participation in professional development and subsequent productivity.

Research, Development, and Dissemination

Policymakers and developers charged with the responsibility of designing and implementing professional development incur a variety of related costs, and resources must be set aside for these purposes. As teacher professional development initiatives increasingly reflect the kinds of recommendations made in the research on effective practices (Hawley & Valli, 1998; National Commission on Teaching and America's Future, 1996; National Foundation for the Improvement of Education, 1996), they will become more varied and flexible to conform with the strengths and needs embedded in particular contexts (NASBE, 1998). This implies an additional need for developers and policymakers to effectively disseminate useful information and assistance that can help local practitioners make informed decisions about what types of approaches to adopt and how to effectively implement them. For instance, information systems coordinated at more macro levels (e.g., state, federal, professional associations) could be designed with the goal of providing the best, most up-to-date research on effective approaches to professional development and the conditions under which these initiatives are most effective. This implies a new expanded role for these more central levels of authority in supporting local decisions about teacher preparation and professional development. These sorts of information systems can be very costly, both in terms of personnel to maintain the systems and technology to organize and disseminate the information to local decision makers.

Distribution of the Cost Burden

Support for teacher professional development comes from a variety of sources. These include federally sponsored programs, state education systems, school districts, schools, teachers and teacher candidates, professional associations, colleges and universities, and a variety of external sources. Support from all sources (whether captured in budgets or not) must be included in estimates of the total costs of professional development.

Assessing the distribution of the cost burden is an important step in understanding the full cost of the initiative and how that cost is shared by various individuals and organizations. The case of tuition and fees for professional development provides a good example of how cost burdens can be shared and shifted. Tuition and fees can be viewed as a source of revenue used to purchase program-related components like personnel, transportation, equipment, and materials. While the costs of tuition and fees are generally shouldered by the students themselves, some public policy initiatives shift this cost burden to others. For instance, loan forgiveness programs designed to attract prospective teachers into the profession shift the burden of repaying student education loans from the student to some level of government (generally the state or federal government). Another example is district-sponsored teacher preparation programs designed to recruit and prepare teachers for service in large, urban areas lacking an adequate supply of high-quality educators. These programs often cover the cost of coursework associated with the teacher preparation program (e.g., by providing the courses themselves at no expense to the student, or paying university tuition for program requirements). Furthermore, many of these districts pay salaries or stipends to students for their ongoing service in the schools throughout the course of the professional development program. Such compensation can be seen as offsetting the costs of the participant time invested in the preparation program. Understanding how the cost burden is distributed across individuals and organizations can be critical for local decision makers as they design, plan, and implement teacher professional development initiatives that fit with the resources and needs of their local communities.

DIRECTIONS FOR FUTURE WORK

The previous section described the wide array of cost elements associated with preservice and inservice teacher professional development. The discussion gives rise to a number of issues in need of further consideration, mapping the way for future work in this area. I outline the next steps below.

Applying the Cost Framework

The next step in this research is to apply the framework to specific initiatives to test and further clarify it. In particular, this chapter describes a number of cost elements that need additional consideration. For instance, the inclusion of future salary obligations as a cost of professional development has been questioned. Similarly, how to best handle the cost of time that teacher candidates invest in their preparation programs needs further attention. Using the framework to consider costs of particular approaches has a two-fold contribution: (1) it will help to clarify and guide decisions about some of the more ambiguous and controversial cost elements currently included in the framework, and (2) it is a good starting point for acquiring better information on the costs of different approaches to professional development.

Exploring Economic Trade-offs

In addition to estimating the costs of teacher professional development, investigating the economic trade-offs associated with different approaches to professional development is a pressing issue. As described above, a diverse set of approaches characterizes preservice and inservice teacher professional development, and new innovations continue to emerge. The cost elements outlined in this chapter can serve as a framework for estimating the costs of different, sometimes competing, approaches to the professional development of teachers. Reaching a better, more comprehensive understanding of the costs associated with these approaches allows decision makers to recognize the array of resources devoted to teacher professional development, and even compare the resource requirements of alternative approaches. In addition, more sophisticated analyses are needed to weigh the trade-offs embedded in policy choices related to the design of teacher professional development. In other words, there are many competing approaches to the professional development of educators, and policymakers need to think hard about which make the most sense in terms of resource allocation decisions.

The focus of this type of investigation could range from broad models or programs of professional development (e.g., professional development schools vs. more traditional approaches) to discrete practices that support professional development (e.g., substitute teachers vs. overstaffing schools with more regular teachers). Regardless of how the analysis is focused, the emphasis would be on the economic trade-offs (costs and effects) associated with the designated alternatives. This type of project presents a number of serious challenges. One involves the specification of the alternatives to be compared. Another relates to the difficulty of capturing and measuring all of the costs and effects around the different approaches or initiatives.[14]

Comparing Education Professional Development Investments with Other Fields

Finally, the costs of teacher professional development should be compared with the professional development costs associated with other fields (e.g., social workers, nurses, and employees of large private corporations). A comparative analysis such as this would help to gauge investment levels across different professions and sectors of the economy. Furthermore, it is likely that lessons from other fields could be applied to education in terms of strategies for designing, funding, and implementing effective professional development.

NOTES

1. This work was prepared as part of The Finance Project' s Collaborative Research and Development Initiative on Financing Professional Development in Education with financial support form the Ford Foundation. I am grateful for the insightful comments of a number of individuals, including Carol Cohen, Cheryl Hayes, Randy Ross, David Monk, Jack Jennings, Eric Hirsch, Randy Hitz, Judith Renyi, Allan Odden, Sarah Archibald, and members of The Finance Project's advisory panel on the financing of professional development in education. Any remaining errors or oversights are my own.

2. Given the current separate and distinct delivery systems of preservice, induction, and inservice teacher professional development, the usefulness of this comprehensive approach is debatable. However, in an effort to be as inclusive and comprehensive as possible, I include all three stages of professional development.

3. Darling-Hammond (1990) distinguishes between alternative routes to certification, which do not change the standards, but introduce other options for attaining them, and alternative certification, which changes the standards under which certification is granted.

4. Policymakers interested in teacher retention have focused attention on high-quality teacher induction programs, which generally involve special provisions for novice teachers such as intensive mentoring programs, periodic assessments, and ongoing targeted support. Although teacher induction programs are often recognized as a distinct phase of professional development, they are included in this section since they typically occur during a teacher's first several years of service.

5. This framework is the result of an effort to coordinate my work supported by The Finance Project with related work being conducted by Allan Odden and Sarah Archibald through CPRE. Preliminary frameworks independently developed for both projects were modestly adapted with the goal of agreeing on a shared framework. The cost categories described here, with the exception of the final two, represent the resulting common framework. The final two categories are included only in the Rice framework, which aims to capture the full economic cost of professional development initiatives.

6. Future salary obligations relate only to the preservice component of professional development. There is some debate over whether this category should be considered as a cost of teacher professional development, or whether it is a general personnel cost that simply coincides with particular types of professional development. These issues are discussed further below.

7. The loss of earnings is what economists refer to as "foregone earnings." This cost can be quite substantial because it includes the benefits that could be had by using those earnings in productive ways (e.g., investing the capital).

8. Issues such as this give rise to the need for cost-effectiveness analyses of different alternatives. To the degree that the costs are lower and effectiveness is not compromised, greater efficiency is served. This is an empirical question. Goldhaber and Brewer (1999) report no difference in the achievement of students who had teachers with regular versus alternative certification. Darling-Hammond (1990), however, argues that traditional

teacher certification programs are preferable to many of the alternative approaches.

9. Because the opportunity costs of a set amount of teacher time would presumably not vary across these different scenarios, these factors relate more to the distribution of the cost burden (e.g., expenditures versus teachers' donated time).

10. Some of this seemingly donated time may actually be compensated. For example, in systems where teachers receive bonuses when students achieve certain standards, teachers may choose to "donate" time to professional development activities designed to improve the likelihood they will receive a bonus.

11. Training refers to one-time professional development opportunities (e.g., single-day workshop, summer institute), while coaching refers to ongoing interactions (e.g., mentoring, collaborative planning).

12. It is important that costs be accounted for only once in the analysis (e.g., including the cost of university faculty under both "trainers and coaches" and "tuition and fees" would constitute double-counting this cost category).

13. Randy Ross and David Monk were instrumental in helping me think through the complexities associated with future salary obligations as a cost of teacher professional development. This component of the framework applies only to inservice professional development.

14. Evaluating the effectiveness of teacher professional development presents serious challenges. Possible indicators include participation/seat time, the ability of the teacher to successfully use the instructional/management strategies taught in the professional development experience, and eventual student achievement resulting from participation in professional development.

REFERENCES

American Council on Education (ACE). (1999). *Transforming the way teachers are taught.* Washington, DC: Author.

Center for the Study of Teaching and Policy (CTP). (1998). *Policy and excellent teaching: Focus for a national research center.* Seattle, WA: Author.

Darling-Hammond, L. (1990). Teaching and knowledge: Policy issues posed by alternate certification for teachers. *Peabody Journal of Education, 67*(3), 123–154.

Education Commission of the States (ECS). (1997). *Investment in teacher professional development: A look at 16 districts.* Denver, CO: Author.

Elmore, R. (1997). *Investing in teacher learning: Staff development and instructional improvement in Community School District #2, New York City.* Washington, DC: National Commission on Teaching and America's Future, Consortium for Policy Research in Education.

Goldhaber, D. D., & Brewer, D. J. (1999). *Does teacher certification matter? Teacher certification status and student achievement.* Paper presented at the annual meeting of the American Education Finance Association, Seattle, WA.

Hawley, W. D. (1987). The high costs and doubtful efficacy of extended teach-preparation programs: An invitation to more basic reforms. *American Journal of Education, 95*(2), 275–298.

Hawley, W. D., & Valli, L. (1998). The essentials of effective professional development: A new consensus. In L. Darling-Hammond (Ed.), *The heart of the matter.* San Francisco: Jossey-Bass.

Holmes Group. (1986). *Tomorrow's teachers: A report of the Holmes Group.* East Lansing, MI: Author.

Little, J. W. (1993). Teachers' professional development in a climate of educational reform. *Educational Evaluation and Policy Analysis, 15*(2), 129–151.

Little, J. W., Gerritz, W. H., Stern, D. H., Guthrie, J. W., Kirst, M.W., & Marsh, D. D. (1987). *Staff development in California: Public and personal investments, program patterns, and policy choices.* Policy Analysis for California Education (PACE) and Far West Laboratory for Educational Research and Development (Policy paper no. PC87-12-15, CPEC), San Francisco.

Miles, K. H., Bouchard, F., Winner, K., Cohen, M. A., & Guiney, E. (1999). *Professional development spending in the Boston public schools.* Boston: Boston Plan for Excellence.

Miller, B., Lord, B., & Dorney, J. (1994). *Staff development for teachers: A study of configurations and costs in four districts.* Newton, MA: Education Development Center.

Moore, D. R., & Hyde, A. A. (1981). *Making sense of staff development: An analysis of staff development programs and their costs in three urban school districts.* Chicago: Designs for Change.

National Association of School Boards of Education (NASBE). (1998). *The numbers game: Ensuring quantity and quality in the teaching work force.* Alexandria, VA: Author.

National Center for Education Statistics (NCES). (1998). *Toward better teaching: Professional development in 1993–94.* U.S. Department of Education, Office of Educational Research and Improvement (NCES 98-230), Washington, DC.

National Commission on Teaching and America's Future. (1996). *What matters most: Teaching for America's future.* New York: Author.

National Education Commission on Time and Learning. (1994). *Prisoners of time.* Washington, DC: Government Printing Office.

National Foundation for the Improvement of Education. (1996). *Teachers take charge of their learning: Transforming professional development for student success.* Washington DC: Author.

Rice, J. K. (2000). *Recent trends in the theory and practice of teacher professional development: Implications for cost.* Manuscript prepared for the National Partnership for Excellence and Accountability in Teaching.

Rice, J. K. (2001). Fiscal implications of new directions in teacher professional development. *School Business Affairs, 67*(4), 19–24.

Rice, J. K., & Brent, B. O. (in press). An alternative avenue to teacher certification: A cost analysis of the Pathways to Teaching Careers Program. *Journal of Education Finance.*

Ross, R. (1995). *Effective teacher development through salary incentives (An exploratory analysis).* RAND.

Sparks, D. (1995). A paradigm shift in staff development. *The ERIC Review, 3*(3), 3–4.

Stern, D., Gerritz, W. H., & Little, J. W. (1989). Making the most of a school district's two (or five) cents: Accounting for investment in teachers' professional development. *Journal of Education Finance, 14*, 368–379.

Sykes, G. (1996). Reform of and as professional development. *Phi Delta Kappan, 77*(7), 465–467.

INDEX

Studies in Leading and Organizing Schools, pages 235–239
Copyright © 2003 by Information Age Publishing
All rights of reproduction in any form reserved.

235

W